ROCKAWAY

ROCKAWAY

SURFING HEADLONG INTO A NEW LIFE

Diane Cardwell

Houghton Mifflin Harcourt
Boston   New York
2020

For information about permission to reproduce selections
from this book, write to trade.permissions@hmhco.com
or to Permissions, Houghton Mifflin Harcourt Publishing
Company, 3 Park Avenue, 19th Floor, New York, NY 10016.

hmhbooks.com

Library of Congress Cataloging-in-Publication Data
Names: Cardwell, Diane, 1964– author.
Title: Rockaway : surfing headlong into a new life / Diane Cardwell.
Description: Boston : Houghton Mifflin Harcourt, 2020.
Identifiers: LCCN 2019045702 (print) | LCCN 2019045703 (ebook) |
ISBN 9780358067788 (hardcover) | ISBN 9780358307136 |
ISBN 9780358311270 | ISBN 9780358067825 (ebook)
Subjects: LCSH: Cardwell, Diane, 1964– | Women surfers—United
States—Biography. | African American surfers—Biography |
Surfing—United States—Biography. | Women journalists—United
States—Biography. | African American journalists—Biography. |
Divorced Women—United States—Biography. |
Rockaway Beach (New York, N.Y.)—Biography.
Classification: LCC GV838.C34 A3 2020 (print) |
LCC GV838.C34 (ebook) | DDC 797.3/2092 [B]—dc23
LC record available at https://lccn.loc.gov/2019045702
LC ebook record available at https://lccn.loc.gov/2019045703

Book design by Chrissy Kurpeski

Select text excerpts from the essay "High Water"
first appeared in the January 2013 issue of *Vogue*.
Written and used by permission of the author.

Several chapters include portions of "Rising Tide of Money Erodes
a Long Island Holdout" and "Surfing Headlong into a New Life,"
both by Diane Cardwell, which originally appeared in the *New
York Times* on July 2, 2010, and on May 31, 2015, respectively, are
copyright the *New York Times* and used here by permission.

Map by Chrissy Kurpeski

Printed in the United States of America
DOC 10 9 8 7 6 5 4 3 2 1

Contents

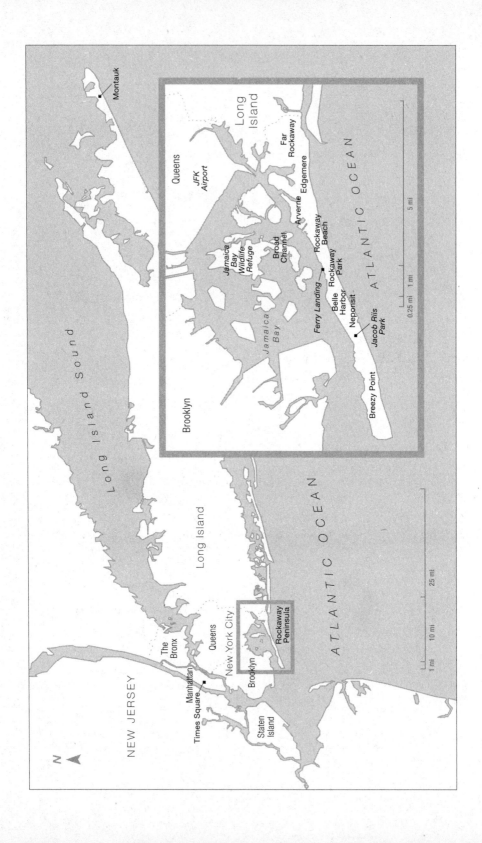

Prologue:
Over the Falls

FEBRUARY 2013

Still I must on; for I am as a weed
Flung from the rock, on Ocean's foam to sail
Where'er the surge may sweep, the tempest's breath prevail.

— LORD BYRON, *CHILDE HAROLD'S PILGRIMAGE*

IS THIS HOW IT ENDS?

The thought burned through my head, surprising and unbidden. I was straddling a surfboard in a thrashing ocean, breathless and struggling to stay upright, my arms so tired and aching I could barely lift them. Looking up, I saw my friends waiting for me on the shore, but they and the palm trees lining the cliffs all appeared to be receding. I'd been trying to get back to the beach for what felt like an eternity, and every time I took a moment's rest the heaving aquamarine waters tugged me farther away from the stretch of sand I needed to reach. I felt overwhelmed and small, as if in the clutches of a liquid bully tossing me this way and that, while wind whipped my dark, wet curls against my cheeks, salt spray stung my eyes, and surging water plugged my ears and gushed into my mouth and up my nose. The current was pulling me parallel to the coast, where bulkheads of razor-sharp coral and rocks could shred my flesh like a cat-o'-nine-tails. As my body started to fail, it dawned on me for the first time that I might not make it back.

Just an hour before, I'd been relaxed and happy. I'd arrived at the beach near the northwest corner of Puerto Rico with a friend, a feisty, green-eyed brunette I'd met back home as I'd haplessly tried to learn to surf over the past few years. She was not only my regular buddy in the waves but also one of the first new friends I'd made in a decade—part of the social life I was building as I slowly emerged from the wreckage of a divorce. Rented boards in hand, we were excited to escape the February chill of New York City and the rubble-strewn mess of my neighborhood in Rockaway Beach, still in recovery from the battering of Superstorm Sandy. Standing under the canopy of fanning leaves in the dirt parking lot overlooking the beach, we ran into a few friends from Rockaway who had just finished their sessions. Sure, it was a little choppy, with the swirl of the current making spirals of white foam amid the translucent peaks, but the waves were weaker than they looked, one of them said, and not much to worry about.

"Watch out for the current, though," another friend told us. "Make sure you don't let it take you out to the left. Just paddle at an angle the other way."

Maybe I shouldn't do this, I'd thought, eyeing the waves as they reared up and twisted before violently crashing toward the shore. But I'd quickly silenced that voice. As long as I kept to the right, I'd be fine. I'd always been able to handle myself in the ocean at home on the East Coast, and I was aching for the balm of wild water on my skin—I just couldn't resist.

Plus I needed this break from the rest of my life, which felt in shambles. Over the past five years I'd been lashed by loss after loss

—my marriage, my father, my chances of bearing a child. I was, in every sense of the word, adrift.

Surfing, despite my distinct lack of aptitude and struggles to find my balance in the ocean, consistently brought me joy and a sense of purpose. On a surfboard I could feel powerful and free and in tune with the universe, if only for an instant. The rest of the time I felt the opposite.

And now there was a clear and present danger confronting me. After I had stepped into the warm, inviting water sliding over the sand, I had focused so intently on charging through the walls of foam lining up in front of me that I hadn't noticed the current, stronger than I realized, taking me exactly where I didn't want to go: to the left.

So despite my efforts to paddle back, I was now stuck "outside" —the term surfers use for the zone beyond where the waves are breaking—and far from where I could safely return to shore. My surf buddy was nowhere to be seen in the water, having probably, and wisely, ditched the effort sooner. *It doesn't matter how many people you're surfing with,* I thought. *In the end you're alone, just you and the ocean.*

What if I can't get in by myself? I wondered as I contemplated my predicament. I closed my eyes and saw an unlikely fever-dream pastiche of lost-at-sea images: sunburned survivors found in life rafts, having subsisted on raw fish, birds, and their own urine; old-style paintings of half-nude women, shipwrecked and flung upon the sand; headlines about teenagers who'd fallen prey to rip tides, seemingly every year, in the Rockaways; the *Andrea Gail,* buffeted by mammoth seas before sinking; Gilligan and the Skipper losing control of the S.S. *Minnow* on what was supposed to be a three-hour tour.

I peered at the beach. I was even farther from my friends, who now looked like stick figures on the sand. *Can they tell I'm in trouble? Can they call in a rescue? Can I hold on long enough, or will I get swept out to sea? Are there sharks out there?*

Resting, I tried to tamp down the rising sense of dread, but I couldn't keep other kinds of doubts from creeping in. Maybe I was just not meant for this. If I'd so wrongly assumed I was ready for this ocean, I might very well have been wrongly convinced that I could actually have a roll-with-the-swells surfer's life—that I could, in middle age, pivot from my get-ahead, career-focused existence to something that seemed more meaningful. Maybe it was too late for that, just like it was too late to save my marriage, too late to get pregnant, too late to find another great love. I was clinging to a rented surfboard and maybe to a rented life—one I could dip into from time to time but couldn't really make my own. I looked around and took in the spectacular beauty of the place, seeing how close to and yet still so far from safety I was. What a ridiculous place to die.

Suddenly something in me snapped. *So what?* So what if I didn't have the answers, or a partner, or the picture-perfect life I thought I was building? I'd bought, not rented, this new life, and now I had to live it. *You got yourself into this mess, and it's up to you—and you alone—to get out of it.*

I sat up and took a deep breath as I arched my back and stretched out my chest, squeezing my shoulder blades together and shutting my eyes against the brilliance of the sky. Overcome, I yelled out, "No, not now," words that were immediately swallowed by the water's roar. I flopped back down on the board and began pulling my arms through the chop, hardly able to hold up my chest and head but willing myself to ignore the soreness and near paralysis settling into my shoulders, arms, and back. "You can do this," I chanted, over and over, like a mantra, cackling at how insane and uncool I must have looked—a million miles away from one of those sinewy surf babes I was trying to become. "Dig deeper!"

Eventually I cast an eye toward the shore and saw the stack of logs that doubled as stairs between the beach and the parking lot and realized that I was almost where I needed to be. Looking out toward the horizon, I noticed waves cresting and threatening to break, waves that looked like they could swallow and pummel me. I needed to get beyond them, where I could maybe catch one or slip back in between them. One began rising up beside me, so I slowly spun the board around and headed toward it with what little strength I had left, thinking I could punch through the lip.

But the ocean had a different idea. As I began sailing through to the other side, I felt a force, like the hand of Poseidon, grab the tail of my board, spin it around, and thrust it down the crumbling face of the wave. Water churned and rumbled around me as I gripped the edges of the board and lifted my chest, hoping that would keep me afloat and off the ocean floor.

As I hurtled along, the curtain of water swaddling my head parted and I could see that I was speeding toward the shore, where my friends were jumping up and down, yelling and gesturing for me to stand up and actually surf the wave. But I had noodles for arms and nothing left to launch my cramping body onto my feet. I was missing a shot at the very thing I'd traveled for: a ride on a wave, my skin bathed in sunlight and droplets of warm water. It was a disappointment, but I barely had the energy to care. As I neared the beach, I rolled off the board in exhaustion and relief, dragged it out of the water, and dropped it in the sand, then hunched over to rest my elbows on my knees. I stayed there, panting, and listened to my heartbeat slow as the waves crashed and receded somewhere behind me and a sense of security returned. I'd survived the ordeal with no real harm—at least not to my body. I would live to surf another day, and that, in this moment, was all that mattered.

‖‖

PART I

AT SEA

I suddenly realized that I was no member of
the crew — simply a blind passenger.

—FREDERICK KOHNER,
GIDGET, THE LITTLE GIRL WITH BIG IDEAS

1

First Light

IT WAS SUMMER AND I WAS DESPERATE FOR A WAY OUT of the city. Under normal circumstances I'd have had summer plans already: a weekend share somewhere with my husband, visits with friends upstate, or a long trip vineyard-hopping in France or Northern California or hiking and kayaking in Canada or Maine. But I was nearly three years divorced and this summer was mine, all mine, and looking really empty. As I sat at my desk in the third-floor newsroom of the *New York Times* in midtown Manhattan, bundled in a scratchy wool cardigan against the air-conditioned chill, I peered through the glass skin of the building at the people striding along the sidewalks below and at the buses winding up through the maze of ramps stacked above the Port Authority transit terminal across the avenue. It seemed that everyone was on the move.

I'd been a reporter at the *Times* for nearly a decade and had a new beat covering the city's hospitality industry for the Metro desk.

I'd convinced my editor that since so many of the restaurateurs, hoteliers, business executives, celebrities, and others from that scene would be heading out of town for the season—especially to the east end of Long Island—I should follow the annual exodus for my next article. But I hadn't yet found a specific story idea good enough to justify the expense of a trip, so I was on the phone fishing for leads with Jim, a longtime colleague who spent summers in Montauk, the remote and quirky fishing village at the island's prow.

"Ooooh," he said, "I know what you should write about—it's such a good story—but I almost don't want to tell you. I just kind of don't want to draw attention to it."

"Oh, c'mon," I said into my headset, "you've got to at least tell me what it is. If you don't want me to write about it, I won't, but if it's such a good story somebody else, like the *Wall Street Journal,* is going to figure it out and do it first."

"Yeah, yeah, okay, you're right," he said. "Plus I know it's kind of crazy to think I can keep anything about Montauk under wraps." I heard a deep inhale and then his voice dropped low, as if to arrange a parking-garage rendezvous to spill state secrets. "The Montauket's for sale. They're asking, like, $17 million."

"What's the Montauket—and is that a lot of money for it?"

"Oh my god—the Montauket!" Jim said, his voice back to normal volume. "It's a big deal if it sells."

The Montauket, it turned out, was a scruffy bar and motel perched high on a bluff overlooking Fort Pond Bay on Montauk's northern coast that had been considered for generations to be the best place in the area to watch the sunset. Though the End, as the town is known, is technically an unincorporated hamlet that's part of greater East Hampton, it had long eschewed that gloss and instead clung fiercely to its maritime history, blue-collar ethos, and hippie surfer vibe. But as wave after wave of development replaced mildewed budget lodgings with whitewashed boutique hotels catering to the fashionable set, the Montauket had become the last bastion of the townies, Jim told me, and a kind of stand-in for the place's soul.

It was, as Jim said, a good story, and, since the Fourth of July was approaching, a good time to tell it, as editors always wanted a fun, summery piece to run near the holiday weekend. Which was why, on a Saturday afternoon a week or so later, I sat at the bar of the Montauket breathing the salt air of the bay and scribbling in a reporter's notebook. I took in the framed portraits of fish and sea-scapes on the walls, drinks listed on chalkboards, and heavy wood beams crossing the ceiling. There was a cigarette machine near the entrance, a jukebox in a corner, and a manual cash register behind the bar that was actually in use, not just for show. The place was practically empty, but a young man and woman were out on the back patio, hardly able to keep their hands—or mouths—off one another.

The bartender, an efficient, no-frills woman in a black tank top, leaned her head out through an open window toward them. "I'd tell you to get a room, but we don't have any," she yelled. "I'm sick of looking at you licking each other like ice cream cones." She came back in and passed by me on her way to another task, rolling her eyes and shaking her head. The whole thing was feature-story gold.

A few hours later the sunset crowd descended. I stepped outside and watched them quickly fill the picnic-table benches and patio chairs under the soft glow of string lights and the descending sun, masked by cottony clouds hovering over the calm ripples of the bay. The jukebox blared Springsteen's "No Surrender" and a man in cargo shorts and a CLAM POWER T-shirt held aloft his Amstel Light, bellowing along, "No retreat, baby!" I slipped back inside the bar and, scanning the tightly packed room, spotted two men who appeared to be in their sixties. I introduced myself in the hope that they could tell me some of the history.

"How long have you been coming here?" I asked.

"Since the seventies," said one of them, a retired contractor with thinning dark hair and a button-down shirt. "It was an old man's bar, and I was a younger man then. Now I'm the old guy."

The place, they told me, was a popular spot for fishing vacations among Jones Beach lifeguards once the season ended, and a favorite of Billy Joel's.

"It used to be like time stopped here," said the other man, a white-haired guy in a coral polo shirt and khakis whose family had begun spending summers in Montauk in the 1920s. "Everything was held in place, like a picture of Roosevelt." Now, he said, because of the trendy hordes that routinely swamped the town, "we're just trying to hold back the floods."

I looked around at the crowd as the occasional raucous laugh shot through the din of weekend-night voices ricocheting off the ceiling. Outside, streaks of persimmon and periwinkle, the dying embers of sunset, hovered at the horizon's edge. I wondered what would become of the time-capsule charm here if a sale went through —whether the rough edges would get buffed away by the inexorable march of money, much as it had in so many quarters of the old Manhattan where I had grown up in the 1970s and '80s. The owner of the place, a petite woman with a slim hoop through her eyebrow whose family had run it since 1959, when a relative won the right to buy it in a poker game, had told me earlier that afternoon that, money aside, it was simply time to move on, to try something new.

I thought I knew what she meant. With my marriage over, I was still wrestling with the lingering feeling that I was waiting for my real life to start. I'd rented out the elegant townhouse I'd shared with my ex-husband, Eric, in Brooklyn and moved to a small apartment in a tenement on an unloved stretch of Bedford-Stuyvesant and, emerging from the slag heap of the divorce, was trying to sally forth on a path of my own, wherever it might lead. Maybe someday I'd again get to feel like that couple on the deck. Back in my twenties, when I started dating Eric—tall and broad-shouldered, with dazzling green eyes—we, too, couldn't keep our hands off each other in public, and made out all over downtown Manhattan. But those days were long gone, and for the moment, getting used to being single for the first time in almost twenty years and not feeling miserable was enough.

I woke up the next morning in my room at the Beachcomber, a complex of shingled Sea Ranch–style efficiencies separated from the Atlantic by Old Montauk Highway. I felt good about how the reporting had gone: I'd covered all the bases I needed to and thought I had a firm handle on the character of the town and the Montauket's place in it. But I felt a nagging itch as I made my usual morning brew of espresso with a splash of cream and filled a bowl with yogurt and granola. I hadn't gotten the perspective of any surfers. I was a little nervous about what kind of reception I might get at the main surfing beach, given the reputation surfers have for territoriality and a kind of antiestablishment worldview, but I decided to head over anyway to a stretch of the coast called Ditch Plains before making the drive back to Brooklyn.

Shit! I thought as I sped along the sunbaked highway, seeing too late the small white pole marking the road to Ditch. *That was it! Why do I always have to be this way?* I was irritated with myself for yet again screwing up a straightforward trip. I had learned to drive late — at thirty — and some fifteen years later still couldn't navigate very well on my own. I was always missing a turnoff or heading the wrong way and having to double back to get on the right path. Luckily, within a few minutes I came to another intersection, so I returned and wound down the street, buoyed by how pretty and familiar it seemed, like the back roads of Cape Cod, where I'd spent summers as a child. My parents, Depression-era strivers, hadn't been well off, but my father, a midlevel executive at a small savings bank, had an uncle who lived in Hyannis, near the mouth of the Cape. My mother was a public school teacher, so as soon as classes let out she would whisk me and my older sister up there for the summer.

As I made my way toward Ditch, the weathered cottages and shingled houses that peeked from behind stands of scrubby pink or white rugosa roses reminded me of the ones we'd seen every day on our way to the beach. I rounded bend after bend with warm sunlight streaming through the trees onto my bare shoulders under the open sunroof until I finally saw the East Deck Motel, a collection of attached spartan rooms where I'd been told the surf spot was, and found a place to park.

It was my first visit ever to a surf beach, or break, and I had no idea what to expect. I walked back to the motel and through its parking lot to the dune above the beach, where a tan camper selling food stood at the entrance. Just beyond, a couple of people in wetsuits were sitting on a bench, with surfboards lying next to them.

When I finally made it to the sand, what I saw in the glittering indigo waters below stopped me cold. Surfers, dozens of them, were propelling themselves before mellow knee-high waves, hopping easily to their feet, and then rolling lazily along, skipping and cross-stepping up and down the length of their boards. One woman, her skintight black wetsuit shiny with water and her long dark hair glistening in the sun, looked like some sort of enchantress of the break as she moved toward the shore, incanting a spell as she waved her arms up and down and swung her hips to the same rhythm.

Dumbstruck, I felt as though I'd stumbled upon a secret tribe of magical creatures—fairies and nymphs frolicking in a hidden bay. I couldn't believe this was surfing, a sport to which I'd never given much more than a glancing thought. Growing up, I figured you had to be insane to want to ride those heaving walls of water they showed on *Wide World of Sports,* the competitors' bodies mere specks sliding down (and down and under) the giant turquoise seas. Then, too, the popular image of surf culture—those laid-back stoners and tattooed dudes—wasn't so appealing to me. I'd grown up inside Manhattan's pressure cooker of ambition and possibility and, as I traversed my young adulthood, preferred to blow off steam with a night at the disco rather than a day at the beach.

But far from the skyscraper-high monsters I'd long seen on TV, here were waves small and inviting, nudging their way slowly out of a sequined sea and ushering the riders along. I stood there for what must have been an hour, transfixed. My eyes would steal away from time to time to rest on the rainbow of surfboards, a few of which looked like something Frankie and Annette might have ridden in *Beach Party,* stretched across the dune; or on the guy strumming a guitar under a makeshift tent fashioned from driftwood logs and fluttering cloths; or on the packs of lithe young women in bikinis sunbathing amid a scattering of bonfire remains.

But my attention was repeatedly drawn back to the wizards of the waves. *This is surfing?* Then another, quieter voice rumbled up from deep inside: *Maybe I could do that.* I almost chuckled at the thought of myself, a once timid and not-so-athletic girl from Manhattan, surfing, but I could feel it taking hold.

A tingling in the skin across my cheekbones broke me out of my trance, signaling the beginnings of a sunburn. I'd stayed longer than I meant to, and I hadn't even talked to anyone yet. But since I had a tight deadline, I figured I should skip interviewing the surfers and get going so I could beat the afternoon traffic back to my sweltering apartment in Brooklyn. As I walked through the parking lot and to the street, I noticed a yellow cottage with a handwritten FOR RENT sign in the window, which jumped out at me as if it were flashing red neon.

Kismet, I thought as I stared at it, my heart beginning to race and my brain suddenly feverish. I wondered what it was like inside, imagining myself walking over to the beach with coffee in the mornings, spending my days in the waves, boiling lobster at night. I'd visited Montauk only once before, years ago, when I had come out for a cold early-spring weekend with Eric to see the seals that had been returning to a rock outcropping near the lighthouse after a long absence. I fell for the place then — the dark-blue waters and comfortable, worn-around-the-edges aura felt familiar to me, more nautical and rusty, like Cape Cod, than the manicured Hamptons.

God, I'd love to spend time here, I thought. And then I walked on.

It's probably too expensive, I told myself, *or available when you aren't.*

What will you do out here all by yourself?

How will you learn to surf? You don't have a board or a wetsuit and you don't know anything about how to get them.

What if you spend all that money and then it rains?

I was almost to my car when I stopped and turned around, shutting out all those negative voices. *How many times have I done this very thing,* I wondered, *talked myself out of trying something because it's unfamiliar or scary or might push me outside the box where I've convinced myself I belong?* Over the years at work I'd shied away from pursuing foreign correspondent postings, believing that I lacked the gumption needed to excel. In my social life, I'd avoided industry mixers and gallery openings and even cocktail parties where I might not know many people, telling myself that I was awkward and lousy at making small talk. But I was itching to break those habits, be different in the world, get over those insecurities—or at least stop letting them get in the way.

"No," I said aloud, muttering, "just go take down the number."

So I walked back and stood on the edge of the lawn and began writing. Suddenly the front door opened and a friendly woman with reddish brown hair beckoned me over.

"Are you interested in the house?" she said as I approached. She smiled and shook my hand.

"I might be. But it depends on when it's available and if I can afford it."

"Well, come in and let me show you the place," she said, moving aside into the living room. As I crossed the threshold onto the flat blue carpet, it was like traveling back through time. The place was simple and spotless, a ranch-style cottage like so many I'd seen before. There were two cozy armchairs in front of a television and a couch draped in a light floral quilt off to the side.

"I don't know how many people you might have here, but that opens to a bed," she said, gesturing toward the couch.

"It may just be me, but that's good to know."

We walked to the eat-in kitchen, where she showed me the collection of pots, pans, dishes, and appliances, and then through the living room to the bathroom and two bedrooms, which were stocked with all the linens, towels, and basic toiletries I'd need.

"Oh, and here," she said, pulling open the shiny brown wood slider on one of the bedroom closets, "there's a big pot in case you want to cook lobster."

"Wow, this is great. I'd barely need to bring anything."

"Thanks. It's been in my husband's family for years," she said as we headed back to the kitchen, which opened onto the backyard. "We've been having the same people every summer—some of them for twenty years," she added. "But this time a few have dropped out."

"Do you live out here?"

"No, we're further in on the island. Let me show you the back."

"So, do you surf?" I asked as we headed out and stood by a wood picnic table and benches.

"We don't, but my daughter does. Do you?"

"No—not yet," I said, laughing. "But I was watching them over at the beach and I'm thinking I might want to come back and learn."

"Well, the house would be great for that."

She quoted me a price for the week that was just within my reach. I kept looking around, trying to spot the drawback that was making this little paradise attainable, like cannibals lurking out in the shed or the gates of hell hidden behind the fence. Instead I saw an open yard rimmed with spiky grasses where I could imagine whiling away the evenings, happily exhausted from the beach, with something sizzling on the grill perched on a metal stake in the ground.

"I have two weeks open," she said as she pulled out a small notebook and flipped to a list written in pencil. One of them was the week before Labor Day, which I'd already scheduled to take off. Kismet indeed.

"It's a lot of money, but I think I can swing it," I said, as if willing it to be true simply by speaking the words. "Can I think about it and let you know sometime next week?"

"That's fine."

I knew I could scrape together the cash, but I wasn't sure I could really afford it. I'd only recently gotten myself out of the financial hole I tumbled into after the divorce by failing to recalibrate my spending to one income rather than two, and I wasn't at all sure I should be indulging in a summer getaway. But it felt like too good an opportunity to pass up—and like the universe was trying to tell me something, even if I had no real idea of what I was getting into.

I was certainly used to the beach—as a kid I'd spent my days on the bay side of Kalmus Beach in Hyannis, endlessly playing and splashing in the water, sifting sand for tiny shells, leaping from rock to rock on the jetty, my tangle of dark frizz streaked reddish blond from the sun and my tanned skin going so dark it made my brown eyes seem lighter. I was by nature curious, though cautious and shy, and often took so long to get into the water—edging near the shore, dipping first a toe and then maybe a foot before retreating from the tide, only to start up again—that my mother would leave me alone to perform my ritual until I finally made it in. Then she would suddenly appear by my side, or dispatch my sister—seven years older and courageous, a natural athlete and champion swimmer—to watch over me as I ran and jumped and patted water on the top of my head.

"Why are you doing that?" she asked me one day.

"It's a trick," came my four-year-old response.

I started learning to swim that summer when my mother taught me how to float. I could still see her standing in the water in a black one-piece and tortoiseshell Wayfarers with forest-green lenses, cradling me faceup in her arms. "Arch your back, and keep your arms out," she said as I looked up at her face, a canvas of patience and delight framed by curly light brown hair against a gauze of cloud wisps and a baby-blue sky. The water gently prodded my rib cage and head as she relaxed her arms, allowing me to sink a little before lifting me up, again and again, until I finally stayed up on my own. "See!" she said, her laughter like the tinkle of capiz shells. "You're floating!" It was the most miraculous thing in the world.

I loved being in the water, and as I got older I continued to swim at that beach—and do handstands and flips and all sorts of maneuvers I was afraid to try on land—even after my parents bought a modest ranch in a development near a pond in Mashpee, about twelve miles away. But waves and what you could do in them never piqued my interest. I didn't like the forceful waters of the ocean side at Kalmus. I wanted to swim, and those waves just got in the way and stirred up seaweed that spooked me when it brushed against my calf or thigh, conjuring visions of spiny sea creatures or tentacled jellyfish prepared to strike. And the guys I saw struggling to set up and launch their windsurfers made all that rigging seem cumbersome and tedious, a hindrance to the carefree good time I was after. Those other people could keep their waves. I had no use for them.

But in Montauk I'd seen something I hadn't much contemplated: a water sport that let you be *in* the ocean rather than on it, with nothing more than the board to mediate. That's what I loved when Eric introduced me to kayaking, that sense of being part of the inlets and streams and mangroves as I paddled through them. And surfing? Well, that looked like it could be even more fun.

As I got into my car and began driving back home, I felt like I was leaving a great first date. I kept replaying the images of the surfers in my head—their swivels, their glides, their turns—and imagining what it would be like to be them.

But while I whizzed along the parkway, past the densely planted trees and stone overpasses, I started getting discouraged about the whole enterprise, worried that it was more than I should take on. Even if it was possible to rent equipment and take lessons, I thought, I was unsure about the expense and how to find a good instructor.

Then I remembered: *Jim surfs! Maybe he'll know where to go.*

This is exactly the sort of thing you should be doing, I thought as I got to Brooklyn, passing the automotive repair shops, contracting suppliers, storefront churches, and cocktail lounges that cropped up along Atlantic Avenue. In the years since the marriage had fallen apart, I'd struggled to figure out how to vacation on my own. Most of my friends were married with children and went on family get-aways, and though I wasn't entirely without a sense of adventure, the idea of negotiating long trips by myself did not turn me on. Two years earlier I had gotten a much-needed escape from the scene of my domestic disaster in the form of a yearlong journalism fellowship at Stanford in California. Before I left, I treated myself to a group class in digital photography in a small town on Lake Como in Italy, where I kept fantasizing that I'd somehow meet George Clooney, who has a house there, and begin a romance that would solve all my problems. He was, from my perspective at least, age-appropriate, and he admired journalism, so I figured we'd have some actual basis for connection. Of course I never even caught a glimpse of Clooney during the week I was there, but I did find the shared photography enterprise helpful for breaking through my natural reticence among people I don't know well and for creating a structure through which to explore a new place. If I took the Montauk rental it could be similar, I reasoned, as I'd have the surfing project to help me organize my time and maybe even meet people.

As I approached my block, passing the castlelike Bedford Union Armory, its red-brick facade glowing in the early evening sun, I decided to do it. Later that night I crawled into bed and snuggled into the pillows, unable to stop smiling as I thought about the week in Montauk and how much fun it could be. I closed my eyes and re-played what I'd seen that morning, those beautiful, graceful people sliding through the waves, so powerful and so free. When I finally drifted off to sleep, it was with visions of myself dancing on a shimmering sea.

2

Hooked

JULY–SEPTEMBER 2010

ON A LATE-JULY MORNING ALMOST A MONTH AFTER MY reporting trip to Montauk, I was getting dressed for the office, sticky with sweat from the sun beating into my un-air-conditioned apartment, and realizing that I was craving the feeling of water lapping at my feet. The weeklong surf vacation in Montauk was more than a month away, and I could sense the sunsets beginning to quicken and suddenly wanted a day at the beach.

A few hours later I was at an outdoor press conference in midtown Manhattan for the ceremonial opening of a new hotel, fretting over which of the beaches accessible by public transportation I should visit the coming weekend, Coney Island or Jacob Riis, in the Rockaways. I watched the mayor, Michael Bloomberg, deliver congratulatory remarks amid ferns and potted bamboo and then join the hotel developers and other grandees to snip a leafy green plastic vine draped across the entrance in place of the typical red ribbon, part of promoting the building's environmentally friendly features.

After a question-and-answer session with the media, the group broke up and the mayor, surrounded by aides and security, hustled off to a black SUV. I headed toward the entrance for a tour and reception and said hello to Adrian Benepe, commissioner of the Parks Department, whom I'd interviewed a number of times over the years but hadn't seen in a long while.

"What are you covering these days?" he asked, his short hair as dark and tidy as his jacket and tie.

"Bars, hotels, and restaurants — the hospitality industry," I told him. "It's a lot of fun, but honestly," I said, laughing, "I feel like I would have been a lot better at it when I was younger."

"I know what you mean — I'm at events almost every night, raising money for Parks."

And then I thought, *I should ask him where to go this weekend.* As czar of the city's beaches, Adrian was in a position to know.

"Maybe you can help me with something," I blurted.

"Sure," he said.

I told him about my struggle to choose.

"Are you driving?"

"No, I can get to either one by subway — or mainly by subway, at least."

He took a breath as if to speak and then stopped. A few awkward seconds of silence passed, and it occurred to me that maybe I'd done the wrong thing in asking him to put one beach he stewarded ahead of another, like asking a parent which child they prefer. I was about to say, "Never mind," and withdraw the question to let him off the hook when he said simply, "Coney Island is very crowded."

Thank god I kept my mouth shut — Rockaway it is! I thought, excited and relieved to have a destination and a new adventure. Though it had been years since I'd gone to any city beach, I had been to Coney a number of times, often for work, covering local politics, but also for the occasional weekend day trip. Not so with

Rockaway, as the collection of neighborhoods dotting the Rockaway Peninsula at the city's southern edge is sometimes known—it was practically the frontier.

Sunday morning arrived, and at seven-thirty, armed with coffee, a towel, water, and reading material, I stepped into the near-deserted Brooklyn streets cloaked in that special summer smell of spoiled milk and stale urine to begin the long trek to the Rockaways. I was on a mission not just to sink my toes into the sand before July ended but also to recapture one of the many leisure-time casualties of my wrecked relationship. Eric and I had often had a car, one parental castoff or another, during the fifteen years we were together, and we found time to head to Maine or Long Island for at least a few days most years. Early on, we even snagged a tiny converted hay barn near the beach at the cheaper end of the Hamptons for an enchanted summer, during which a trio of driftwood-colored rabbits stood up along the driveway one misty morning as if to salute as we left the house.

But that was a long time ago, and without easy access to a vehicle and with my will to travel attenuated by unhealed wounds and loneliness, it just hadn't occurred to me to try to get out of the neighborhood until that week. My experience with the beaches that dot the city's 520 miles of coastline was limited, despite my New York City upbringing. Cape Cod had given me my first taste of true independence and a precious respite from the urban constraints of my youth, when my life was defined by the dangers, both real and imagined, that lurked outside our apartments, first in Harlem and then on the pre-gentrified Upper West Side. It was New York's bad old days of high street crime, and I was rarely allowed out alone, and then always given strict instructions on which blocks to avoid. My parents, like many others, also made sure I had "mugger money" in my pocket—at least five dollars, so as not to make potential assailants angry enough to hurt me or my friends. But at the beach I could wander off for hours by myself to play in the water or examine the dunes, get thin, salty potato chips at the concession stand, or hang out with my summer friend, a local girl with long blond hair and pale-gray eyes whom I'd met there during one of my solo meanderings. It was a relationship that existed entirely in the sand: I'd run into her year after year, and she'd show me the best places to dig for clams or to find the tiniest seashells. I had what felt like a radical freedom at the shore—an association I never lost.

As I got older and couldn't travel that far come summer, I looked to nearer beaches, which in my twenties became backdrops for a different kind of abandon. At my first job in journalism, I'd become close friends with a guy named Jonathan, a tremendously talented writer and editor who was tall, charismatic, cute, stylish, and fun—one of those rare people who could make just about any situation feel like a fabulous party. Even in an office full of artsy young strivers at a short-lived but influential magazine called *7 Days,* he stood out, his long blond hair swinging from side to side as he strode about, a collection of thin bracelets encircling his wrist and a faint scent of patchouli in his wake. He'd grown up in a big, boisterous Irish Catholic family in South Jersey, so we'd go "down the shore" to Stone Harbor or Avalon or Cape May from time to time, but we also shared rentals in the Hamptons. We'd spend our weekend days at the beach or lounging in some chic friend's backyard or pool and our nights cooking dinners or heading out to house parties, art and fashion events, or dance clubs, fueled as much by our own exuberance over feeling young and optimistic as by anything else.

Eric, whose parents were Latvian refugees from World War II, had grown up in a suburb of Buffalo but had developed a love of the mountains and woods, and a few of my friends from *7 Days* had country homes upstate or had moved there. Attracted by the mix of sweet old farmhouses, a burgeoning food and wine scene, and the cultural sophistication of the writers and artists we were getting to know, we began pursuing a weekend life in the Hudson Valley. The beach was nice but so limited, we thought—what would we do once the cold weather came?—and well beyond our means anyway. Here was an area where we could do things year-round, we reasoned, whether kayaking or hiking or cross-country skiing, a place where I could garden, raise chickens and cows, and pursue photography, a place where we could even imagine growing old. It was a picture I grabbed hold of and refused to surrender, envisioning how our life together would play out there: entertaining friends and family, frolicking with dogs and children, visiting vineyards and restaurants, summer-stock playhouses and museums. It would be relaxing yet lively, rustic but urbane. The beach retreated into the background.

That vision hadn't come to be—not the weekend house, not the lasting marriage, not the hobby farm, not the children. So there I was, on my own, riding two trains and a bus to get from Bed-Stuy to the Rockaways, still wondering just how and when I had let myself get so derailed. Once upon a time, I remembered, I had been a fabulous young girl about town, pursuing my own interests and dreams, feeling like I had nothing but options before me. Hadn't I wanted to travel the world, taking pictures and learning and writing about this place and that, their cultures and their foods? Hadn't I wanted to make documentaries and movies and television shows? Hadn't I thought about becoming a real estate developer—or learning to sew and designing my own clothes? I'd had all those notions and yearnings at one point or another, but I hadn't pursued any of them, and, as I molded my aims to Eric's and tied myself down to mortgage payments and credit card bills in pursuit of a fantasy domestic life, I'd let them all wash away like the sands of an eroding dune.

Well, maybe I can't have any of that, but I can still have the beach, I thought as the bus made its way along Flatbush Avenue, the sprawling commercial artery that runs like an enormous strip mall across Brooklyn to its southern edge on Jamaica Bay. I felt a kind of warm fellowship with the multiracial array of excited young people who surrounded me on the bus with their beach chairs, boom boxes, and coolers. Whatever our differences of origin, situation, or experience, we were all up early on a summer morning, chasing the joy only the beach can bring. And it struck me that I was taking full advantage of the one good thing about lacking a partner or child: I owed my time and energy to no one but myself.

As the bus passed through a forested stretch, I suddenly got a whiff of sulfur and realized with a start that we must be near the marshes and inlets of the bay. Moments later the bus began rattling over a bridge, the sound of its progress becoming a deep metallic hum as the wheels settled into the gridlines of the steel-grate surface. Coasting high above the water, I could see Jamaica Bay, that day a calm sheet of cerulean beneath us, and straight ahead the Rockaway Peninsula, running perpendicular to our road like the top of a *T,* with the vast expanse of the Atlantic Ocean just beyond.

The bus crossed over and wound down to Jacob Riis Park on the ocean side, long known as the People's Beach, where it nearly emptied. Established in the 1910s and soon named for the social journalist who crusaded for the poor, it was largely built in the thirties in order to give city dwellers the same kind of access to the healing powers of fresh air and the ocean as their landed, car-owning neighbors in the suburbs.

As my fellow passengers and I walked through the grand art deco brick bathhouse, its cool floors rubbed smooth by the generations of happy, sandy feet that had come before us, I realized that I'd been there before, long ago, with Eric, under what I imagined were similar circumstances: deciding to get up some weekend morning and head out. Back then it had been early enough—both in the season and in the day—that the park was nearly empty when we got there. It was overcast, and as we walked to the damp gray sand we came upon a young couple lying on a rumpled blanket with a few empty tallboys by their heads. The woman rolled over and looked up at us with a scowl, eyes bloodshot and bottle-blond hair matted against her cheek, as if she'd awakened still drunk and we were to blame.

Now, years later, I was up early again at an almost empty beach, but this time it all looked and felt somehow different—brighter and more welcoming. I found a flat patch of sand near a dune where I could see the ocean. I laid out my towel, baked for a while, splashed and swam in the water, read about the latest in age-defying skin potions, leafed through the weddings and real estate sections of the *New York Times*. I stretched like a cat in the sun and it hit me: I was having a fine old time.

Around noon, hungry and uninspired by the hot dogs and nachos on offer at the concessions, I decided to leave and try to find Rockaway Taco, a hipster place I'd been hearing about. I recalled that my friend Bob, who produced political news at a local TV station, NY1, lived in the area, so I sent him an email. I hadn't seen him in years, but the reply came quickly: his house was only a few blocks from Rockaway Taco, so I should grab my food and come over. After a quick Google search for directions, I was on my way. I rode the Q22 bus past the lavish homes and manicured yards of the wealthy neighborhoods of Neponsit and Belle Harbor, the weathered, wood-shingle siding and front porches of the Capes and Colonials edged in hydrangeas and tiger lilies, and the sun-dappled streets leading to the ocean as in so many beach towns. I got off about ten minutes later at a decidedly less bucolic corner in Rockaway Beach near an imposing brick building that, like several others on the peninsula, housed mentally ill adults.

I waited in line at the taco stand, surprised by the vibrant, eclectic crowd and makeshift cool of the place and its little outdoor dining area with brightly painted tables and benches, a rack of books and magazines, and a reggae soundtrack. I secured two fish tacos and headed around the corner and across the enormous oval parking lot that, along with a huge, pottery-encrusted whale statue, formed the gateway to Rockaway Beach. I climbed the brick steps to Bob's house, a stately white three-story Dutch Colonial with a big wraparound porch overlooking the ocean, where a bunch of professional acquaintances I'd always liked yet hadn't kept up with were hanging out.

"Hey, D, how you doin'?" said Josh, a former reporter who had just started an online news site, coming in for a hug as I reached the porch. "Nice to see you."

"Hey! So glad you emailed—so good to see you," Bob said, emerging from the house with a big smile and fistfuls of wineglasses. "It's been so long!" I couldn't remember when I'd last seen either of them, both dark-haired guys a little under six feet wearing T-shirts and shorts, but they were so easygoing it was almost as if no time had passed at all.

Josh's wife, Iva, was sitting at a round white plastic table, her straight dark hair fanned over shoulders left bare by a white sundress, uncorking a bottle of rosé. "Come, have some wine," she said in her soft, rolling Croatian accent. I took a seat next to her and soaked in the warmth of the greeting, the seaside-blue paint on the porch ceiling, the span of the ocean, and the way the whale statue glittered in the sun.

"That whale looks so familiar," I said. "Like the one I used to see at the old children's zoo in Central Park when I was a kid. But it wasn't covered in mosaic."

"It's the same whale," said Bob, who'd been living there for more than a decade. He explained that it hadn't gotten the tile decoration until it had landed by the shore after the old zoo's demolition. Whalemina, they called her.

I felt the tug of nostalgia—like a slackened thread tightening in my heart, connecting me back to a time when I was happy—as Iva poured me a glass of wine and I pulled my tacos from the bag. "Oh, we had some earlier," she said, her pale-blue eyes going wide as her smile dimpled her cheeks. "Aren't they great?"

Indeed they were, just like the wine she said she'd picked up at the liquor store on the boulevard—surprisingly delicious. *Maybe Rockaway isn't so down-and-out after all.*

"God, these are good," I said, relishing the crunch of the cabbage, radishes, and lightly battered fish topped with spiced mayo. "I got obsessed with fish tacos in California. They have them everywhere out there, and they were practically all I ever wanted to eat. But these are every bit as good as anything I had there."

"Yeah, that place is a great addition to the neighborhood," Bob said. "There's nothing else like it around here."

The couple's young sons were hanging out inside, and Josh, who had been ferrying their sandals and clothing to a car parked in front of the house, cracked open a can of Bud and joined us.

"How are things going with the website?" I asked him. "You just launched, right?"

"Yeah, two weeks ago," he said. "It's a soft launch, so we're not completely out there yet, but so far, so good. It's a lot of work, but we're getting a good response. You should come by the office some-time—I can show you the site and you can meet the team. There are five of us now," he added, chuckling.

"I'd love to do that. But what brings you here—are you guys living here?"

"No," Josh said. "We're in Astoria, but we're out here with the boys almost every weekend in the summer."

Iva added, "They love the beach."

"And what brought you out today?" Bob asked me.

"It's so funny—I just wanted to get to the beach, but I couldn't decide between here and Coney. Then I ran into Adrian Benepe at a press conference and he told me that Coney's very crowded, so I came here."

"Glad you did!" Bob said.

"Me, too," I replied.

While I chatted with the three of them and watched the play of light on the ocean as the sun fell somewhere in the distance, I felt a distinct sense of comfort, as if I could just slip right into Bob's world. Of course I could never live in a place this far from the city, from my office in midtown or my life, such as it was, in Brooklyn. But as I settled into the easy camaraderie and mel-low hospitality of the group, I realized that I was finally in a place where I felt good, where the failures of my past no longer weighed so heavily.

■ ■ ■

About a month later the summer of 2010 was racing to its unofficial close—Labor Day—and my weeklong vacation at the yellow cottage in Montauk was at last under way. I'd been there three days already but hadn't yet surfed. Instead I'd been having a lovely time catching up on reading, hiking along the cliffs and the point overlooking the bright-blue waters, and wandering about the town and the wharf with its old-school bait-and-tackle shops, lobster pounds, and mix of private motorboats and fleets of trawlers and long-liners for commercial fishing.

You wouldn't have known it from the postcard-blue sky and uninterrupted sunlight, but it was hurricane season, the time of year most East Coast surfers live for, when the high winds from storms that originate near the edge of West Africa pump seemingly boundless energy into the seas. Near the beginning that energy creates enormous swaths of sloppy, churning waves, but as it moves through the water over thousands of miles, it arranges itself into smooth, regular lines known as swell. As the swell comes out of deep water and nears a coast, it refracts off the surface of a continental shelf and then runs into obstructions like sandbars and boulders and reefs, which, depending on their shape, configuration, and incline, cause the swell to rear up, or peak, and form the waves surfers seek to ride. Generally speaking, the bigger the storm, the bigger the swell, and the farther it travels without being interrupted before appearing near the shoreline, the bigger and stronger the wave.

Montauk sits about a two-hour drive east from Rockaway. Its location at the very tip of Long Island and its mainly south-facing beaches mean it is well exposed to pick up swell traveling toward it from a wide berth in the Atlantic Ocean, the path of which can be unblocked for thousands of miles. Its coast is lined with coves and bluffs and rocky outcroppings that modulate the way the waves break or shelter them from the wind, which in turn allows them to form the glossy wedges or sinuous tubes that make for quality rides. As a result, Montauk has among the best, most consistent waves on the eastern seaboard, especially in fall and winter. But at the beginning of my stay there, the ocean had been shuddering with the effects of Danielle, the first major hurricane of the season. Rough surf and riptides from the storm had led to two deaths and hundreds of rescues in Florida and Maryland, and even after tracking up the East Coast and out to sea it was still making the waves too big and powerful for a first-timer. With the clock ticking on my vacation, I was worrying that the whole trip was going to end up being a waste on the surfing front, some sort of karmic punishment for my hasty, emotional decision to spend money I shouldn't have.

Then, late on Tuesday afternoon, I got a voicemail from Kristin at the surf school that my coworker Jim had recommended: the forecast looked good for the next day. If I was willing, she said almost apologetically, I could meet my instructor, Sean, on the beach in front of the parking lot at Ditch Plains at five in the afternoon for a whitewater lesson. I didn't know what that meant exactly, but I was thrilled, and a little giddy. I was going to get to surf.

So the next afternoon, after some confusion about which parking lot Kristin had meant, I found Sean from CoreysWave Professional Surf Instruction waiting in the sun on a thin spit of dark-yellow sand running between the dune and the rocks lining the water's edge. He looked to be in his twenties, a stocky guy with thick, sun-streaked brown hair that hung to his chin and a cutoff wetsuit the color of split pea soup.

"Hey," he said, handing me a plum-colored suit. "Have you ever surfed before?"

"Not at all," I told him. "And I've never done any kind of board or wave sport in my life."

"Okay," he said, flinging his hair to the side. "We'll be on the beach for a half hour or so, going over the pop-up, and then basically I'm going to be pushing you into waves the rest of the time."

"Okay," I said, letting the unfamiliar lingo wash over me as I tried unsuccessfully to visualize how it was all going to go. I began getting into the wetsuit, stepping in with the long, zippered opening in front and setting about squeezing my legs through the tubes of unyielding rubber. Since it was near the end of summer, the air was still warm, but Montauk waters rarely make it much past seventy degrees, I'd been told, so I'd need the two to three millimeters of neoprene I was struggling to put on. It was on the lighter end as wetsuits go, but still it felt so heavy and stiff as I tugged it toward my hips it might as well have been a sheet of lead.

Sean eyed my lack of progress. "The zipper," he said, "goes in the back."

"Right," I said, pulling the suit down and beginning the process all over again. Panting and sweaty, I finally got the thing to my waist, at which point Sean told me to stop. I would have an easier time practicing the pop-up—whatever *that* was—if I wasn't fully suited up, he said. "Otherwise you're going to get pretty hot pretty fast. Do you know if you're regular or goofy?"

I looked at him blankly. He chuckled.

"Regular or goofy—left or right foot in front?"

I'd never known there was such a thing as a natural preference to ride a board with one side or the other in front—a phenomenon, I'd eventually come to learn, that's shared in other board sports, like snow- and skate-, although some people ride the different boards differently. We performed a simple test. I leaned forward to see which foot came out first to avoid a fall, and we determined I was regular, meaning I would want my left foot forward and my right in back, wearing the leash.

To show me the pop-up, Sean lay down on his belly in the sand with his legs straight behind him and then, in slow motion, demonstrated what I would try to do in the water: a kind of push-up followed by tucking the left leg up under my chest and between my arms while rotating toward the right into a low sideways lunge and sliding the right foot in to stand about hips'-width apart in a crouch. When he put it all together, it seemed, in yoga terms, a little like springing from a baby cobra through a plank into a modified warrior position. I told him as much, and he chuckled again.

"Kind of," he said. "Now you try."

I lay down, put my hands next to my rib cage with my arms like chicken wings, and strove to replicate what he'd done, but I kept getting tangled in myself. No matter how hard I thought or talked or tried my way through the various steps, I couldn't seem to make enough room under my midsection to bring my leg forward, or to pivot at the right time or angle. After five or six attempts, I started getting closer, but I was still coming up off-center.

"You twist like that," he said, showing me what I'd done wrong, "and you're off the board."

Huffing—and huffy—with frustration, sweating under the late-afternoon sun, I tried again and again and again, to little avail. Eventually I landed one right. "Give me two more like that, and we'll head in."

"One," I countered, gasping and spitting sand. "If we keep this up, I won't have anything left for the water."

I hit the next one and he agreed to let me try for real. I pulled the wetsuit up and over my sticky body, fighting to push my arms into sleeves that seemed to stretch forever, like taffy. I finally got the suit on and zipped up the back, feeling rivulets of sweat trickling down my spine. Sean grabbed the board, a long, spongy expanse of blue foam, and headed into the water, pointing out a few of the larger rocks peeking through the swirling current that we'd need to avoid. I followed, slipping and tottering over the slick, rocky bottom, seeing peril wherever I looked. I was barely in up to my shins when a knot of dread developed in my stomach at the prospect of slamming into the stones. *What have I gotten myself into?*

Finally I caught up to Sean and the board. "Hop owhown!" he said with a toss of the hair.

"What?"

"Hop owhown," he repeated, gesturing to the board as it dodged and weaved in the ocean chop.

Oh, I thought, the knot of impending doom pulling tighter. *"Hop on." He's just being playful with the accent—he must think I'm an idiot.*

I felt unsteady even just standing there with the waves and current pushing and pulling at my legs and midsection, but with something more like a heave and a grappling shimmy than a hop, I climbed onto the board as Sean held it. "When you get up," he said as he towed me out just to where the waves were breaking and turned the board around to face the shore, "if you feel like you're going to fall, try to fall back and flat. No diving headfirst."

Before I could work up a panic over the possibility of braining myself on the bottom, he was telling me to get ready. My heart started pounding. This was it: my first wave. I lay there as I'd practiced in the sand, with my feet back and together and my chest up, looking out at the dune that rose between the narrow beach and the dirt parking lot beyond it. "Here you go," Sean said as the board began to slide forward and suddenly accelerated. "Get up!" he yelled. I did, and just as he'd predicted, I was promptly off the board and in the foam—but, miraculously, not on the rocks.

I felt vaguely victorious. I hadn't gotten to my feet, but at least now I wasn't afraid to fall—which was good, since that's what I proceeded to do, over and over as Sean pushed me into wave after wave and I scrambled to get up, only to roll off one side of the board or the other. There was nothing unpleasant about it, though I was beginning to think I'd have nothing to show for my efforts at the end of the lesson but a head and belly full of seawater along with an aching lower back and blazing shoulder muscles.

It went on like that for maybe twenty minutes until finally Sean pushed me and I felt the board charge forward. I took a deep breath, pushed up with my arms, coiled my body, snapped my feet under me, and stood up and rode. It was fantastic. For an instant I jacked into a mysterious engine whose thrust allowed me to glide on the ocean itself, as if the board no longer existed and I was a waterborne Hermes with sea spray instead of wings at my heels, channeling all that energy from the depths to fly toward the shore. And then, just as suddenly, my weight shifted and there I was again, falling back into the water.

It hardly mattered. My body was flooded with adrenaline and my heart was trying to break free of my chest. It was a powerful high—cosmic, euphoric, liberating, addictive. And, yes—oh, yes —I wanted some more.

I got a tiny bit more that day, and then again the next afternoon when I returned for a second lesson, but it soon dawned on me just how far I was from being like the wave dancers I'd seen earlier that summer. Not only did I lack the flexibility to fold my five-foot-ten frame quickly into a surfing stance, but also I had little of the upper-body strength needed for paddling and launching all of my 170 pounds onto my feet. I felt lumbering and spastic, too exhausted and throbbing with pain to get through much more than an hour of the lesson—and that was with Sean doing most of the work.

I had little reason to hope I would ever be able to master the sport, and yet I was smitten, a sorry combination I confessed to Kristin, a small blonde in a skimpy bikini who came by the beach at the end of my second lesson. "It takes a long time to build up those muscles," she said, the brim of a baseball cap shading her ocean-blue eyes, "but you'll do fine. We've had people out here for lessons who showed no ability to surf—and I mean *no* ability—but they stuck with it and they're surfing now. It will come."

I stared at her, the fading sun turning her trim figure to gold, and decided to believe her, if for no other reason than I desperately wanted what she was saying to be true.

Weeks later I was obsessed with trying surfing again. It didn't matter that I'd sucked at it; I just couldn't wait to get back in the water and have that feeling of *glide* all over again. *Surfing,* I wondered, *where have you been all my life?*

I wasn't entirely unathletic growing up, but I wasn't sporty either. As a kid I hated the zero-sum-game aspect of competition, so I avoided it and opted for dance as my phys ed as soon as I could. My mother nurtured that avocation, even though it was to my father's eternal disappointment that I never pursued track and field, swimming, basketball, golf, or tennis as he'd wanted. It was a shame, in his eyes, that I'd wasted what he felt was a genetic prize of height, passed down, apparently, from his father and uncles but skipping him along the way. Call it a lack of discipline, but things I couldn't pick up quickly I abandoned.

Achievement was the reigning narrative in my house. "When you put your name on something," my mother told me in elementary school, "it means you've done the best you can do," and that narrative represented both oppression and liberty. There was never even a question whether I'd go to college, following in the footsteps of three generations on my father's side, beginning with my great-grandfather, who was born a slave in Virginia but graduated from Hampton in 1874, later attending Oberlin and becoming a teacher. The ties to education and the belief that it was the best way to punch our way through the limits imposed by racial discrimination were tight. My mother hadn't gone to college by the time she married—she'd gone to work straight out of high school to help support her mother, a widow—so my father, a 1950s traditionalist in many ways, took over caring for my infant sister at night so that my mother could get her bachelor's degree at City College. I accepted the importance of education as a given, but my parents scrimped and saved so that my sister and I could attend fancy private schools with the help of financial aid. The expectations for success felt like a lot to live up to.

At the same time, I had figured out early on that achieving in school could give me the parental latitude to do what I wanted. As long as my grades were good, I could goof off with my friends or work on plays, dance performances, and the school newspaper—pursuits that fed my artistic, dramatic side and made me, surprisingly, one of the cool kids.

I loved all of it, but I had another motivation for wanting to avoid going home for as long as I could: my father was, as he might have put it, a boozer. I never knew what awaited me when I came home and he'd be three, four, maybe five enormous martinis into his evening. When he was sober, he could be funny and fun-loving. He was a quintessential charmer who was good with a story, quick with a joke, and a keen reader of people. When he was drunk, all those traits hardened into a weapon that he would use, with uncanny aim, to probe and eviscerate my weak spots, leaving me crying so hard sometimes I felt I would never stop.

"You're a *hedonist!* An *ingrate!*" he would yell, warning that if I didn't shape up, I'd never amount to anything, wasting all that he had sacrificed on my behalf. Compared to him, I didn't know what it was to struggle. I had it so easy. What he could have done with all he'd given me! All he asked for in return was academic achievement and obedience, "and is that *so goddamned much to ask?*"

On some level it wasn't—and I pretty much did what I could to comply. But for him, nothing short of perfection would do. I stood with him one afternoon on our concrete terrace, proudly showing him the ninety-seven I'd gotten on a math test. "Why isn't it a hundred?" he asked, smiling but not really joking as the paper flapped in the breeze. It was clear that if I wanted my life to go on with any kind of peace and joy, failure would not be an option, a lesson that became a kind of organizing principle for everything I did going forward.

So what am I to do about surfing? The only way I could achieve even a basic competence would be to practice, but that alone presented a challenge. Surfing wasn't like jogging or even tennis or golf, where equipment and facilities—public courts and courses, driving ranges, the concrete walls of handball courts against which to hit a ball—were readily available. Aside from the somewhat difficult matter of buying and storing a wetsuit and a board, there was the need for a large body of water with rideable waves, something in short supply in the middle of New York City.

Despite all that, I was determined to figure out how to take the lessons I sorely needed. I lived far from the ocean and had a demanding day job and only intermittent access to a car. I owned a barely used silver Honda SUV that I'd bought in California and loved, but it spent most of its time on the Upper West Side with my sister, who lived in the apartment where we grew up. She hadn't left home for college but instead attended St. John's in Queens, where our father had gone, and then followed in my mother's footsteps to become a gifted public school teacher. After getting master's degrees in education at Bank Street and Harvard and specializing in early childhood development and teaching, she was now back in New York, pursuing her doctorate at CUNY. Given her studies, she didn't have a lot of extra cash or time, and she was managing the care of our father, a widower then in his nineties who could barely see and needed help with basic daily functions. The car had been an offering on my part to lighten her burden—make it easier to grocery shop, run errands, escape to the Paramus, New Jersey, malls where my mother had taken us on weekends—as well as assuage my guilt over not doing more to help.

It occurred to me that there must be someplace closer to Bed-Stuy where I could take lessons—maybe Long Beach or somewhere else not too far out on Long Island that I could get to by train. Late one night tooling around on the Internet, I came across a business called New York Surf School, located near an A train stop in the Rockaways.

The *Rockaways*? I hadn't even noticed there was surfing when I was blithely eating fish tacos at Bob's earlier in the summer. The neighborhood where the school taught was near his, and I couldn't believe my luck in finding it. It appeared to be one of only two programs anywhere close to Brooklyn. They taught kids and adults in individual and small-group sessions, it wasn't break-the-bank expensive, and I could get there on the subway. The school's low-tech website felt friendly to me, and I saw pictures that included lots of smiling female students, some who even looked near my age. I figured I'd splurge on a few private lessons and then maybe try out the groups. After I paid online, I texted with a guy named Frank, who ran the school, to schedule my first session for a Saturday a few weeks later.

I woke up at about seven that morning to a storm raging outside the window behind my bed overlooking Atlantic Avenue, even at that hour a clogged, multichannel artery of speeding cars and trucks. Charcoal clouds stained the pearl-gray sky, rain bounced hard off the concrete alley downstairs, wind whipped tree limbs over the metal mesh fence that separated my building from an empty lot. I texted Frank, wondering if the lesson would still be on and if I should start heading out.

"We surf in the rain!!!" came the response, though he suggested I wait a little to allow it to let up. *Of course you do,* I thought, burrowing back under the covers. *You're going to be wet anyway.*

An hour later I slipped out of bed, pulled on a bathing suit, got dressed, and packed a towel, underwear, and a water bottle into my bag. *I can't believe I'm doing this,* I thought with a kind of mad excitement as I began making a smoothie and espresso to take with me, surprised that I wasn't using the excuse of bad weather to talk myself out of going, that I was actually following through. Part of me ached to climb back into bed. But a bigger part was pushing me out into the wet, convinced that what lay beyond the soggy walk past the discount shops, food markets, storefront churches, and the old Slave Theater to the A train would be something to help fill the yawning chasm of my solitary weekend. That alone made it worth the foray.

The rain had nearly stopped, but it was still cold and gray by the time the train climbed the tracks from underground and headed toward an elevated station, marking the passage from Brooklyn to Queens. I'd been traveling for forty minutes already and I still had a whole 'nother borough to go. I watched as the train wound through the outer urban landscape, row after row of two- and three-story houses, a jumble of pentagons, squares, and triangles rendered in brick, stone, and vinyl siding.

We headed past Aqueduct Racetrack, crossing high over the Brooklyn-Queens Expressway toward Howard Beach and Kennedy airport, and it hit me how far I was from the city I knew. It wasn't even the same Rockaway I'd visited over the summer: instead of going toward the wealthy, suburban west end near Jacob Riis, this time I was aiming for the center of the peninsula, connected to the rest of the city by a different bridge and train trestles that led to the more densely populated high-rise neighborhoods that rub shoulders with Long Island. Suddenly the landscape shifted, with strands of marsh grass and scrub brush poking up between the train tracks and becoming thickets lining the passageway as we crossed into the wildlife refuge that surrounds Jamaica Bay. I caught glimpses of houses built on docks, boat hulls stretching over backyards, ducks and swans floating behind a fleeting screen of tree branches and vines just beginning to hint at turning from green to gold and russet as we rumbled through Broad Channel. Finally the Rockaway Peninsula came into view.

I suppose I should have known there could be surfing there. If you imagine the entirety of Long Island as a giant fish, with Brooklyn and Queens as the head swooping underneath Manhattan and the Bronx toward Staten Island and New Jersey to the southwest, its body and tail would stretch one hundred miles northeast into the Atlantic. Montauk would sit at the southeastern tip of its tail, and the Rockaway Peninsula would form the bottom of its jaw, with Jamaica Bay filling its open mouth. The underside of that jawbone would rest against the ocean, unprotected from the Atlantic's might —the last barrier between the city and the sea.

Swinging east toward the enormous Far Rockaway housing developments that appeared in the distance, the train trundled past the brick apartments of a public housing complex and the small-scale, new-urbanist dwellings of Arverne by the Sea, a sprawling urban renewal project that was transforming vacant lots between the train trestle and the ocean into something reminiscent of *The Truman Show*. At last we screeched to a stop at Beach Sixty-Seventh Street, where I disembarked, my butt, hips, and legs stiff from sitting so long. I gingerly descended to the damp, deserted street and made my way past traffic lights hooded in tattered black plastic to a patchwork of white- and beige-sided houses with aqua- and celery-colored doors and huge piles of dirt that loomed behind blue plywood construction barriers. At last I came to a narrow path of sand that led between wind-whipped juniper bushes up and over a hill to the beach.

"Hey, howya doin'?" a dark-haired man in a black wetsuit called out as he hustled up the dune and approached me. "Are you Diane?"

It was Frank. He was neither young nor tremendously athletic-looking, but he was enthusiastic, with an easy smile, thinning salt-and-pepper hair, and kind hazel eyes. He directed me up to the boardwalk and down to the beach, where I found the other student who had made it out that day, a slim young woman with dirty-blond hair, and an instructor named Kevin, a wiry, fair-skinned, fair-haired fellow with a no-nonsense manner.

The summer season had already ended and there were no concessions or bathrooms, so after selecting our gear from a tangle of wetsuits, booties, and gloves on the sand, my fellow student and I suited up on the beach. She pulled her own nimble-looking, off-white board out of a protective sleeve and headed into the water with Frank while I stayed back with Kevin, going through a brief warm-up, a few basics of water and board safety, and the pop-up. He said he'd be pushing me into the waves, but he wanted me to paddle to help get going.

We walked over to the board, which lay in the sand like a toppled megalith. Eleven feet long, it was at least two feet wide, maybe four inches thick at the center, and covered in a dense chartreuse-colored sponge soft enough to keep me from hurting myself—or anyone else who might get near me. Most surfing injuries result from haphazard contact with a board or fin, my instructors told me—someone else's or your own. Surfboards, generally fashioned from a Styrofoam-type material that's cut and planed and sanded before being wrapped in tough layers of fiberglass cloth and resin, are engineered to be lightweight but hard, and need surprisingly little force to cause a whole lot of hurt.

But this was a beginner board, no doubt about it, with each of its elements aimed at staying safe and making it easier to catch waves and remain steady in them. The overall size—known as volume in surf-speak—would help it float, meaning it would take less paddle effort to get it moving than a shorter, narrower, thinner board. The fat, smooth curve of the side edges, called rails, along with the rounded tail and nose, would make it easier to keep the beast traveling along a line, especially given the soft, "mushy" waves that Rockaway was known for. All of that surface area in the water, though, would make it harder to execute sharp turns and would create drag as it moved, slowing it down—which wouldn't be so bad for someone just starting out. Except for being a surfboard with fins and a leash, it had practically nothing to do with the thin, curvy shortboards professionals tend to use, their sharper rails, more extreme slopes, elaborate fin setups, and pointier ends all meant to help build speed and allow for more radical maneuvers on bigger, faster waves that rise at steep angles or form hollow curls.

I had been on a long soft-top in Montauk, too, but this thing seemed even more hulking—the Big Green Monster, I'd already named it. I leaned over to grab it, but its sheer size and weight daunted me, and it slipped from my hands to land back in the sand with a thud. "Let me get that for you," Kevin said, smiling and smoothly hoisting it under one arm like a light jacket. "It takes some getting used to."

We made our way into the gray-brown water, which was choppy

but not rough and seemed lacking in much of what had been scary in Montauk. Rock jetties sectioned the ocean along that stretch, but the bottom was almost entirely sand. We walked out, with Kevin guiding the board, showing me how to hold it near the nose and punch it through the waves as they crested.

We were about waist-deep when he turned the board toward the shore and told me to climb on. Again I struggled to haul myself into the proper position. Kevin said that instead of grabbing the rails and trying to pull myself across, I should put my hands flat on the top of the board, called the deck, and push up through my arms and chest to create the room and momentum to launch myself on top. I looked at him, uncomprehending.

"Here, I'll show you," he said, demonstrating what he meant with feline ease. "It keeps the board a lot more stable that way." Then I tried. I understood exactly what he'd done, but, like seemingly everything else in surfing, I just didn't have the strength or coordination to pull it off.

After a couple of tries I managed to belly-flop onto the board, like a flounder. Kevin stood in front of me, holding the nose, pale-blue eyes scanning the horizon. "Okay, here it comes," he said, stepping around the side of the board and guiding it forward. "Start your paddle, please."

I began to stroke, windmilling my arms through the water, but it felt like I was at a standstill. "Keep paddling," he said. Finally the board started to slide forward and sharply accelerated. "Up-up-up-up-up-up-up!" he shouted.

I stopped stroking, pushed up from the board, and for just a second stood, still looking down at my feet on the chartreuse deck, gray water swirling around me as I defied the physics of my normal life and recaptured the childhood feeling of *wheeeeee* that was once as accessible as a playground slide. And then I splashed into that water as the board continued to hurtle toward the shore. But just as in Montauk, that tiny moment was exhilarating. I could barely remember ever feeling that free.

We went on for a few more waves, and then Kevin decided to move us out a little deeper, closer to where the other student sat on her board with Frank near the end of the jetty, where the waves were cresting and beginning to roll across the section before breaking. A wave started to rise behind her. She turned toward the shore, fell flat on the board, and paddled furiously. I could see the wave lifting the tail of her board as Frank leaned in over her, screaming, "Paddle harder! Give it all you got!"

If she caught it, I realized, we would be in her path, but Kevin didn't seem concerned. "Do we need to get out of the way?" I asked.

"Don't worry," he said. "She's not going anywhere."

She wasn't, it turned out—*How did he know that?*—but neither was I. I was getting to my feet, but I could stay there for only a second or two before tumbling off the board. It wasn't at all scary or painful, but I was beginning to feel frustrated and wondered if I would ever manage to get a longer ride. I was running out of stamina, too, with my arms and shoulders aching from my efforts. We took a break, heading back to the beach so I could rest and have some water. I didn't have too many more attempts in me, I told Kevin, so he suggested I stop trying to paddle and just concentrate on getting into a better standing position.

We went back out and that did it. By the time we were done I'd gotten two solid rides, swooping along the wave toward the shore, standing on the Big Green Monster long enough to look up and see the line of oceanfront homes getting closer as I went. I was elated.

I was also exhausted. "I'm not sure I have the strength to get this wetsuit off," I told Kevin, laughing as we walked up the beach.

"That's how you want to feel," he said. "You never want to leave a session looking back at the ocean."

Words to live by. We got to the neoprene pile, and as Kevin began packing up, I slowly pulled off the wetsuit, noticing that even though it was heavy with water, it felt more pliant than when I'd put it on. Shivering in the damp air, I wrapped my towel around me and headed up to the boardwalk, figuring it would be easier to change out of my bikini on the benches, their wood warped and dark-green paint blistered by the elements. I brushed the sand from my feet and dried off as best I could—which is to say not well—and then, loosely swathed in the towel, pulled off my bathing suit and pulled my underwear and clothing over my moist, grudging flesh, imagining that I was inadvertently giving the good people of Arverne a late-morning show with the occasional flash of boob or butt cheek. Finally decent, I put on my socks and shoes, feeling the grind of sand granules between my toes, packed up my bag, and made my way back to the A train.

As we clattered through Queens, I felt a soreness settling into my body that I could tell wasn't from any kind of damage. Instead it was the hard-won, righteous soreness from going all-out chasing after something that I'd decided, entirely on my own, I wanted to do. I was proud of myself for not chickening out, for not, as usual, letting the fear of failure stop me.

The train headed back into Brooklyn, shaking, rattling, and rolling through the tunnels, speeding past the tile-clad stations named for some of the city's early leaders and landowners, and I clung to that feeling even as I sensed it slipping away. I had made some progress during the lesson—not much, but some. I was seeing just how big an effort surfing would require, and I was trying not to get disheartened. We pulled into Nostrand Avenue, and I slowly stood up from my seat and walked to the platform. As I climbed the stairs into the still-gray afternoon, feeling the strain in every overtaxed muscle, tendon, ligament, and joint, I realized that if I wanted to surf, I would need to unlearn my father's lesson: failure would have to be an option—again, and again, and again.

3

Run Aground

SEPTEMBER 2010

A FEW WEEKS LATER, JUST OVER THE CUSP INTO FALL, I was about to get another shot at improving my surfing. A friend who'd been part of the old life in Brooklyn that had so painfully slipped from my grasp was getting married over the weekend at the family estate of his bride-to-be in East Hampton, so I'd booked another surf lesson for the day after the wedding in Montauk, where I'd be staying. I'd taken Friday off from work so I could drive out early with another friend, Jen — my original connection to the groom, with whom she'd grown up in New England — and have a little time to chill before heading out for drinks with the other early arrivals and folks coming from the rehearsal dinner.

In my bedroom Thursday night, I stared at the fancy clothes strewn across my bed, contemplating what to choose for the wedding. I'd had few recent opportunities to wear any of them

—the swingy featherweight black silk shift, the shimmery champagne-colored number you could wrap in several ways, the beaded, sugary pink dupioni minidress I'd bought at a vintage shop in college, which still fit—and I was full of mixed emotions. I was excited to go surfing again, happy for the bride and groom, and looking forward to reconnecting with Jen, whom I'd gotten to know a decade earlier when she was the press secretary for a public advocate candidate in New York City and I was a baby political reporter at the *New York Times* covering the race. But I was also a little mournful, yearning for the robust, built-in social life I'd had when I was part of a couple.

When Jen and I first met, I was less than a year into trying to transform myself professionally from being a magazine editor tied to an office desk to being a reporter who spent her time out in the world. I wanted to gather and tell stories myself rather than midwife other people's explorations—but I also wanted to wrap my work life more easily around Eric's, since he was hell-bent on a career that involved foreign travel and potentially relocation.

I was lucky enough to get the chance to make that transformation at the *Times,* but it was such an intense, public undertaking that I was terrified I might not be able to pull it off. Both older and less experienced than most of my reporting colleagues, I felt like I was starting out all over again, tossing aside the reputation I'd built up over the years as an editor. I knew I'd never recover from the humiliation if I wasn't successful—I couldn't imagine continuing to work at the *Times* wearing the scarlet *F* of failure—so I threw myself at the job with everything I had. As a result, I was often wrapped up in work, overwhelmed with stress, and in the throes of a freak-out over how to approach strangers on the street, write a story in forty-five minutes or less, and handle the relentless intrusions of my editors, known simply as the Desk. At the same time, Eric had become the foreign policy director at Bill Clinton's post-presidential foundation, a dream job after years of toiling away at a series of small international nonprofits, but one that kept him overseas much of the time and practically sucked him inside his BlackBerry when he came home.

I sensed yet couldn't face that something between us was withering, that there was an ineffable emotional connection that we weren't tending. But as we floated atop the Brooklyn housing bubble, trading one beautiful brownstone apartment for another, it all looked so right that I kept convincing myself I could make it *be* right, that we would find a way back to the closeness and intimacy we'd once had. Eric seemed committed to us, too, and after ten years of dating, in the fall of 2002, we finally wed.

Not long after, our real estate machinations allowed us to buy a brick townhouse in Carroll Gardens, the culmination of a dream of gracious living I'd had since childhood. The block was relatively charmless—it was nearly barren of trees and dead-ended in an oil depot that sat on a polluted and moldering canal—but inside, the house was lovely. It had hundred-year-old floors the color of maple syrup, white stone mantels, pressed-tin ceilings, and a big garden out back. Living there was to be the beginning of a homier life together. It was a place we could fix up, and one where maybe we could start a family. One night, over wine in the front parlor, which we hadn't yet figured out how to use, much less decorate, we decided I should go off the pill and let nature take its course.

I'd hit the jackpot, I thought. I had somehow landed a handsome, charming husband who liked the same things I did—a garden filled with vegetables and flowers, vintage-modern furnishings, high-end food and wine—and wanted to stay with me forever. I'd never need to date again, I crowed to myself, to go out there in search of a man who'd actually be attracted by my nerdy, gawky ways.

We spent weekends in the suburbs or Manhattan, prowling for furnishings and kitchen notions, or out in the garden, hacking away at misplaced juniper bushes and awkward trees, replacing them with roses and vegetable beds. Jen, a tiny, whip-smart, hilarious brunette, was part of that, too. She and I had become fast friends during that

2001 campaign and later neighbors when she moved in with a boyfriend around the corner from Eric and me. We saw them regularly, out in the neighborhood or at our place or theirs, often with a coterie of the interesting and connected literary, political, and nonprofit folk who populated the area.

Yet Eric and I continued to drift apart. I can't say exactly where we went off the rails, but I know it didn't help that both of us kept paying too much attention to our jobs and social lives and not enough to each other or to making a family. It wasn't that things ever got actively bad: even when we were snappish we mostly managed to enjoy each other. That allowed us, or at least allowed me, to mistake having a good time for being happy. But it turned out that we were all along letting a collection of slights and disappointments accrete like barnacles on the hull of our romance, slowing the momentum until we could no longer move forward together.

In the end it was Eric who figured it out first and triggered our demise. It was 2007, I was forty-two, and we'd finally gotten serious about having children. Unable to conceive on our own, we'd started down the road to IVF by picking a fertility center and taking a few preliminary steps, like providing a sperm sample and making sure my fallopian tubes were unblocked. Eric had just been offered a new job overseeing the sustainable development arm of a global mining financier based in Vancouver, a job that promised a saner work life and that I thought could give us a chance to right our ship. I was in the kitchen getting ready to make a celebratory meal that involved center-cut pork chops and a bottle of our favorite champagne when he came home.

I opened the champagne and poured us both glasses. We had a toast, and then I pulled the chops from the refrigerator. "We need to talk," he said behind me, tightly. I turned to face him. "I don't want to try to have a kid right now. I think we need to work on our relationship."

"Okay," I said, feeling confused, but not much more. "What does that mean, exactly?"

"I'm not happy," he said. "Are you happy with the way things are?"

"Well, not entirely, but I thought we would be able to make things better once you changed jobs."

"I know, but I feel like we're in crisis."

"I don't know that we're in crisis. Things maybe aren't great, but I feel like we can fix them."

"I think we should go to counseling. And I just don't want to try to have a kid until we get things sorted."

I stood there with my champagne, feeling stupid, with a furious bile starting to bubble up from my gut and burn the back of my throat. While I'd been happily shopping and planning a nice evening to usher us toward the next phase of our shared enterprise, he'd been going over in his head how he was going to tell me we were on the brink of falling apart. *How could I not see this coming?* I wanted to hurl the flute across the room, make the shattering crystal a sonic expression of my shattering heart. Instead I drained the glass and poured another one. "I don't think I can cook now," I said, putting the chops away. "We'll just have to go out."

We finished the champagne and then kept drinking at a little Italian place a few blocks away. I told him that I'd go to couples counseling, even though I had the suspicion that it would simply make an inevitable breakup a little kinder.

"I mean, what do you want?" I asked at some point, my head hot and buzzing with anger, hurt, and alcohol. "Do you want a divorce?"

"I don't know."

I looked at him, the broad planes of his face illuminated by a flickering votive candle between us, his eyes in shadow, darkened pits sunk into his skull and unreadable to me. Suddenly the entire room seemed to recede behind him—the exposed brick walls, long wood bar, and small tables brimming with other Brooklyn couples folding in on themselves. I knew I needed out, needed to be anywhere but here, going through the motions of a normal dinner with this man on whom I'd staked my future but who now didn't know if he wanted to be with me. "I've got to get out of here," I said, standing up, choking back tears. "I just can't be around you right now." I turned and walked unsteadily to the street, wondering where exactly I was going, crying into the night. I'd just walked out on my husband, leaving him stunned and uncomfortable in a restaurant where we were regulars—and I certainly couldn't handle going home.

So I walked: up and down the commercial strip, through a few of the tree-lined blocks I'd always thought were pretty, over to the Gowanus Canal and across a cobblestone bridge to the edge of Park Slope on the other side. No longer crying, I stared at the water, at the bundle of wood pilings jutting up at its edge, and at the snaking path of the current in the moonlight as it fed south along the industrial waterfront toward the harbor. How many years I'd invested in this neighborhood, I thought, chasing after an imaginary life, and for *what*? To end up rejected and alone, rattling around the house, where the beams of sunlight refracted through leaves outside the six-foot parlor windows onto every beautiful detail—the vintage floorboards, the plaster moldings—would be like arrows pointing toward all I had reached for and lost. If we split up, there would be no babies, no dogs, no fantastic backyard dinner parties of prime local meats and homegrown produce with our oh-so-entertaining and like-minded friends and their kids. *And then who will I be?*

I'd been with Eric for so long that I couldn't see what life would be without him, couldn't fathom having to try to date. I'd never been very good at it when I was young, and now I felt headed out to pasture: too old for most men near my age, and possibly unable to bear a child. He'd have no trouble at all finding someone else, I thought bitterly. He's a guy, after all—successful, attractive, younger, and still fertile. The trees rustled overhead. It was as if they were laughing at me.

It should have been obvious that night that it was over, but it took me months to accept it. Eric moved to Vancouver for the job but came back every few weeks for our couples counseling as we debated whether I should join him there. On a gray morning in November, during one of his increasingly rare returns to Brooklyn, we stood together in the kitchen, gazing out over the back deck at the one tree we had preserved in the garden: a dogwood that bloomed a dark and extraordinary green-veined pink, fading to white over a few spring weeks. The garden was misty and quiet except for the familiar and hopeful chirping of birds. Standing next to Eric, I turned and leaned in to kiss him, and he presented me his cheek.

We separated for good soon after that, committed to treating each other as well as we could in ending what had once felt like a tremendous shared love. Distraught and embarrassed, I could barely reach out to my friends. It wasn't just the dissolution of the marriage and the prospect of disappointing my father that shamed me—"Diane, you've made me very proud," he had said at the wedding, the only time he ever did so—but my own inability to see it coming. I had always thought of myself as emotionally clear-eyed and resilient, someone valued by relatives and friends for my independence and stability, rather than as one of those women who loses her way in an unhappy relationship. But that's exactly what I was, and I couldn't get over how unclearly I had seen myself, like the anorectic girl who registers only flab in her reflection. I spent many nights seeking solace in the company of good wine alongside a bamboo steamer of dumplings or a bowl of meatballs at the bar of one hipster boîte or another, always making sure I had a book to read, trying to project a vaguely Parisian image. It was just a cover, a thin veil barely masking the fact that I was a sad and lonely woman with no one to go home to, feeling too unloved and pathetic to try to start up with anyone new. I'd wake up and cry each morning, with the sensation that my body was too heavy to drag out of bed, every muscle trying to curl itself back into the mattress. *How could I let this happen?* I'd think. *Why didn't we try to fix it earlier?* And, *When will I stop feeling like such a loser?*

In fits and starts—and with the help of regular therapy sessions

—I eventually did begin participating in my life again. I started dreaming of an escape in the form of a John S. Knight fellowship at Stanford, which at that time awarded journalists an academic year to study whatever they wanted, and began laying the groundwork with my editors to apply. By the spring I'd begun to feel stable enough to start sharing my ordeal with friends. One day I stood outside City Hall—I was by then the bureau chief in charge of covering the mayor—looking south at the swaying grasses, sprightly flowers, and spray of the park's fountain sparkling in the sunlight, with a BlackBerry stuck to my ear, and told Jen how Eric and I had let our relationship fray and were divorcing. She listened, asked probing yet sensitive questions, and gave me sympathy and comfort. Conversation stopped for a moment and I heard a sharp intake of breath. "So," she said, "would now be a bad time to ask you to be one of my chuppah holders?"

I burst out laughing. Of course it was, and yet it wasn't. I loved Jen, and since she was genuinely happy to be marrying the man who seemed like the right guy to settle down with, I was happy for her. And miserable though I felt, I was thrilled she wanted me to be part of the inner circle of her future.

At Jen's wedding reception, on a historic farm in Massachusetts, I found myself standing in the dark near a stone fountain with Ben, a friend I'd met through Jen who also lived in Brooklyn. I'd always enjoyed talking with him, but we'd both been married—happily, I wrongly presumed in both cases—and then suddenly, at the wedding, we weren't.

That night, as I looked up at him in the hazy nimbus of candles and starlight, I noticed how lean and firm he was, the fineness of his features, how his straight light-brown hair swooped down over his brow. The deep, satisfying rumble of his laugh. I could feel a kind of electric nervousness between us, and I had the distinct impression that something could happen that night. But he had to get going, he said, to make the drive back to Boston, where he was staying.

Nothing happened for almost a year, during which I'd see him from time to time at some Brooklyn gathering or other. But after one of them, when we'd run into each other at a book reading and then headed out with a group for dinner, he emailed, suggesting we have a drink. *Is this a date?* I wondered as I walked from my house to the bar, leaves and branches of the stately oaks and London plane trees gently rustling overhead. *My god, he's cute,* I remember thinking as I looked across the cramped little wood table at him. We spent most of the time dissecting our failed relationships, but it wasn't obvious to me that it was indeed a date until he told me about a recent medical emergency when doctors had had to replace a tube he'd had inserted during college to relieve pressure from a benign tumor near his brain stem.

"So you have—wait, is it a stent or a shunt?" I asked him. "My father had to have one of those put into his heart to keep a valve or something open."

"That's a stent," he said, chuckling. "I have a shunt."

"And it goes from your brain to where, exactly?"

"Here, I'll show you," he said, reaching across the table to grab my hand and trace the tube, surprisingly thick, that ran beneath his skin from his head down into his neck and chest. I was simultaneously taken aback and sucked in by the sudden intimacy of it— here, finally, was man-flesh beneath my fingertips—but I was also so long out of the dating game that I just didn't know how to respond.

Luckily, I didn't need to. He walked me home, and in front of my stoop in the sodium glow of the streetlights, he kissed me. It was chaste as kisses go, but so soft, tender, and urgent I almost swooned.

Over the next few weeks we had a number of great dates and progressively steamy make-out sessions. When we eventually did have sex, it was fine—Ben certainly did his part to enhance the proceedings—but I just couldn't stay inside myself long enough to focus and really enjoy it. It was the first time I'd even been naked with someone other than Eric since my twenties, and it was almost as if I were Annie Hall in bed, persuaded to skip her customary precoital joint — sitting outside my own body and watching the proceedings, thinking, *Well, now, fancy that.*

Nothing much ever came of our entanglement. We liked each other, sure, but I had gotten the fellowship and was about to head off to California for the better part of a year, which put a damper on things. We stayed friendly after, but the romance was just not to be.

. ■ ■ ■

Two years later Jen was divorced just like I was and had moved to Boston. I, too, had given up my lingering claims on the neighborhood we'd shared in Brooklyn and had sold the townhouse. She was flying into JFK for the East Hampton wedding and staying with me in Montauk. Friday morning, as I sat at the curb of a dingy arrival area at the airport, worrying over a Google Map printout of the maze of onramps and feeder roads and minor arteries that would get us to the highway, I heard a sharp *rat-a-tat-tat* on the passenger-side window and looked up to see Jen, a big, excited smile on her face that made her mahogany eyes scrunch up and instantly dissolved my anxiety.

"Oh my god, remember when we first met and I almost killed you?" she said, laughing as she climbed in and pulled out her phone to help shepherd us on our way. When we'd met during that long-ago political contest, she had come to pick me up in Brooklyn in the campaign's rickety eggplant-colored van at the crack of dawn to attend a press conference in Upper Manhattan. We'd had some tricky merges onto the BQE and the Major Deegan Expressway, but I'd never truly felt like my life was in danger. Now we were whizzing out to the End, both with wrecked marriages behind us and no real prospects ahead. But at least the road through Long Island was straight and clear and open, and by noon we'd arrived in Montauk and stopped for lunch at an old family-owned lobster pound overlooking Fort Pond Bay.

"So have you been in touch with Ben at all?" I asked her when we were seated with beers and lobster rolls at a white plastic table on a dock.

"No, I haven't been in touch with much of anyone lately, but I think he'll be there tonight."

"Yeah, I haven't seen him in almost a year. He picked me up in Bed-Stuy and we drove to some incredibly delicious hole-in-the-wall he knows in Flushing. Little Hot Pepper, I think."

"Ben always had good taste in food."

After lunch we headed to the Beachcomber, where I'd stayed at the beginning of the summer. We hung out on our oceanfront balcony and previewed our outfits for the weekend. She was due that evening at the rehearsal dinner, and she called a taxi for the trip to East Hampton so I could have a break from driving. After a nap and a leisurely shower, I drove into town to a restaurant I'd discovered during my week there. Not quite ready to deal with everyone, I hadn't tried to connect with any of the other early arrivals, preferring to be by myself with a plate of wild striped bass and a glass of rosé from a winery a few towns over. I liked the whole group a great deal, a collection of smart, politically engaged progressives whom Jen and the groom had gotten to know through literary, activist, and education networks. But they were all so coupled-up, as I had been when I met them, and I needed to steel myself for the endless conversations about married life and childrearing that by definition, though not intent, excluded me, and to be prepared to answer questions about my postdivorce self with all the hope and cheerfulness the occasion called for. I still didn't have a very good answer for why my marriage had disintegrated—or whether or how I planned to try to have a kid—and just the idea of talking about any of it deflated me, dredging up the mortifying sense I still carried that it was a grand disaster of my own making. We were gathering to wish the happy couple bon voyage as they set sail on what we all genuinely wished would be a lifelong journey, and it just wouldn't do to bring along a big sack of shit labeled SELF-PITY.

I looked around the restaurant, noting the dangling Edison

bulb fixtures, tropical beach-shack decor, and chatty crowd of well-exfoliated young couples and sunburned families in khakis and sweaters and bracelets made of braided string. It was a familiar role for me, the loner observing the crowd, to all appearances part of the scene, but not quite. That was how I'd often gotten by while growing up in a tumultuous household, watching, conciliating, retreating, holding in all the tension while others set theirs free. It was also how I'd spent much of my time as a journalist, especially over the past several months on the hospitality beat: out among the patrons of the city's hangouts but on the outside, watching snippets of other people's lives unfold. But, I reminded myself, I was at the start of something new and pursuing a sport I'd never even considered before, and that was giving me hope: hope that there was still something out there for me, that I could find happiness again.

Things could be a lot worse, I thought as I surrendered my barstool and made my way to the car. *This does not suck.*

Twenty minutes later I was sitting in the darkened car across the street from the pub in Amagansett where the bride and groom and rehearsal-dinner folks were to meet up with the rest of us. The dinner was running late, so I was stalling before heading inside, worrying that I wouldn't know anyone and wanting to avoid awkward small talk. Some little internal voice, though, was prodding me to just get out and face it. No amount of hesitating was going to change the fact that I had to navigate my life on my own, and I might as well get on with trying to enjoy it.

I was about to climb down from the driver's seat and head into whatever awaited me when I saw Ben. He was getting out of a small red hatchback parked in front of me and stood for a few seconds until an attractive blonde appeared by his side. He casually draped his arm over her shoulders, and the two of them slowly crossed the street toward the bar. I was long over our dalliance and pretty sure I had no real interest in him, and yet that sight sent a shockwave through my system, a rolling sensation of sadness and longing and deprivation that pinned me to my seat.

Breathe, I told myself, *just breathe.* I don't know how long I sat there—five minutes or twenty—before I felt I could go in and face them all. It wasn't so much him that I was craving but what he and she and seemingly everyone at the wedding had except for Jen and me: someone else in their lives, someone to understand them, hold them, love them, listen to them, fuck them, advise them, help them, support them. I didn't, and had no concrete reason to believe I ever would again. It was lousy to be single, and no matter how much I kept telling myself I was going to be okay on my own, and better that way than with the wrong man, no matter how many times I ran myself into a weeping, heaving exhaustion with Whitney Houston wailing into my earbuds "I'd rather be alone than unhappy," I was so full of want right then I felt I could explode. I couldn't help but wonder, *When, when, when, when, WHEN do I get to be the girl on someone's arm again?*

■ ■ ■

Sunday morning I awakened to a raging hangover, my head throbbing, body sore, tongue sticky with paste. The wedding, at the bride's oceanfront family estate at the end of a long driveway off an exclusive lane in East Hampton, had been a beautiful, elaborate affair and, despite my trepidation, a great time all around. People had been so interested to hear about my newfound obsession with surfing—and to share tales and frustrations about their own beloved activities—that I hadn't had to talk about my relationship status at all. But there had been free-flowing champagne, which I, like Liz Imbrie, one of the journalist outsiders in *The Philadelphia Story,* had never had enough of, so I predictably drank way too much.

Now I climbed gingerly out of bed and looked at the ocean. The weather was overcast and misty, but I could just make out some rough, medium-sized waves. I was due at my surf lesson by nine, so I didn't have much time. Jen was curled up on the sofa bed, reading, and said she'd be okay by herself there for a few hours before we went to the final brunch reception and then back to Brooklyn. I made some espresso, ate half a bowl of granola, grabbed some water, and got into the car.

I drove along the highway and through town, the road still damp in the heavy morning air. I turned right toward the beach, made my way to the East Deck Motel, and pulled into a driveway across the street, where I was to meet my instructor, John.

I walked past a long surfboard lying in the yard of a big brown split-level and knocked. "Hey," a guy said, peering through the screen door. "You must be Diane."

"Yes," I said with a start, realizing that he was so hot I would have a hard time looking at him. I had noticed him teaching another student when I was out with Sean in Montauk earlier that summer but had been so freaked out in the water that I hadn't registered quite how good-looking he was. He had thick sandy-brown hair pulled back in a short, low ponytail and broad, high cheekbones bronzed from a summer in the sun. He stood about my height, with brown eyes and a chiseled chin hovering above the mounds and hollows of his bare, heavily muscled shoulders and chest, all leading down to what seemed like a half-healed scrape on his rib cage, just above the waistband of his sweatpants.

Look away! I heard myself screaming in my head. *Get ahold of yourself!* I did, taking a deep breath, willing myself to focus on why I was there.

"Let me get you a suit and I'll meet you outside."

He came out and noticed the board in the grass. "Oh, wow, I didn't realize he dropped it off!" he said, excited, handing me a wetsuit. He knelt over the board and picked it up, turning it this way and that, running his fingers over its shiny surface to land on a repaired spot that looked like a smudge of ivory in a pale-blue expanse on the bottom. "Wow, he did a great job. I can't wait to get this back out in the water."

John headed inside as I pulled off my T-shirt and cutoff denim skirt and began to struggle into the wetsuit. He was back out in what seemed like an instant, having traded the sweatpants for a gray wetsuit pulled up to the waist. We chatted as I tried with middling success to keep my eyes focused on my task and away from his chest. He was Kristin's cousin and had grown up elsewhere on Long Island, a family friend of her partner, Corey from the surf school. The house was his grandmother's, so he was able to spend summers there and had been surfing since childhood, he said as he pulled up the top of his suit. "We were just really lucky to have this," he said more than once.

We walked across the street and through the dirt parking lot to the beach. He grabbed two big soft-top boards from an array leaning up against a dune and headed into the water, waiting for me about shin-deep to catch up and take one of them. The water was cold and choppy and I felt unstable on the rocks, but some combination of my hangover fog and the smidgen of progress I'd made at the lesson in Rockaway was dulling the edge of my fear.

"I know this was supposed to be a whitewater lesson," he said as I tried to ferry the board out into the slop. "But I don't believe in that. We're going outside."

I wasn't well versed in surf terms, so I thought we were already outside, but I soon realized that he meant something other than outdoors: rather than stay closer to the beach and try to catch the foam from waves that had already broken, we would go beyond that, "outside," to catch the waves as they peaked, as I had done with Kevin in Rockaway. But with John on a surfboard rather than standing in front of me in the water, I realized that I'd have to handle myself and the board on my own. The old dread-knot began to coil in my belly. The waves suddenly seemed bigger and more menacing than what I'd been on before, as if they could work me over as I tried to get through them. But before I had time to chicken out, I was flat on the board, following instructions to push up with my arms to get over the crests, and frantically paddling behind John, waves slapping my face as I went. Outside wasn't too far, I was happy to realize, and before long I was sitting next to him in the water, wheezing, and definitely more alert than when I'd rolled out of bed.

We quickly established a rhythm, with me straddling the board facing the shore and him sitting parallel to me, facing out to the ocean. As the waves would rise from the surface, he'd tell me when to lie down and paddle, spinning his board around and paddling alongside and just a little behind me. As the water lifted the tail of my board, he'd give me a small shove and yell for me to stand up. Surprisingly, it was going relatively well, despite the low-level ache in my head and occasional roiling of my gut. I was getting to my feet and every so often coasting for a good three or four seconds—an eternity, it seemed, in comparison to my first trip out here.

It was thrilling and fun, and though I was still too new to it all to focus on much beyond my feet and the board, I was loving the feeling of gliding over the ocean surface, propelled by that magic motor from the deep, and I didn't want it to stop. I could see the nose of the board cutting a path through the gray peaks ridged in white, rising and tipping over and swishing around me.

Eagerly I thought, *Maybe I'm starting to get the hang of this.* I wondered if I would soon be able to rent a board back in Rockaway and go out to practice by myself.

I asked John if I might be ready for such a step. "Not yet," he said. "You can't paddle fast enough to catch waves on your own."

A sobering assessment, but true. Even with him helping, my energy was flagging, my arms starting to feel like putty. I got up on the next wave and rode it until it broke, the sudden pulse of the water tossing me off. I came up and got a hold of the board to realize that John had hung back and caught the next wave: he was sliding toward me and then beyond, stepping lightly and gracefully up and down the length of the board, somehow steering it this way and that through the foam washing over the rocks. He was like some sort of aquatic twinkle-toes. I had no idea what he was up to, but I wanted to be able to move like that, too.

"Come on, let's get back out there," he said as he came back toward me, where I was standing hunched over my board, waiting for the sting of overuse to stop spreading through my shoulders as I struggled to stay upright in the whitewater.

"I need to rest for a minute."

A wave broke just in front of us, and the onslaught of its churn almost swept me off my feet.

"Okay, we can hang out here," he said sharply, water streaming from his head, "but we're just going to keep getting pounded. You can rest out there."

Irritated, I considered turning around and just heading to the beach, but something shifted for me, just as it had after I'd spotted the yellow house in June. *Don't quit just because it's hard. If you want this, you're going to have to keep trying.*

Determined to ignore my throbbing trapezius muscles, I got back on the board and paddled out, coughing up the saltwater draining from my sinuses into my throat as I made it back to where we'd been sitting. I was still struggling to sit upright in the unstable conditions, but I managed to regain my breath and a wisp of composure while John surfed a few waves. After a while I told him I was ready to try again, but probably only a few more times. He got me into a breaker, but I could stay up for only a moment. Disappointed, I thought I should try for one last wave before ending the session.

We waited for what seemed like an eternity. Finally a suitable wave gathered behind me. I paddled, he pushed, and I jumped to my feet. Riding along, I managed to stay up even as the wave broke and to coast practically all the way to the shore. As I got close to the beach, I remembered John's warning not to ride all the way in, to avoid snagging the fin or scraping the board on the rocks lining the shallows. I looked down. It wasn't too rocky yet, and the board was moving so slowly that it seemed I could just step right off. But suddenly something wiggled beneath me. I lost my balance and, trying to stay upright, quickly pivoted my body seaward. My feet, however, stayed planted, as if they were glued to the board. I felt torque and then a mild pop in my left knee that instantly became a ferocious, radiating pain as I tumbled awkwardly, lurching and spinning until I found myself, inexplicably, sitting astride the board facing out into the ocean, pantomiming a howl, and grasping my throbbing joint.

John barreled toward me from outside, paddling on his knees, yelling, "Are you okay?"

"Not yet," I said, straining to get the words out through the bilious ache. "I think I did something to my knee."

"Can you walk?"

"I think so. But I don't know why it's getting worse."

I stood up, and he took the board and deftly carried both his and mine to the shore as I hobbled onto the sand. I could indeed walk, but not for long and not at all well.

"I'll take you back to the house and you can get out of the wetsuit," he said, propping the boards back up against the dune. "Do you need help?"

"I think I'm okay," I said through gritted teeth, unwilling to surrender to the tiny jackhammers chiseling away somewhere deep in the joint, and wholly unprepared to handle physical contact with John. If I hopped on the good leg for a few paces and then just barely touched down with the bad one, I was finding, I had a shot at making it to the car without passing out.

I hopped and limped slowly through the dirt parking lot, passing a lush thicket edging the path, as John occasionally stopped to wait for me.

"You sure you're all right?" he asked.

"No, but I will be," I said, one of my stock, optimistic responses to injury. And I believed it, that I would be all right, even as I stood in John's grandmother's yard and peeled off the heavy, wet rubber to reveal a rapidly swelling knee that would no longer bend without agony. I wrapped a towel around myself and climbed into the car, using my hands to gently fold my double-sized leg into position, grateful that I wouldn't need to move it to work the pedals. I opened the sunroof and wheeled back down the road, worry beginning to creep in. *I hope I haven't done any real damage.*

I brushed it off, choosing to bask in the endorphin glow of the waves I'd ridden and focus on figuring out how to make my body more surf-ready. It wasn't just that I couldn't paddle fast enough. I couldn't do anything well enough in this sport that I'd stubbornly latched on to with a conviction born of nothing but conviction. The mind was more than willing, but the flesh—oh, the flesh was going to need a lot of work.

4

In the Shaping Bay

OCTOBER 2010–MAY 2011

IT WAS LATE OCTOBER AND I WAS LYING ON A PADDED table in one of the many small beige treatment rooms of a physical therapy clinic near Columbus Circle in midtown Manhattan while a young woman wearing a white polo shirt and khakis jiggled my kneecap and pressed gently around it with her fingertips. The pop I'd felt as my knee twisted at my last surf lesson in Montauk turned out to be a sprain of the medial collateral ligament, a fibrous rope that connects the bottom of the thighbone to the top of the shinbone and plays a major role in stabilizing the knee. It's a common enough injury, especially in contact sports, and is usually the result of a blow or a sharp twist that overstretches or even begins to tear the connective bands. The doctor wasn't overly concerned, but the ligament still hadn't healed after four boring weeks of using a cane, diligent RICE—rest, ice, compression, elevation—and gentle exercises like lying on my back and repeatedly flexing my knee against the floor, so he'd finally sent me to PT.

The young woman continued pressing, and I suddenly felt a click and a sense of relief as something settled into place.

"What was that?" I asked.

"There are all these little sacs at the joints that help keep everything moving," she said, "and sometimes they get an air bubble around them and it can inhibit normal function. Just makes things feel stuck. That's what that was—getting the air out."

Like a fart.

Over the last few weeks I'd come to approach these sessions with a mixture of enthusiasm and dread. I liked learning about the inner workings of my body and getting back on a path toward the fitness and physical confidence I'd had in my youth, back when I was a decent dancer—balanced and graceful, with an ear for the music and enough ability to contort myself into most positions the choreography called for. The dance studio had been one place where my height felt like an asset, giving me the long lines dance teachers and choreographers find praiseworthy, rather than a thing I'd always tried to minimize, whether by wearing flats or by standing with one hip thrust to the side so I could be roughly on the same level as everybody else.

I'd stopped dancing in college but had tried to remain active, going for the occasional run along the river near campus or swimming laps in a pool. Except for the height, I'd always been fairly comfortable with how my body looked, but wanted to keep pushing what it could do. Shortly after I graduated, I was in a car accident that left me with a concussion, a broken cheekbone, a wrenched back, some cracked teeth, and a lingering sense of my body as fragile, a thing I needed to handle with great care—a sense of vulnerability I never shed.

Once I'd recovered—and found myself weak and closing in on 190 pounds—I slowly got fitter, intermittently swimming, running, and working out in the gym. As a result, the exercises I performed out on the shiny maple rehab floor felt as comfortable as an old shoe: leg lifts and step-ups with my ankle tethered to one or another color-coded elastic band, bright pops of cheer in an otherwise colorless environment.

But then there was the hands-on segment: agonizing, allegedly therapeutic manipulations that felt anything but and left me on occasion with bruises stippling my thigh. Contributing to my pain, my therapist said, was tightness in my quad and iliotibial, or IT, band, something that plagues a lot of people who run, which was about the only real exercise I'd been doing before the injury with anything approaching regularity. Another thick connector that aids in stabilizing the knee, the IT band travels from the pelvis down the outer thigh and across the knee to the shinbone and isn't easily loosened up. The prescribed cure is to roll these rigid muscles and fibers against a stiff foam tube at home and submit to massage treatment at the clinic, both of which hovered at the edge of my pain tolerance.

"When you find a spot that hurts," the therapist told me as she showed me how to roll, "just stay on it."

"For how long?" I asked.

"At least two minutes. More if you can take it." I could barely tolerate one.

No pain, no gain—in exercise it was a mantra I believed in, but PT stood for personal torture, pure and simple, and the only way to get through it was to stay focused on the imaginings that distracted me at work and animated my dreams at night. In them I would glide across a satin celadon curtain, barely conscious of the board beneath my feet, the foam of the breaking wave tickling my heels as it propelled me on and on and on. Given how slowly I was progressing with the knee, I would probably have to wait until spring to try realizing that vision, but by then I wanted to be ready. I was convinced that my injury and most of my problems in the sport —my inability to paddle, my lack of stamina, my lousy pop-up —stemmed from being weak and stiff, byproducts of putting in long hours at my desk, talking on the phone, writing, and typing. I wasn't entirely out of shape, but I was nowhere near where I needed to be.

The surfers I'd stumbled upon in Montauk had made it all look so effortless, so easy, as if their boards were magic carpets motoring them across the water, but I had come to see how deceptive that image was. "People learn to surf very quickly when they surf every day," my first instructor, Sean, had told me in Montauk. They also learn quickly when they start learning young, he might have added, since it just gets harder to teach the body new tricks as it ages.

That's true for any activity, but perhaps more so for surfing, which engages muscles practically from head to toe with combinations of motions that just don't come up in daily routines or in many other sports. As in swimming, paddling relies on muscles big and small in the arms, shoulders, chest, and back. The pop-up requires the strength and flexibility of a yogi, while steering the board demands the power and agility in the lower body—waist, hips, butt, legs, feet—of a basketball player or skier to maintain balance and position while rotating, arching, and shifting your weight around the board to extend the ride. With the heavy emphasis on paddling and springing, surfing is particularly challenging for women, who don't tend to pack the same kind of upper-body strength as men. Sports researchers comparing small groups of male and female surfers have found that women tend to pop up more slowly, a result, the researchers concluded, of less maximum strength and a lower speed in applying it—essentially deficits of force and power. Sure, an elite athlete like Tom Brady can pick up surfing later in life. But I couldn't even execute a proper push-up on my living room floor, much less in rapidly moving water while jumping up and pivoting to land in the right spot along the center line of the board.

Determined to fix that, I got in touch with Jonathan, my friend from my job at *7 Days,* who worked out with a trainer a few times a week. Jonathan said the training was the only thing that had stopped the debilitating back spasms that had laid him low over the years and had kept him from injury as he began pursuing tennis with gusto. "Rob's great—he's kind of gentle," Jonathan told me. "He just knows how to push without being an asshole, and he's cute and fun and charming."

That was enough of an endorsement for me. I made an appointment for the first Tuesday in November and, after a morning of work calls from my apartment in Brooklyn, headed to the private gym in NoHo where Rob held his training sessions. It was a little before noon when I got off the F train at the corner of Broadway and Houston and made my way toward Lafayette Street and then up a few blocks to Great Jones. It was sunny and warm for the season—probably fifty degrees—and the bright light was bathing the littered sidewalks, uneven cobblestones, old tenements, and factory-buildings-turned-expensive-apartments in a golden glow. I passed an imposing brick building that served as a shelter for homeless women and peered at a white cast-iron loft building with a blue mansard roof that wouldn't have seemed out of place in Paris. I looked up the avenue past the Greek Revival townhouses of Colonnade Row and the Renaissance-style facade of the Public Theater toward the black steel cube sculpture at Astor Place, thinking about how much time I'd spent at those crossroads.

The office for that first magazine job had been right up the street, not far from the punk-lite bustle of St. Marks Place, where I'd come with friends in high school to buy the fishnets, Sid Vicious buttons, and vintage dresses that made us—high-achieving private-school kids—feel like rebels. Working as an editorial assistant and then a junior editor, I had spent most of my time helping my bosses produce articles, but I also got to dabble in assigning and editing stories of my own. Playing at being a grown-up, I'd take writers and agents to lunch at in-the-know little hotspots and head out after work to book parties and film screenings and beers and burgers with young colleagues, feeling like we were some new incarnation of the downtown publishing folk who had toiled and eaten and drank and smoked in some of the same places we did.

After the magazine collapsed in 1990, a victim of the battered economy following the 1987 stock market crash, I spent much of my leisure time with Jonathan, often hanging out and sleeping over at the sprawling loft on Great Jones that he shared with a brilliant, hilarious writer and actor, a woman named Mo Gaffney. We were all living some version of a creative, freelance life, though mine was significantly less successful than theirs, and we had the luxury of whooping it up pretty much any—sometimes every—night of the week. At a party there in those days I'd even met Rob, the trainer, a charismatic guy with a presence much larger than his modest stature and Mediterranean good looks: dark, wavy hair, warm brown eyes, generous lips, strong jaw.

The whole neighborhood, but that block of Great Jones especially, felt like a horizontal fossil record of my social evolution, each building and stretch of pavement and bar, café, or restaurant an ever-shifting reminder of the personas and aspirations I'd tried on like so many pairs of Doc Martens back when I felt like I had an eternity to figure myself out. I was still throttled by all the disappointments in my professional and personal lives, but my pace picked up as I got closer to Rob's gym, in a building next door to Jonathan's old loft. I was excited to make progress on my curious new endeavor.

I pushed open the heavy industrial gray door, stepped into the lobby, passed the receptionist for an art gallery and rehearsal studios connected to the experimental La MaMa Theatre, and climbed the creaky, listing wood stairs to the second floor, where I was due for my first workout. I'd joined gyms and had trainers before, but I'd never been able to stick with any kind of fitness routine for long, despite how much I loved working up a good sweat. I'd go a few times, or for a few months, and feel great about it, but then I always let something else—like late nights out or looming work deadlines—get in the way.

I reached the top of the dimly lit stairs and opened the door to find something that felt more like an airy dance studio than I'd expected. Light poured in from two ten-foot windows at the back wall, offering a view of trees, fire escapes, and buildings. The floor was covered in white-speckled black matting, and there were just a few machines, along with racks of free weights, balls, ropes, and brightly colored resistance bands against a perimeter of mirrored walls. There was a bank of lockers near a coat rack and a kitchenette with shelves of towels in the front, but there wasn't much in the way of the intimidating weight machines that you'd find in a regular gym.

I waved hello to Rob, who was finishing up with another client. "Hi, Diane!" he called out. "Why don't you get changed and then I'll be right with you." I headed into one of the changing rooms and pulled off my street clothes and shoes and put on my sneakers and standard running outfit: track shorts, sports bra, man's sleeveless ribbed undershirt. When I came out, Rob ushered me into the kitchen to choose a midcentury-modern-style plastic tumbler from a multicolored stack, filled it with water, and directed me over to a corner at the back where there was a treadmill, a stationary bike, and a rowing machine.

He was as handsome as ever, though his easy smile cut deeper crinkles at the corners of his eyes. He was stunningly well built, with the definition in his chest visible beneath his T-shirt. He had developed an interest in sports and fitness early, watching his mother exercise along with Jack LaLanne on TV, and had earned a number of varsity letters. He went on to become a competitive body builder, a two-time Ironman, and a ten-time marathon finisher. After graduating from college with a bachelor's degree in exercise science, he worked as a trainer in gyms and corporate fitness programs before cofounding Great Jones Fitness. Over the years he'd gained experience in handling all sorts of clients, including lifelong jocks, type-A executives, high-strung creative sorts, and—a growing subspecialty —aging adults who'd never worked out but were suddenly afraid of falling in the street and cracking a hip.

"How's the knee feeling?" he asked.

"Pretty good—a little crunchy now and then, but it doesn't hurt if I don't stress it too much."

"Okay, good. Let's start with three minutes on the bike and see how that goes," he said, eyeing my legs and adjusting the seat height to near my waist. "Try that."

I hoisted myself clumsily onto the narrow leather triangle, fumbled with the pedals until I got the toes of my sneakers under the straps, and started pumping. I loathed stationary biking—I found it dull, and my hamstrings and quads were so weak they usually cramped up before I could get my heart rate going—but I supposed I could handle anything for three minutes.

"You don't have a lot of weight machines here," I said, panting lightly and feeling the warmth of exertion starting to pulse up my calves.

"No, we like functional exercises—sometimes with resistance or weights, but you use the muscles in the way you'd actually use them. We just think it's healthier in the long run than working, or over-working, them in isolation the way those machines can."

He asked if and how often I exercised and whether I'd played any sports. I told him that I'd been trying to swim a few times a week at a gym near my office, since I couldn't yet run.

"But I'm not an athlete at all," I said. "I always took dance instead of playing sports growing up."

"Well," he said with a chuckle and shake of his head, "that's athletic."

I suppose it is. I wondered why I'd never thought of it that way as I finished up on the bike and followed him to the middle of the floor. *Athlete.* It just wasn't a label I'd ever considered applying to myself. That was a badge reserved for people like my sister and some of my friends, who brought home ribbons and trophies and patches establishing their progress and victories and achievements, not for awkward, timid, hypersensitive kids like me who spent a lot of time in their heads and could memorize and understand and perform line after line of Shakespeare but never hit a home run, who could tease out the underlying themes in novels and classic mythology but never won a single race.

Rob handed me a four-pound medicine ball and guided me through a warm-up with it, ten reps of various motions to activate the major muscle groups with squats, twists, chops, and swings, ending with something he called "around the world," which involved drawing enormous circles in the air with the ball from above my head down to my feet. If the bike didn't get my heart rate up, this surely did: I was gasping and sweating, my whole body so slick the ball was threatening to slip from my fingers.

"This is just the warm-up?" I said as we both laughed. "Feels like the workout."

"Don't worry—we'll take it slow," he said, putting the ball back on a stand. "Let's try some hip circles."

He showed me what to do, resting his hands against a bar set on a tall metal rack and then lifting one leg out to the side and rotating it around to the back before reversing to return to the side. "Twenty on each side."

It was like the back half of a ballet *rond de jambe*—circle of the leg—in the air, a motion I'd grown up practicing, so it seemed simple enough and at first felt like a nice airy stretch. But the standing leg soon gave me trouble, with the (obviously weak) hip muscles that were working to stabilize everything screaming at me to stop.

I made it through the set, and Rob then guided me through some squats—"Lower, lower, now squeeze the glutes as you come up," he urged—before moving back to the metal rack. "Push-ups," he said as he moved the bar up a notch to rest at a level well above my waist. I braced against it and began to lower myself, already feeling the strain in my chest. "Keep your elbows in, closer to your body," he said. "Keep your head up! Bring the boobs to the bar— don't collapse into it. Good, good!"

"I don't think I can do many more of these," I said after three.

"Can you get six? I'd take that."

"Maybe."

I squeezed out eight, puffing and groaning and gritting my teeth on the last one as my shoulder and chest muscles contracted and nearly failed. He suggested a rest. I took a few sips of water, thinking I would stand there and recover, but Rob's idea of rest turned out to be something else entirely.

He pulled a small plywood board with a narrow beam running beneath it from under the rack of free weights and placed it on the floor. "Here—stand on this, and try to keep it balanced on the center. We'll go for thirty seconds."

I put the water down and stepped onto the board, but I couldn't keep it level, so I rocked from side to side. I looked up at him, frustrated. "I thought you said I could rest."

"It's an active rest," he said with a smile. "Tighten your core, and keep a little bend in the knees." As our half-minute wound down, I began to find my center and keep the board steady for almost the last seven or so seconds. *Not bad,* I thought. *There's something to all this core business.* After another round of hip circles, squats, push-ups, and active rest on the balance board, Rob grabbed a wide yellow elastic loop from a hook on the mirrored wall and then took me over to a bench to sit so he could slip it around my ankles.

"Okay, we're going to do some abductions. Basically you're just going to walk across the floor," he said, demonstrating a kind of crouching sidestep. "Stay low," he said as I stood up and begin stepping across the floor, feeling a little like a crab. "Lead with the heel—don't let those toes go first." The tension on the band didn't seem like much, but after only a few steps I could feel a distinct burning sensation building in the muscles surrounding my hips.

"Eventually we'll get you doing some explosive motions that will help with your pop-up," he said as I reached the front door and swallowed the urge to just keep going and flee to the street. "But until the knee is stronger," he continued, "I don't want you jumping. This will help build some stability in the meantime."

We followed with a set of side lunges—adduction, abduction's opposite—to strengthen my inner thighs, and then rounds of hamstring curls, arm swings with resistance bands he called swimmers, abdominal crunches, and some internal and external rotations for my rotator cuff. I could see how all of them would help my surfing, but by the time we finished I was quivering with exhaustion, even though I suspected he had taken it easy on me, feeling out my mental and physical resolve.

"So how was the workout?" he asked as he set up a table to stretch me out.

"Good—really good!" I said, meaning it as I climbed slowly onto the table. I could tell already that I would be sore in the morning, but I was almost looking forward to it. It wasn't the hurt I enjoyed, exactly, but in my teens I had developed an intimate, almost fetishized relationship with pain, quietly reveling, and feeling a bit superior, in the soreness I sensed the day after a challenging dance class. Those dull aches throughout my body were like talismans I clung to, reminders that I'd stretched a little further, strengthened muscles a little more, maybe gotten a little closer to shedding the five or ten pounds I was always looking to lose. At that age, even anorexia seemed kind of cool (though it obviously wasn't): those skinny girls with a mystical, enviable ability to control and transform their bodies through the sheer will and discipline I felt I lacked. But now I was hoping to take control of my body in a healthier way, one that would transform me into that joyful woman who surfed through my dreams.

■　■　■

"Now that things are finally warming up, we will be going out on Fridays," read the email from Frank at the surf school in the Rockaways. The coming Friday looked "to be a great day to play hookey!!"

Ooooh, that would be awesome, I thought, cataloguing my workweek to figure out if I could take the morning off and surf. It was near the end of April, and I'd just begun thinking it was time to get back in the water. I'd had an emotional roller coaster of a few months, watching my father fight off infections and the failure of various organs before fading away over two bitterly cold weeks near the start of the year, and I was desperate for some saltwater therapy —something to help flush out the pervasive memories of his decline.

I was seeing definite progress in my workouts with Rob, which had practically erased any worries I'd had about my knee. I could crab-walk across the gym—I'd progressed to a green band from the yellow—do a set of squats on the balance board while keeping it steady for the better part of a minute, get through push-ups on the bar even though it was set a few notches lower. But I was eager to see whether my results in the gym would translate into results in the water, so I jumped at the chance to go to Rockaway on Friday and signed up for a private lesson. *Start the weekend out right.*

A little before ten that morning, I descended from the elevated A train platform in Arverne to find that things there were looking up since my last visit. Even though the traffic lights were still sheathed in raggedy black plastic, there was a sprawling new suburban-style Stop & Shop just down the street from the station, and grass was starting to grow behind the white picket fences of the homes leading to the ocean.

As I reached the corner, I saw Kevin, the wiry blond who had given me the lesson on the Big Green Monster the previous fall, near the open back doors of a white van perforated along the bottom with rust. I remembered him saying, "You never want to leave a session looking back at the ocean," as I crossed to him. He was wearing a white T-shirt and a wetsuit riding his hips and standing in front of a block-long weathered blue plywood construction barrier enclosing an enormous mound of brown dirt. Now he called out in greeting, "Hey, how are ya—glad to see you back! Let me get you a suit." He turned into the van to rummage through a cat's cradle of black neoprene piled next to a stack of belly-down surfboards, their black leashes coiled around the upturned fins sticking out of the slick white undersides.

"What do you think, you're about a twelve?" he asked.

"Actually I'm probably a ten, if you have one."

"I do," he said, turning around with a suit in his hand. "Take this one."

"Thanks." I crossed the street, a spur running from a two-lane road called Shore Front Parkway, which was originally to serve as a link in an ambitious network of highways the legendary planner Robert Moses started conceiving in the 1920s to connect the southern reaches of the city to the Hamptons. The grand plan never reached full flower, and the two-mile stretch that locals sometimes called "the road from nowhere to nowhere" was the only part ever built on the peninsula. I headed up the sandy, juniper-lined path and splintering steps to the boardwalk and saw the school's leader, Frank, on the beach, racing up toward me.

"Hey, howya doin'? Good to see you, good to see you. You're booked for a private today, right?"

"Yes—and psyched to get in the water!"

"Great, great. I just gotta get some more boards, but go ahead down and suit up and we'll get you going."

I joined the small group of students in the sand to begin struggling into the wetsuit and saw that Frank's emailed prediction about the conditions had turned out to be spot-on. It was warm and sunny—maybe sixty-five degrees—and the waves were relatively smooth and peaking in the thigh- to waist-high range. The swell making those waves was traveling largely from the southeast, headed straight for the coastline, which angled to face that direction. The wind, coming from the west and southwest, wasn't very strong—maybe eleven miles per hour—so even though it was essentially blowing across the fronts of the waves as they moved, it was only enough to flick at the faces and lips, adding what surfers sometimes call texture. If the wind were coming from the same direction as the swell and toward the shore (called onshore), it would blow over the backs of the waves and have the effect of flattening out the tops, making them mushy and more difficult to catch and ride. But if the wind were offshore, or blowing directly into their fronts, it could help them stand up longer before breaking and keep the peaks sharp and the faces smooth, a condition called "clean" or "glassy."

I watched as the humps formed, sometimes one after another in groups of three, sometimes randomly out of nowhere, along what seemed to be the same latitude between the shoreline and the horizon. I'd done enough weird-hour Internet reading to understand that this reflected the location of sandbars out there—long underwater hills heaved up and packed down and groomed by the endless movement of water to and fro—and that what I was seeing on the ocean surface matched the contours of the seabed beneath. But I couldn't quite wrap my brain around a new concept I'd recently come across. What I was watching as the waves appeared, rose, and crested wasn't really water moving but something Jack London once described as a "communicated agitation." He was referring to how energy travels through the water without displacing it, a transfer through vibration from molecule to molecule until that energy reaches a critical point near the shallows that finally tips the water over—potential energy becoming kinetic energy in that last moment. "The water that composes the body of a wave does not move," London wrote in 1907, observing and eventually trying surfing in Waikiki on Oahu. "If it did, when a stone is thrown into a pond and the ripples spread away in an ever-widening circle, there would appear at the center an ever-increasing hole. No, the water that composes the body of a wave is stationary. Thus you may watch a particular portion of the ocean's surface and you will see the same water rise and fall a thousand times to the agitation communicated by a thousand successive waves." I got it, but not wholly: I hadn't made it to physics or calculus in high school, so it all felt a little too trippy to hold in my head.

However it all works doesn't matter—there are waves to ride. I quelled the urge to jump up and down with glee, knowing I needed to (a) not look like a crazy person and (b) conserve all my energy for the lesson.

"Lookin' good, lookin' good out there," Frank said as he, Kevin, and another guy came down to the beach with some equipment and a few more boards, shiny red, yellow, and blue vinyl-clad soft-tops that ranged in length from eight to ten feet, which they laid in the sand. "I think you'll need booties today, but not gloves."

There were maybe ten of us there that day, and after we picked out thick black boots, Kevin led us all through a warm-up—shoulder, hip, and knee circles, lunges, and side stretches—and began introducing the other students to the pop-up. Frank, who'd been applying textured black traction pads to the decks of the surfboards, called me over. "You don't need to go through that. Why don't you get started with Simon here?"

"Okay, cool," I said, turning to meet my instructor, a short, slope-shouldered, bald guy with electric-blue eyes that practically glowed against his sun-bronzed skin.

"Nice to meet you," he said. "Frank, which board should we take?" He had an accent I couldn't quite place, with *board* coming out as *boowaad*. It wasn't exactly old-school Brooklyn like Frank's, but it sounded like some amalgam of Long Island, Boston, and the Jersey Shore.

"That one," Frank said, pointing toward the Big Green Monster with his chin. "You're good on that, right?" he asked me.

"Sure," I said, nodding. "I need that stability."

Simon grabbed the eleven-foot board, easily hoisting it onto his shoulder, and led me out into the break. It smelled fresh and briny as I dragged my legs through the cold blue-gray water, feeling a slight chill as it seeped through the neoprene skin I was wearing, though I quickly warmed up as it began to work. Wetsuits commonly insulate against the cold by trapping a thin layer of body-heated water inside; tiny bubbles of nitrogen in the rubber foam keep that heat from escaping. We chatted a bit about how many times I'd surfed (just four!) and what I felt I needed to work on (everything!) before he stopped and turned the board toward the shore. We tried a few waves—I paddled, he pushed—but I couldn't quite get to my feet.

"Let me see something, Diane," he said as the next wave approached and he moved toward the back of the board. I felt it accelerate, pressed through my arms and chest, and sprang up, but only got to my knees, with my weight over my heels, and ended up rolling off the back of the board as it shot up in the air and smacked flat on the water.

"*There's* your problem!" Simon shouted with the enthusiasm of a man who'd discovered gold. "You're not moving your toes!" The accent surfaced again—"Ya nawt movin' ya toes"—as he threw his hands in the air and leaned toward me. "You know, I'm here trying to come up with something to help your surfing, and that's *it! You've got to move your toes!* Your toes gotta move toward the nose when you pop up!"

We tried again—*toes to the nose, toes to the nose*—and it worked: I was up on my feet, staring down at them, encased in black rubber on the chartreuse deck, marveling at the feeling of the ride and how the board just kept on moving. Abruptly the wave broke and, like a liquid bronco, tossed me off. I felt a rush of cold water up my nose and over my skin as the wetsuit flushed, a hazard of midquality gear that allows a new layer of water to suddenly replace the warmed one. "Okay, that'll wake you up!" I said as I surfaced, coughing saltwater and feeling an ice-cream headache stab my forehead. It dissipated by the time I retrieved the board and hauled it back to Simon, and I managed a few more rides, but I found that as often as not I was falling off the board just as I got up or as a breaking wave heaved me off.

My energy fading, I told him I could use a break.

"Okay, we can stay here until you're ready to try again," he said. "Do you have access to a pool?"

"I do, actually. I've been working out with a trainer to get my strength up, but I also try to swim at the gym near my office."

"That's good. You should be doing as many laps as you can," he said, squinting up at me, the sunlight turning his eyes into pale opalescent slits. "It'll help a lot with your paddling and your stamina. That's what I do—I just come out with fins and swim as far as I can, either uptown from where I live in Rockaway Beach to like One-oh-Eight, One-Sixteen and back, or downtown toward Far Rockaway."

"Oh, where do you live?"

"Over on Eighty-Seventh, behind the projects."

I did a quick calculation: that meant he was swimming roughly two to three miles in open water—worthy of a full triathlon.

"Wow, you must be in terrific shape."

"Well, I'm an old guy, so I gotta keep working at it," he said, looking at me sideways with a sly grin. "I see how some of these young hipsters coming out to the Jetty look at me, think I can't really surf like they can." His voice grew loud and intense and percussive as he talked faster. "But I just watch and bide my time, wait for the right one, and I end up riding the waves *they can't even make!* I don't like to go to the Jetty all that much," he said, looking out to the horizon as he wound down. "Too crowded and aggressive."

"Where's the Jetty?"

"Up by Ninetieth Street. It's the main break."

Right by Bob's house. I was certainly not ready to surf there, given the Serengeti-like atmosphere Simon described—predators warily eyeing and circling and judging one another, ready to pick off a weak straggler like me. But maybe someday.

"This is a nice wave coming," he said. "Are you ready?"

"Yes, but I think this might be my last one," I told him as I lay down and, on his signal, paddled and caught it. Again—*toes to the nose*—I got to my feet and watched as the board moved through the water. I heard Simon shouting, "Ride the wave, not the board," and realized that he was right: I'd been so focused on standing up and staying *on the board* that I hadn't been paying attention to staying *in the wave*. I looked up and along the wave, trying to divine how it would unfurl toward the beach and how I might stay with it. It was shaped like a wedge sloping toward the direction I was going, and I could see that it made a kind of diagonal line toward the shore. I kept looking at it and somehow naturally followed it almost all the way to the sand until I leaned back to fall flat.

"See, that was so much better," Simon said, wading toward me.

"It was," I said, giddy and laughing as we walked to the beach. "But I have no idea what I did."

"You turned! You got set in the wave and you *turned*. That's what you need to do to ride it."

"Okay. But how do I turn? That one just happened."

"Well, the first thing is just to look where you're going." He dropped the board in the sand and struck a pose: legs maybe hips' width apart, knees facing forward and slightly bent, torso facing off to the side, with the arms stretching loosely in the same direction. "That helps set your weight the right way. But you also have to adjust to steer," he said, contorting a knee and ankle in and down toward the ground, a position that looked so unnatural and ill-advised that a sympathetic twinge of pain shot through my leg. "And when you get good, you can cross-step to stay in the right place on the wave." Still in a crouch, he stepped sideways, slowly crossing one foot over another. "But that's an advanced move," he said. "You'll need to get the basics down first."

"Okay, I'll start focusing on that next time." *Every time I think I'm getting somewhere, I realize how far I've still got to go.*

We walked over to the pile of gear and array of surfboards, where I plopped in the sand to pull off my boots and begin peeling down the wetsuit. I was exhausted and could feel the unwillingness of my muscles to move that would soon transform into aches. But I was calm and content in a way I hadn't been for months, as if a pressure valve inside my chest had finally turned, allowing the hot, bitter remnants of my losses to slowly seep away.

■ ■ ■

About a month later I was back at the beach, waiting for a lesson to start. I'd taken a few more one-on-ones with Simon and then, at Frank's suggestion, signed up for group lessons, buying a discounted pack of five so I could afford to come out at least once a weekend. I'd continued my workouts with Rob, and as promised, we'd been doing more "explosive" exercises, compound moves sometimes described in the fitness trade as plyometric or ballistic, depending on the sequence of motions and whether they employ throwing or swinging weights like a medicine ball or kettlebell. My routine had begun to include the squat thrust—a sort-of half burpee that involves squatting, putting the hands on the floor, jumping back into a plank, and then jumping forward to a squat before standing. The exercise is meant to help build power—essentially the ability to exert maximum force quickly—by targeting a type of muscle fiber known as fast twitch, which is good for performing springing motions like the pop-up. Those fibers are part of why cats, for instance, can leap onto a kitchen counter with no windup, or why Serena Williams can serve in excess of 120 miles an hour and dispense with many of her opponents in just a few strokes.

Frank arrived, hustling down from the boardwalk with some unfamiliar new suits over his arm: navy blue with aqua insets and plum with orange, still wrapped in plastic.

"Shorties!" he said, fanning them out on the sand and starting to take the plastic wrapping off. "Pick your color, pick your size."

I found a ten in blue and held it up, exclaiming, "Oh my god, it's so cute!" It was like a regular wetsuit, though thinner, with a high neck, long sleeves, and a zipper up the back, but it had no legs to speak of, like a thick leotard with a boy-short bottom. I was a little skeptical that it was going to have enough coverage to keep me warm, but I was excited to try it out.

"I think you're going to like those," he said.

I already did. It was a whole lot easier to get into without the legs, which often seemed to be the least cooperative part. I grabbed the Big Green Monster and dragged it toward the water by the leash, not talking much with the other students, five or six twentysomethings who seemed to have come as a group. I felt a tingle run up my spine as the water washed over my feet and slapped at my legs but quickly adjusted and was soon sitting on my board just outside the breakers, feeling the gentle rise and fall of the waves and the pull of the westward current. At least at that point I felt pretty stable straddling the board, I realized, something that hadn't been true even a few lessons ago. The rest of the group filled in around me as Kevin and another guy took up positions from which they would guide and push us into the waves. After we'd all gone a few rounds with each instructor, I saw that Kevin was free and paddled over to him.

A wave came almost immediately. He pushed me into it, and just as he said, "Up-up-up-up-up!" I sprang and heard my feet hit with a quick, rhythmic thud—*ba-DUM*. I knew instantly that I was on the sweet spot of the board even though I wasn't looking at it, because I felt perfectly balanced and steady, as if I were weightless and suspended over the water as I flew toward the beach. I watched the wave, following its line of energy toward the charcoal-gray boulders of the jetty across the break as I neared the sand, actually doing what Simon had urged—riding the wave, not the board—and feeling miraculously, shockingly, like I was an organic extension of the ocean, a bona fide part of the ecosystem.

I saw Frank just in front of me on his way out toward the group. "Lookin' good, lookin' good," he called out before diving under the wave.

Getting close to the shore, I fell off the board, hauled the Big Green Monster toward me by the leash, hoisted myself back onto it, and paddled over to Kevin, who was standing with Frank.

"That's the most solid pop-up I've seen you do," Kevin said. "It looked really good!"

"It *felt* really good!"

"That's the thing about getting out of those heavy wetsuits," Frank said. "You get all that water weight off your legs. It's like trying to surf lugging around an extra twenty, thirty pounds."

I hadn't realized the suits could hold quite that much water, but it was true that I felt unfettered with my bare legs in the sea, no longer sluggish and spastic but increasingly mobile and at ease. I got into another wave, took it almost to the shore, and then paddled back to Kevin.

"You know, you caught that one on your own," Kevin said, smiling, his pale-blue eyes gone nearly clear in the sun.

"*I did?* Oh my god, I can't believe it—that's actual progress!"

"Absolutely!"

It was a small step, but it felt like a major triumph. The ability to catch waves on my own would mean the ability to surf on my own —to discover and guide my experience—rather than forever needing someone to stand by my side, telling me when to go and giving me that little nudge.

I fell off just as I popped up on the next one—and the next one and the one after that. As I clambered back onto the board to try yet again, Frank looked over at me sympathetically and said, "That's the thing about surfing: it's simple, but it's not easy."

Exactly, I thought as I settled onto the board and collected myself for another try. Everything about surfing always seemed so clear, so simple, when explained or demonstrated—even attempted, sometimes—on dry land. But once I was in the water, the whole enterprise became an entirely different thing: slippery, mysterious, and exhausting. After falling off a few more waves, I finally got one and took it all the way to the shore. There were still ten or fifteen minutes left to the session, but I was tired and could no longer feel my feet and wanted to leave on a high note. So I got out of the water, wrestled the Big Green Monster up the beach, and sat down to watch the other students. One of them, a brown-skinned woman I hadn't seen earlier, with two short braids under a navy bandanna, paddled into a wave, jumped to her feet, and sailed in at an angle almost parallel to the shore as if it were the most natural thing in the world—a good long ride with nary a wobble in sight.

She came out of the water and up the beach toward me, put down her board, and sat next to me while she took off the leash.

"You looked great on that wave!" I said.

"Hard-won," she said, laughing, water dripping from the ends of her braids as she shook her head from side to side. "Hard-*won*. November, I didn't catch anything. December, I didn't catch anything. I started back up again in March—didn't catch anything. April, same story. So today feels really, really good."

"Wow," I said, thinking, *I don't know that I would have kept up with surfing through such a lousy winter.* "That's great that you stuck with it, then."

"Yeah, it was frustrating, but I'm glad I did."

"I know the feeling! I had a better day today, too. But I think at least half of it is these cute wetsuits!"

"Oh, definitely—getting out of those full suits helped."

We sat there for a few minutes as I felt a ripple of relaxation flow through my body, as if it were pushing out the tension and making every fiber lie flat. We watched the rest of the group as they took their last waves and headed up the beach, all smiles and laughs and high-fives, the sunlight dancing on the water, the currents swirling around the rocks.

||||||||||||||||||||||||||||||||||||||||||||||||||||||||||||||||||||||||||||||||||||||||||||||||||

PART II

FIVE FEET HIGH
AND RISING

I did not consider, even passingly, that I
had a choice when it came to surfing. My
enchantment would take me where it would.

—WILLIAM FINNEGAN,
BARBARIAN DAYS

5

Taking the Plunge

JUNE–OCTOBER 2011

THE BAR IN THE LOBBY OF THE CARLYLE HOTEL ON THE Upper East Side was humming with piano music and an early-evening weekday crowd: distinguished-looking couples in blazers and high-necked dresses, packs of up-and-comers in dark suits and ties, young men and women in the studied, casual, yet sexy garb of a date. It was, as my father might have called it, a swank joint. A fixture of monied Old New York, it was bathed, appropriately enough, in the sepia tones of an antique photograph, as much from the amber lighting, chocolate leather banquettes, and gold-leaf ceiling as from the murals that covered the walls in shades of mustard, ochre, and aqua. Ludwig Bemelmans, famous for his series of Madeline children's books, had painted them in the 1940s, depicting a fanciful vision of Central Park in which elephants ice-skate along with humans, well-dressed rabbits drink wine at a bistro table, and a male giraffe doffs his hat in greeting to a female holding a parasol and purse and accompanying her calf.

It was late spring and still cold and I was there having drinks with an old friend named Jay, whom I'd first gotten to know when I was on the road covering the 2004 Democratic primaries for the *New York Times* and he was the press secretary for the campaign of Howard Dean, the former governor of Vermont. A funny, dark-haired, charismatic guy who practically vibrated with energy and a hint of mischief, Jay had always reminded me a little of Dickie Greenleaf in *The Talented Mr. Ripley,* one of those people infused with a glow whose light could make you feel like the most charming, wonderful person in the world. We'd always gotten along, and so I was happy when a year or so later he moved up from Washington for a job at Bill Clinton's post-presidential foundation and quickly became close with Eric. It was a heady time for all of us — I was getting more prominent assignments and drawing accolades from the higher-ups at the *Times,* while Eric and Jay were rubbing shoulders with the world leaders, power brokers, celebrities, and staggeringly rich people who surrounded Bill Clinton. Jay found an apartment near ours in Brooklyn, and so I'd see him regularly for drinks or dinner, at our place or out in the neighborhood. After the divorce, he and Eric remained tight, and though I didn't see him as often, he was one of the few friends closer to Eric who showed an interest in maintaining a relationship with me. It turned out he'd tried surfing years earlier, something he'd never mentioned until I started, and he'd moved to Los Angeles, in part so that he could pursue the sport more seriously. We'd stayed in touch, after a fashion — I'd get an out-of-the-blue message to come have a drink at one or another of our old haunts *right now,* and more often than not I could. This time around he was in town to make one of his routine appearances at the headquarters of his employer, Bloomberg Philanthropies, and we'd made plans to meet.

He'd brought along a colleague of his, an attractive, forthright, and sharp-witted young woman with straight dark-blond hair who had gone quiet once the talk turned to surfing. It was something I'd noticed a few times in Montauk: when surfers are together, it seems, they can't help but go on almost incessantly about the activity, in conversations so abstruse they tend to exclude anyone who's not similarly obsessed.

"So how often are you surfing?" Jay asked, the soft light of our table lamp making his hazel eyes sparkle. He was wearing a white button-down shirt rather than his usual hipster cropped sweater adorned with stripes or a bird, but he looked much the same as he always had, with close-cut hair and carefully trimmed stubble.

"Almost every weekend—at least once, sometimes twice. I'm still in lessons, but I feel like I'm starting to get the hang of a few things."

"Do you have your own board yet?"

"No, not yet. I'm thinking about getting my own wetsuit, but I haven't thought about a board."

"You should. If you want to surf, you should have your own equipment."

"But boards are expensive," I said. "I don't know if I can spend that kind of money."

"You don't have to go out and get, like, a thousand-dollar board, but you could get something decent used. It would just give you the independence to get out there more."

"Yeah, I can see that, but I don't know." I watched the bubbles rise in my glass of sparkling wine, then glanced at Jay's colleague, unable to think of a way to draw her into the conversation but also unwilling to let the subject go. Jay looked at his phone resting on the table, picked it up, and started typing. It was just like the old days, when he and Eric were constantly tethered to their BlackBerrys, not letting certain emails or texts or phone calls go unanswered as they tried to fit their lives around the hydra-headed needs of a powerful man. I'd been that way, too, for a number of years: always on call, no matter where I was—cooking dinner, at a friend's birthday party, in transit, getting a pedicure—for some crucial interview

I might need to conduct, to write and file a fast story if news suddenly broke on my beat, or to answer questions from the copyeditors who loomed over every reporter's evening and weekend plans. But I had a less newsy beat now—I was still writing features about the hospitality industry and was about to move on to a weekly column about residential real estate for the Metro section—and could pretty safely silence my phone for a social engagement. I could, for the first time in a decade, I realized with a thrill, leave my work largely at work and actually *be* wherever I was.

So I kept prattling on about the board, knowing that Jay was at least half listening. "I mean, my apartment's kind of small and I don't know where I'd keep it. I wouldn't even know what to get," I said, feeling the words come out in a rush. "I still have a lot to work on, of course, but I'm not exactly a beginner, so I don't want to just get a beginner board, I'd want something I could grow into, but I don't know enough yet about what style of surfing—"

"Look," he said flatly, cutting me off and fixing me with an unsmiling stare, "you're never going to get good until you buy a board and surf every day."

My body jerked as my spine stiffened, as if I were snapping-to, and I could feel my face getting hot with a quick, defensive irritation. *Who is he to tell me what to do? What does he know of my ambitions?* I'd had to recalibrate my expectations down so many times already that I wasn't even aiming to be good anymore, just competent, and that phrase, *get good,* was like a poke in my rib cage—an unwelcome reminder that no matter how much I practiced, *good* might still remain beyond my grasp.

"Well," I said, struggling to keep my voice light, "I don't know that my life will ever let me surf *every* day, but maybe I'll think about a board."

Jay kept staring at me, still not smiling. "Listen," he said, "there's a lot of people in L.A. who I'd say surf, like, *culturally,* you know. They talk about it a lot, it's a big quote-unquote part of their life, but they don't actually surf that much. And when I moved out there,

I met this group of guys who, like, *really* surf. And they said, 'This is an amazing thing—*if you do it*. Look, you can culturally surf or you can surf, but if you're going to *surf*, you gotta have your own equipment, and it should, like, suck as little as possible.' They really took me under their wing. When I got out there, I bought a seven-foot board and just struggled with it. Then I met this guy who's a former pro surfer who's now my buddy. I surfed with him one day and he told me, 'You're better than you think, but you need a bigger board.' So he went with me to the surf shop and helped me figure out what was right for me at that point, which was a ten-foot board. Maybe somebody at your surf school could help you figure out what to get."

"Maybe," I said, the irritation gone. As I'd listened to him, it had come to me that he wasn't so much trying to tell me what to do as he was sharing some newfound wisdom—a signal that he took my surfing seriously enough to want to help me get better. Plus he was right. I'd been caught up in the idea that I needed to be further in my development as a surfer—more proficient, more sure of the style I wanted to pursue—before buying a board, as if it were a long-term, locked-in investment. But what Jay was suggesting made a lot more sense: get something that would serve my needs now, that would give me the freedom to get into the water on my own schedule rather than relying on lessons. I wasn't sure I would actually buy the board immediately, but I recognized that if I wanted to advance I'd need to, and sooner than I'd thought.

Several weeks later I was walking along the ocean in Rockaway Beach on my way to Bob's. I'd already taken a surf lesson with a small group of other not-quite-beginners, and by noon it was so warm and sunny that I'd wrapped my multicolored tie-dye beach towel—a souvenir from my first surf trip to Montauk—around me like a sarong and decided to walk the mile to his house barefoot on the boardwalk. Hungry for fish tacos or whatever he might have going on the grill, I felt a serene joy gazing out at the water, a soothing, translucent celadon with smooth, undulating waves, the sun

beating down on my shoulders, arms, and legs, turning the water droplets on my skin into dusty speckles of sea salt. I passed the
tidy, small-scale homes of Arverne by the Sea and then a series of
huge 1960s apartment complexes that had each subsumed three or
four city blocks to plop clusters of thirteen-story tan — or tan-and-
rust-striped — brick buildings around manicured lawns and parking lots. As I reached a block where the brick behemoths gave way
to a hodgepodge of older homes and bungalows built when Rockaway was the city's premier summer resort, I saw a through street
and came off the boardwalk. I was thinking I'd head over to the
main boulevard to pick up a few bottles of prosecco, which had become one of my regular contributions to the social gatherings Bob
hosted on his porch nearly every weekend. And there, in my path
as I waited at the intersection to cross the street, stuck in the grass
traffic median bisecting Shore Front Parkway, was a sign advertis-
ing an open house for one- and two-bedroom condos in a modern
six-story building that stretched across the block on the other side
of the road.

I felt like I should keep walking — I wanted to get to the fun at
Bob's soon — but Jay's words came back to me: *You're never going
to get good until you buy a board and surf every day.* I had been trying to find a new place to buy in Bed-Stuy — in my dreams another
brownstone with an apartment I could rent out to help pay the bills.
I was so focused on pulling myself together and building the perfect nest that I hadn't put any effort into dating: I was stuck on the
idea of a permanent, expandable home, one that could accommo-
date me and my gardening impulses for now and, maybe someday,
the child or two I might bring into my life through some manner
of high-tech pregnancy, adoption, or falling in love with a hot divorced dad. But what if I could have a little weekend place, too? I
had briefly flirted with buying a place on Bob's block the summer
before but hadn't been able to commit at the time, feeling that both
the house and a beach life were beyond my reach. But this time,
with money from the sale of the house I'd owned with Eric sitting

in the bank, I felt I had real possibilities. I stared at the big, brown-framed windows and balconies in the taupe concrete-block facade, imagining how they made the most of the sunlight and ocean view and fantasizing about waking up there, grabbing a board off the terrace, and crossing the street to surf at sunrise. And although I suspected I couldn't pull off having two homes on my own, it couldn't hurt to look, even if I wasn't dressed for real estate hunting.

I tightened my towel around me, brushed the sand from my feet, and slid on my sandals to walk to the building, where a pleasant woman with short brown hair, tanned skin, and a crisp white blouse met me just inside the entrance with a stack of listing sheets and an offer to show me around.

"What kind of apartment would you be looking for?" she asked.

"I hadn't been looking until I saw your sign out there, but something small, I think. I'd be using it on weekends and maybe sometimes during the week if the surf forecast looks good."

"Oh, you're a surfer. We've had a lot of interest from surfers, given the location, right on the main break."

"Well, I'm not quite a surfer yet," I said, laughing. "I'm still learning." *Surfer*—it was like *athlete:* a label I still couldn't quite apply to myself. I didn't think I was like those cultural surfers Jay's buddies disdained, but neither did I feel I was good enough to claim the identity.

"Well, I can show you a one-bedroom on the second floor and, if you're interested, a two-bedroom on the fourth. And there's deeded parking available."

We walked into the bright, airy lobby, which looked straight through to a landscaped, furnished courtyard out back—a common area for residents to lounge and cook out, she said—and took the elevator to the second floor. The building had been completed just a few years before. "There are no restrictions on subletting," she said as we walked down a nondescript hallway, "so you could easily rent it out if you want."

We reached the apartment, and as she opened the door, light

flooded the hallway. I could practically hear a church choir holding an extended "Ahhhhh" as I walked in, squinting at the ocean shimmering beyond a wall of floor-to-ceiling windows. I couldn't even see the street, just the water, as if we were on the deck of a ship.

"Wow, that view!" I said. "It's like the ocean's in your apartment." The place was small, with a kitchen at the entrance that opened onto the living room and balcony and a bathroom and bedroom off to one side. But with pale wood floors, stainless-steel appliances, and glass mosaic tile, it felt contemporary and fresh and beachy, and I could immediately see myself being there.

I walked to the living room windows and out onto the balcony, noting the span of the beach and the main surf break right across the street, with its jetty punching out into the water, a big boulder in the middle painted yellow with the Parks Department's green leaf logo on it. There were about a dozen surfers in dark wetsuits out, no doubt sizing each other up and jostling for position as they stalked waves between stints of bobbing in the water, looking like black rubber stoppers. *One day I'll be out there, too.*

"The only real drawback," I said after we'd gone through the rest of the place, "is being right on Shore Front. I'd be a little concerned about street noise and traffic."

"There's rarely a ton of traffic here, but why don't I show you the two-bedroom? It's up a little higher and looks over the side street."

The difference in being two stories up was surprising. Not only was the apartment bigger—I could have a separate home office! Room for guests!—but also the higher perspective showed so much more of the peninsula's sweep. It was as if the maps and old photographs I'd been looking at online as I tried to learn more about the area's physical orientation and history had sprung to life. I was fascinated that there could be a place and a way of living I'd known nothing about in a city I thought I knew so well. Now I could begin to see where parts of it had played out and how the neighborhoods fit together.

The peninsula, I'd recently learned, had been a summer destination for ages. For at least hundreds of years before the first solid record of contact with Europeans in 1524, quasi-nomadic bands of Lenape Indians spent their summers at the beach, fishing and gathering oysters before moving inland to harvest crops and find winter campsites. When Europeans began establishing year-round settlements there in the seventeenth century, they called the whole peninsula Rockaway or Rockaway Beach, thought to be a corruption of a Native word, Reckouwacky in some spellings, meaning "the place of our own people," or, alternately, of Reckanawahaha, or "the place of laughing waters." But as more settlers moved in, they built farms and estates that grew into villages, with clusters of hotels, rooming houses, cottages, and even tent colonies for summer visitors. As the peninsula expanded, both in population and size, as landfill widened and lengthened it, the neighborhoods and villages took on new names, some that were descriptive, others that memorialized the property owners who developed them. There was Seaside, Belle Harbor, and Breezy Point, known locally as "Breezy," as well as Far Rockaway at the peninsula's far eastern end. There was also Arverne, where I was taking surf lessons, derived from the way the landowner Remington Vernam signed his checks: R. Vernam.

The Beach House, where I was looking at apartments, and Bob's place were in what still carried the name Rockaway Beach, near the center of the peninsula in an area called Hollands on the old maps. That name had nothing to do with Rockaway's Dutch colonial history, in which settlers were able to acquire—some would say swindle—land from the Native Americans after Peter Stuyvesant, the last Dutchman to lead the colony of New Amsterdam, became their official protector in a 1656 treaty. Instead it derived from the Holland family, successful mid-nineteenth-century businesspeople who bought and moved to sixty-five acres in Rockaway Beach. They started out farming and running a hotel and eventually helped establish a school, church, and railroad station. Standing on the fourth-floor balcony of the Beach House, I could look west, or uptown, toward the neighboring community of Rockaway Park, where millions of visitors had once thronged to the long-defunct restaurants, bars, bathhouses, and hotels lining the boardwalk. Amusements had sprawled from ocean to bay, including a steeple-chase, casinos, theaters, carousels, and a grand roller coaster. There was even a huge building overlooking the Atlantic called the Pavilion of Fun. Now the neighborhood was filled with dwellings, some for at-risk youths or the aged and infirm, along with a scattering of restaurants and shops.

By the time I finally got to Bob's with the prosecco about a half hour later, my head was churning with real estate ambitions and I was setting my sights on having a primary home in Brooklyn and a weekend place in the Rockaways. It may well have been an insane aspiration, but I liked the idea of reenacting a primordial rhythm of the city, one that thrummed through history and moved not only some of the earliest New Yorkers but also Gilded Age high society like Astors and Vanderbilts, literati like Henry Wadsworth Longfellow, Washington Irving, and Walt Whitman, and regular folk who'd make summertime pilgrimages to this place for relief from the sweltering inner city. That's how Frank at my surf school had gotten his introduction to the sport: he grew up in Brooklyn, and his family had come to Rockaway every summer, though he hadn't begun surfing in earnest until he was twenty-one.

Arriving at Bob's, I dropped off the prosecco, threw a sundress over my now-dry bikini, and ran over to Rockaway Taco for my food fix. Well fed and excited, I was sitting on the porch with Bob and Iva, Josh's wife, on a weekend visit as usual, as bubbly about the condos as the sparkling wine in my glass.

"I don't know if it makes any real sense to try and do this," I was saying, "but god, I'd love to have a way to be out here more."

"It sounds great," said Iva, who worked for a public relations firm that represented major real estate clients, "and if it's new, it's probably got a tax abatement to keep the monthly charges low."

"Right, it does—though I do worry about what will happen

once it expires in twenty or thirty years," I said. "I kind of like knowing what sort of income I need to make."

"Well," Bob said, "that's a long time from now, and you could always sell it if it got to be too much."

Just then Bob's tenant, John, a tall, broad-shouldered guy with reddish brown hair, wire-rimmed glasses, and freckles, emerged from his apartment, which took up the back half of Bob's first floor and had its own entrance on the porch around back. "I've got some really nice dark rum for floaters if you're getting frozens," he told Bob, who was getting a pitcher off a plastic bar cart.

"Great! I'll be back in a minute," Bob said, heading down the steps and across the street as John disappeared around the back of the porch.

I looked at Iva, confused. "Floaters? Frozens?"

"I guess Bob is getting some drinks," she said, laughing.

A few minutes later Bob emerged from the bar that sat on the ground floor of a three-story building just across the parking lot and returned with the pitcher, now full of a white frozen concoction. "I got us piña coladas—I hope that's all right," he said as he came up the stairs.

"They'll just sell them to you by the pitcher?" I asked, surprised at the ease with which liquor had left the pub. I could hardly imagine such a thing happening in Brooklyn or Manhattan, where patrons were fairly strictly prohibited from, say, taking a beer to the sidewalk if they stepped outside for a smoke.

"Oh, yeah, we do this all the time," he said, pouring the coladas.

John returned, bearing a bottle of caramel-colored rum. "Anyone want a floater?"

"Thanks, but I think I'll try it as is for now," I said as he stepped back to pour about an inch of the rum on top of his and Bob's glasses. I wasn't a big tropical cocktail drinker, but I'd had a few piña coladas over the years and I wanted to see how this one compared, especially to those my sister had perfected as we were growing up.

When she was in college, our parents would occasionally cloister themselves in their bedroom at the back of our apartment so she could have free rein in the living room and kitchen when she had friends over. She'd whip up a big batch of drinks in the blender and let me taste the virgin mixture before setting out the spiked slush, which she'd serve with potato chips, Lipton onion soup dip, and a Tavares soundtrack so she and her friends could practice their Latin hustle moves before heading out to the disco.

I took a sip. It was delicious, the sweet chill of coconut and pineapple taking me back to those giddy evenings when I'd gotten a taste of young adult fun. "Oh my god, this is so good!" I said as John held up the bottle and cocked an eyebrow in my direction. "Sure you don't want some?" he said, with a devilish grin. "It's really nice rum."

"Why not?" I said, holding up my glass. And who was I turn it down? I wanted the good time to keep rolling on, to enjoy the land's-end, outlaw spirit that seemed to pervade the place still, decades after the fleets of saloons and dance halls had closed down. I swirled the rum around in my glass and took a sip, its burnt-sugar kick filling my nose and hitting the back of my throat. "That *is* really nice rum," I said, catching a glimpse of Whalemina's pottery mosaic sparkling in the descending sun.

■　■　■

"It's just not breaking," Kevin was saying one clear, cool Saturday morning as a group of us stood on the sand in Arverne in our wetsuits, scanning the ocean for the waves promised by the forecast, which had yet to appear. The familiar humps of swell were rising every so often in the smooth teal surface, but they just kept moving toward us as if they were logs rolling on an underwater conveyor belt, without peaking to make ride-worthy waves before eventually spilling onto the shore. The problem wasn't the swell, which was enough to make for decent waves in the knee- to waist-high range, or the wind, which was light and offshore, but yet another factor I was coming to understand played a big role in determining conditions: the tide was too high.

All I'd known about tides growing up was that they had something to do with cycles of the moon and that high meant the water was swallowing the beach—which seemed to be when my father would take my sister out surfcasting—and low meant it had retreated, exposing the deposits of seaweed and inland pools where you could sometimes find unusual shells and beach glass. With waves, though, I was learning that the tide level—essentially how deep or shallow the water was at any given distance from the shoreline—would enhance, diminish, or entirely shut down my ability to surf, a peculiarity that largely has to do with fluid mechanics and friction.

When swell moves out of the ocean's deep water and approaches the shallows that hug the coast to start forming waves, the interaction between the water and the seabed slows the progression, but not at the same rate within the wave. The bottom of the wave, which is closer to the seabed, slows more quickly than the top, an effect that intensifies as the water gets shallower. At a certain point—when the water depth is, on average, 1.3 times the height of the wave—the top of the wave outruns the bottom and spills over, or breaks. With a high tide that morning, the water was just too deep for our waves to peak, so until some of it retreated, there could be no surfing.

"Let's head out anyway," Kevin said. "There are some things we can work on while we wait for the tide to drop, like spinning the board around and talking about etiquette."

Etiquette? My utter confusion must have been plain on my face. Kevin chuckled and then explained: "Etiquette—you know, the rules about how you surf with other people so no one gets hurt. When it's okay to go for a wave and when it's not. That sort of thing."

It was early October, and I'd been coming out to the Rockaways

for surf lessons most weekends for months. I no longer felt like a
flailing beginner. I'd graduated from the unwieldy, eleven-foot Big
Green Monster to a marginally more maneuverable ten-foot board.
I was getting to my feet more often than not, and I was, when I
stood in the right spot, riding the waves (not the board). Every so
often I was paddling into waves on my own, as long as an instructor was there to advise me. I'd fallen in with a handful of women—
about a half dozen of us, ranging in age from midtwenties to mid-
forties—who regularly took group lessons together. One of them,
a fun, energetic lawyer with hair almost as orange as the cute Mini
convertible in which she'd given a few of us rides to or from Brooklyn, had also started an email chain with the subject line "Surfing
ladies of Rockaway!" to help coordinate our visits. "Hello all! Who's
planning to surf this gorgeous weekend?" she'd recently written.

But the idea that there was an etiquette to catching waves threw
me for a minute. In the lessons we would spread out across a section
of the break, clustered in twos and threes near an instructor standing in the water, who would call us over one by one to guide us into
the waves. There were rarely many other surfers out there, so there
wasn't anyone else you might run into. But then I realized—*duh*—
that the real world of surfing would not mimic the orderly, managed progression of a lesson. Of course there had to be some sort
of accepted standard for who got to go on a wave and when. I just
hadn't thought about it yet.

There were about five of us that morning, and we followed
Kevin into the water and then through a few rounds of paddling
drills, stroking our way back and forth across the break, trying to
reach down and under the board toward its center before pulling
back with as much power as possible to keep charging forward, almost like tracing the double-C logo of Coco Chanel. I could feel
the momentum build and then hold as I cut easily and smoothly
through the water, my back arched, chest up, ahead of the pack and
just behind Kevin as I aimed for one jetty or the other. The sun was
long up but still low in the sky, dancing on the water in patches of

bronze and brass. I felt strong and in sync as I paddled laps around the break, noting the periodic roar of a plane overhead, on its way to or from JFK Airport. By the time Kevin gathered us together to sit upright on our boards, I was barely even winded.

"Okay," he said, "let's work a little on spinning the board around. When you're out on your own, you want to sit facing straight out to the waves so you can see what's coming, so it's important to be able to turn your board around really fast so you don't miss the wave.

"First you want to grab the board with one hand and get all the way back on the tail, like this," he said, scooting his butt back so that he was now sitting deep in the water with the nose of the board sticking straight up, nearly parallel to his chest. "Then you want to circle your legs in opposite directions to turn the board." He did a quick pivot, adding, "It helps if you also push with one hand," as he dropped his free arm into the water, circling it and pivoting further.

Then it was our turn to try. "Get plenty of room between you, and maybe try just spinning the board from a normal sitting position," he said. We spread out and began to work on turning. At first I couldn't figure out how to coordinate the motions as I circled my legs toward one another, which had the effect of making the board wobble and rock rather than rotating. I tried the opposite direction, still to no avail. I looked over at Kevin, throwing up my arms and shaking my head as if to say, *What am I doing wrong?*

He paddled over. "Think of your legs kind of like eggbeaters," he said, pantomiming the motion with his hands, "and move them kind of one after the other." I did as he said and suddenly I was spinning around, though at a much slower speed than he did. "Play around with it," he said. "Add the arm, go the other way—figure out what feels right to you."

After I'd practiced for a few minutes along with the other students, who also seemed to be getting the hang of the slow turn, Kevin suggested we start trying to move back on the board. "Remember," he said, again showing us what to do, "grip the board, get back as far as you can—it just makes it that much easier to turn."

Maybe easier for him. I reached down and grabbed the rail with my left hand, then heaved my butt toward the tail. But instead of landing at the end of the board, I just kept going, my weight off-kilter and sending me rolling back and to the side and then underwater, with the board on top of me. I surfaced and burst out laughing at my ineptitude, only to see two other students doing exactly the same thing.

"That's gonna take some practice," I said, still laughing, to a slim twentysomething woman with long jet-black hair and dark-brown eyes as we clambered back onto our boards.

"I know," she said, laughing as well. "Everything always looks so easy when he does it!"

"And then it's just *not*. We'll get it, though."

"We will!"

That was the thing about surfing—in those conditions, at least, at that break, with those women: it didn't matter how many times you had to try something, how many times you fell. It might be frustrating or irritating, but you weren't going to get hurt. It wasn't like skiing or skateboarding or anything else that required balance but that you tried to learn on a hard surface. The water was forgiving, and everyone was there to try to improve, help each other along, and have a good time.

We'd practiced our sit-spins for a few more minutes with varying degrees of success when Kevin said the tide had dropped almost enough for us to start surfing. "Let's take a rest out here and talk a little bit about etiquette."

Waves, he explained, have peaks along the crest—sections that appear to be highest along the upper ridge when viewed head-on—which is where they will first begin to spill over before continuing to break across the face, which is called peeling. There should be only one surfer at a time on a wave, both to avoid collisions and to help spread the fun around. So the surfer closest to the peak, Kevin said, has priority over the surfers farther down the line. It was a completely new concept to me.

"It's just one surfer on each wave?" I asked.

"Pretty much," Kevin said. "You can be on the same wave if you're far enough apart, but you have to be sure you both have enough room."

"Well, like how far apart?" one woman asked.

"At least a few board-lengths. But you probably shouldn't try to share a wave unless you know the other surfer."

Another instructor, a round-faced, chubby-cheeked man with dark-brown eyes and wavy dark hair known as Nice-Guy Rich, had joined us. Kevin turned to him. "You and me were surfing waves together last weekend in Breezy."

"Yeah, but you and me surf together all the time," Rich said, "and we both know the rules and what we're doing. Remember what happened with that woman that dropped in on me?"

"Yeah, yeah—tell about that."

"Well, I was up and riding and this woman dropped in—she didn't look around first and just took off really close to me. I tried to go around her but ended up falling on her. She wasn't hurt, but" —he chuckled—"she wasn't too happy about it." He said it with the air of a man who was sorry it hadn't gone well but was sure that he'd done his part to right a bad situation that wasn't his fault.

"So basically, just don't drop in," Kevin said. "And if you make a mistake and you *do* drop in on someone, just paddle over and apologize. Just say you're sorry. It goes a long way toward keeping the peace. Most surfers will be cool with that, right, Rich?"

"Absolutely. But it's better just to wait your turn."

■ ■ ■

Especially since the day was coming when I'd get outside of the cozy, coordinated bubble of instructors and other regular students to surf among strangers, this was good information to have. The Beach House condo, even with its tax abatement, had turned out to be more than I was looking to spend. So I'd gone back to chasing

Brooklyn options: combing real estate ads, going to open houses, running numbers with a mortgage broker, researching property history, negotiating deals, and paying for inspections, only to find some compelling reason not to go through with a purchase. I'd backed out of four or five places before finally giving up, realizing that I was driving myself crazy trying to re-create what I felt I'd lost: the gracious forever home where I could make real the family life I was still hoping for. All along I'd had a picture in my head, an imagined future that required extra bedrooms, Old World charm, homegrown food, and good public schools, and for some reason I was insisting on acquiring the house first, stubbornly convinced that I needed to have the trappings of this imagined life tied down before the life itself—my own stupid, irrational version of *If I buy it, it will come.*

Yet I didn't actually *have* the life, or even any suggestion that I was getting close to it. My romantic prospects were nonexistent. Pretty much all the men I met through work and my social circles were already taken, and my online dating forays had been so fruitless I'd given up on even trying. I was still thinking about having kids, but I hadn't figured out how, or even if, to pursue it.

So I decided to focus seriously on Rockaway, as a weekend place that would feed my surfing habit, make my *right now* work a little better. I kept thinking about my mother, who when I was growing up would never actually use many of the gifts we gave her on birthdays or at Christmas, instead putting them away to save "for good," which for her meant a good occasion, a moment fabulous and special enough to call for an item so nice. Maybe it was a holdover from her childhood deprivations during the Depression, but she'd preserve the silk scarf, pretty purse, or elegant perfume, stowing it carefully on a shelf or in a drawer. After she died, at age sixty-seven, when I was in my early thirties, I helped my sister clean out her closet and bureau, boxing up clothing and accessories that still smelled of her: a mix of Jean Naté body splash and the Maja soap and powder she kept in her drawers. She had been all kindness and fun, the person I was always thrilled to talk to and the buoy who'd kept me afloat in a tempestuous household. I was still railing at the gods over her loss—an awful eleven-month stutter-step to death after she had a stroke following a lumpectomy for breast cancer, which robbed her of her ability to speak, write, or express herself in any conventional manner. I was gutted at the prospect of spending the rest of my life without her, but as I boxed up her things, I was also struck by all the lovely stuff, unused, wrapped in tissue paper or protective plastic: the detritus of a life imagined but unlived, saved for the good she kept looking for that never came.

I knew now that I didn't want to live like that, building my present around a future that could be completely different by the time I got there. I wanted my own anchor in the neighborhood that was beginning to feel like mine. So I connected with an agent I'd met to see if he had anything small for sale. There was very little inventory, he said, but he did have a place he could show me.

As I walked down Beach Ninety-First Street one morning before work to meet him, my heart started pounding. *Could it be?* I had walked through the block once before, taking a new route to Bob's from a surf lesson, and had stumbled across what looked like nirvana: four doll-sized houses packed in a row that abutted a community garden—I could live among gardening surfers! Surfing gardeners!—just three blocks from Bob's, on a narrow alley a half block from the ocean and the main surf jetty. *Why can't I have that?* I'd thought as I'd passed them. As I approached the Realtor, I took a deep breath to keep from gasping. Maybe I *could* have that: he was about to show me one of those homes.

We walked down the alley, a head-high fence covered in Virginia creeper on one side, the near-identical houses on the other. They were all two-story Dutch Colonial Revival bungalows that had to be nearly a hundred years old, with cube-shaped bottom floors and smaller, distinctive, gambrel-roofed boxes on top. We stopped at the third house in, clad in taupe vinyl siding with a white, six-paneled front door.

"Well, this is it," he said. "The owner has tenants living here now, but they're month-to-month, so the house could be delivered vacant."

We climbed the four concrete steps and knocked, which immediately set off a riot of barking inside. "Oh, right—they have dogs," he said.

A small, pregnant blonde opened the door.

The agent greeted her and asked if it was still an okay time for the tour.

"Come on in," she said. "Don't mind the dogs."

We walked into a shallow room that ran the full width of the house, with a gated area at the far end containing the source of the cacophony: four fluffy little white terriers furiously yelping and leaping around and wagging their tails. They seemed more excited than vicious, and it looked like they couldn't get out, so I followed him in.

"This was likely a porch that got enclosed, so this would have been the front of the house," the Realtor said before ushering me through a wide opening that led to the living area. It was small and cramped and included a closet, bathroom, and kitchen. The floors were covered in off-white vinyl tile and the walls were vibrant turquoise, with stenciled capital letters above the kitchen window spelling out the words BON APPÉTIT. Next to the window, which overlooked the community garden out back, was painted a rural vista of the sort you'd see in an old-school Italian restaurant, as if a country lane lined with cypress trees meandered just beyond an arched, stone-framed window right there in Rockaway Beach.

It wasn't at all my style, and the place—home to a family of three at the time—felt cluttered and inefficiently arranged. But even before I saw the two bedrooms upstairs I was hooked. The location and size, 650 square feet in all, were perfect, as were its quirks of old age, right down to the unmilled tree trunks in the basement that had originally served as the foundation. It had obviously been updated, with new concrete piers, insulation, and heat, but the house, like so many around it, hadn't been meant to be inhabited all year long: it was built just for a season, summer, and for a purpose, having fun.

I put in an offer that the seller accepted, brought in an engineer to inspect the house, and this time went to contract. I planned to stay in my Bed-Stuy rental while I regrouped and figured out what might work best for my workaday residence. But once I closed on the bungalow, I'd be able to buy a board and get into the water whenever I wanted, bringing me one step closer to being an actual surfer.

I was thrilled about the whole enterprise, feeling like I had somehow lucked into the place of my dreams. Maybe it was the ghost of Fannie Holland drawing me into the area that bore her family's last name. Like Bob's house, the bungalow seemed to sit within the boundaries of the founding family's land. Shortly after Fannie and her husband, Michael, had moved there in the late 1850s, he had died, leaving her with nine kids, a farm, and a hotel to manage. Somehow she did, and even prospered. More than a century and a half later, perhaps I'd get to claim a small part of that place where a woman suffering from a loss had picked herself up and made a life on her own—maybe even experienced joyful days. It could be my own mini Pavilion of Fun.

6

Chasing Daylight

NOVEMBER 2011

THE SUV SLOWLY MADE ITS WAY FROM THE AIRPORT IN
Liberia, Costa Rica, along dusty roads, past verdant fields, forested
canyons, and jewel-toned waters, before finally arriving, three hours
later, in the beach town of Nosara. I'd been traveling for much of
the day—I'd left my apartment at three in the morning to begin
seven hours of flights, with an hour-and-a-half layover in Miami before the long drive—and I was exhausted. But I was also stoked, as
surfers say: I was taking my first overseas surf trip, a whole week on
my own in the tropics, dedicated to nothing but wave riding at an
intensive surf camp. It felt like the photography course I'd taken on
Lake Como in Italy after the divorce: a deep dive into a personal avocation, completely removed from friends and my regular life, and
not something I would have done when I was married. It was entirely mine.

When I finally got to the Surf Simply resort, back then tucked into a lush hillside near the Pacific coast, it felt like a secret hideaway: eight cream-colored cottages flanking a stone walkway that led up to a main house with an outdoor pool, kitchen, and lounge area all canopied with spiky, fanning leaves, coiled vines, and Technicolor blossoms.

It was a Saturday in the middle of November, raw and cold back in New York but balmy and humid in Nosara at the end of its rainy season, and I couldn't wait to jump in the water without a heavy wetsuit. I was still waiting for the Rockaway house purchase to go through, and I was possessed by the urge to improve my surfing as quickly as I could. I was due to have surgery a few weeks later to fix a persistent case of tennis elbow—resulting not from tennis but from the repetitive strains of gripping a pen and typing—and I wouldn't be able to surf again at least until spring. I was afraid I'd lose what progress I'd made, and couldn't shake the sense that I was stuck in a holding pattern in which I was too dependent on instructors and classes and unable to ride waves consistently, still too insecure to just rent some gear and practice on my own.

But surf camp hadn't been in my sights until a late-summer visit to the Montauket, this time as a customer rather than as a reporter. I was having beers with Jim, the work colleague who had originally suggested the story I'd written about the town, and his wife, Ondine. We stood outside together in a cramped space next to the window that opened from the bar, swaying and shifting and pivoting to avoid the patrons and servers ferrying food and drink around us. As we watched the setting sun turn the sky and water into a flaming pastiche of orange, fuchsia, and navy and talked about surfing, I mentioned how frustrated I was with my sketchy progress. Ondine said that she had gotten her start in surfing when Jim, who had learned growing up while spending summers at the Jersey Shore, bought her a surfboard and gave her a few lessons. "But where I *really* learned to surf was at a camp in Costa Rica," she said. "You go for a week and surf every day, but they break it down and focus on technique that you can take back with you."

I was surprised to learn that places existed where you could get that kind of intensive instruction. It sounded like exactly what I needed. After a couple I met at a lesson in Rockaway told me they had also been to Costa Rica for lessons and liked Surf Simply, I checked it out and decided to go, despite the small fortune it would cost. Maybe like Ondine I'd *really* learn to surf at camp.

After dropping my bags off in the two-bedroom cottage I'd be sharing with another student, I took a quick shower and walked up the steps under the dangling vines and swaying leaves to the rancho, as the staff called the open-air lounge area—part of a courtyard that led to the camp's main building at the crest of the hill —where we were all to have dinner, lulled by the murmur of frogs and crickets and whatever else was out there in the jungle adjusting to nightfall. The pool was off to one side and ringed with patio tables and chairs and a collection of low, cushioned banquettes. In the middle of the rancho was a large wood dining set, a bookshelf, and a flat-panel television mounted on a wall. The full kitchen included a refrigerator stocked with wine and beer, which we were welcome to drink. Behind that was a hallway leading to offices and classrooms and a blackboard with our schedule for the week handwritten in chalk. Pretty much everything we'd need was included —fresh-cooked meals at the rancho, twice-daily surf lessons, theory classes, video reviews, and options for yoga sessions and massages.

Two men were already sitting at the table, so I said hello, grabbed a beer from the fridge, and joined them. They were both Canadians—as were all the other guests, it would turn out. One was a return visitor to the camp, and the other had tried surfing some years ago but had fallen in love with it after a trip with friends the year before to Tamarindo, a busier surf mecca about two hours up the coast, with several schools, waves for all levels, and a party-town atmosphere. "Oh, and that's Evan," one of them added, indicating a rangy dude who was sitting on one of the banquettes in a corner staring at his laptop. "He's already been here a week."

"Wow," I said. "Two whole weeks! *That* would be awesome."

"Yeah, it's great here," Evan said with a grin. "Though last week I was doing the lifeguard course they teach, so I'm looking forward to the surfing."

An athletic-looking guy with a strong jaw, cleft chin, and thick medium-brown hair walked over and introduced himself. It was Ru, the owner, a Brit who had built the resort with his wife, from whom he had now split. *Life really does go on,* I thought, inspired to see someone seeming enthusiastic and happy moving ahead alone. The two other women in the group joined us: my roommate, Carolyn, a young nurse with an open, freckled face and light brown hair, and Jennifer, a tall, lithe park ranger with ice-blue eyes, pale-blond hair, and a preternaturally erect carriage.

Ru suggested we go around the table, introduce ourselves, and talk about our goals for the week. I hadn't been worried about the social aspects of the trip or even about having a roommate. My time in the photo course in Italy and the journalism fellowship in California had reminded me that I adjusted well to structured environments and was able to make new acquaintances easily in them. But I felt my throat tighten at the prospect of having to speak even in such a small and welcoming group. I'd never fully conquered the performance anxiety that frequently made my voice quiver and my hands shake so badly in routine staff meetings that I could barely take notes. So I tried focusing on keeping my breathing steady and slow and on what my campmates were saying.

"My pop-up is fine," one of the guys said, "and my trimming turns are pretty good, so I can usually trim and ride down the line, but I'm not so great at carving, so I'd like to work on that—you know, the carving turns."

I had no idea what he was talking about. Trimming, carving—it was like we were suddenly in cooking school, not surf camp. I could only ever align the board one way or the other to stay in the wave— or ride down the line, as the guy had put it—if an instructor helped me catch it at the right angle to begin with. My actual turning, when I managed it, remained a thing of serendipity. I didn't know how to make it happen. *If everyone else is this far along, how am I going to keep up?* Evan was working on moving from a longboard to a shortboard, a progression demanding such a significant leap in strength, balance, and agility that I wasn't sure I'd ever be able to make it. With less volume than longboards—technically meaning that they occupy less space, a measure usually expressed in liters and corresponding to buoyancy—shortboards require their passengers to work harder to keep them moving through the water. Plus when you're lying on the board, your lower legs and feet extend beyond the tail, so while you can kick to get moving, you can't spring off your toes to pop up.

Jennifer had been surfing off and on for about eight years, but since she lived in the mountains she didn't get to work on her skills very often. "But I do know how to turtle roll," she said—whatever the hell *that* was—as if it were a mystical rite of communing with the sea turtles that nested in a protected reserve some six miles away. Carolyn, I was relieved to hear, was a snowboarder from Alberta who had never surfed before and was just eager to learn. Then the attention turned to me.

"Well, I've been surfing off and on for a little over a year now, but I've only ever surfed in lessons," I said. "So aside from wanting to get more consistent with everything, I'd just like to learn enough so I feel I can go out and practice on my own when I get home."

"That's really, really important," Ru said. "We want you to be self-sufficient and not *need* anyone pushing you into waves."

■   ■   ■

The next morning at our first session, I got a taste of what Ru meant. Dressed in swimsuits and lightweight, quick-drying shirts known as rash guards, we gathered on the steps near a storage locker with two coaches. Kerianne, a golden-brown-haired yogi who'd been a star volleyball player growing up in the landlocked Central Valley of

California, and Harry, a voluble Brit with tousled blond hair and bright-blue eyes, were there to help us pick out boards for the day.

"So what do you usually ride?" Kerianne asked me, opening the locker to reveal about twenty surfboards standing upright in a rack as if at attention. "We have a pretty good range of sizes."

"I'm usually on a ten-foot soft-top."

"Well, here," she said, pulling out a white, hard-shelled board with two bands of aqua stripes running its length and a skinny yellow line centered between them. "Why don't you try this? It's a nine-two," she said, meaning it was nine feet and two inches long.

"Okay," I said dubiously, taking the board, which was surprisingly light for its size. "But I've never been on a board this short."

Kerianne smiled; the board was among the longest in their collection. "You can always try the ten-two if this isn't stable enough, but I don't think you'll need it." It would be my first time on a hard board and I felt a charge, like I was a real surfer, as I carried it down the steps.

We loaded the boards onto a trailer attached to a dune buggy and then climbed up into an open-air truck with back-to-back metal benches and a frame we could hang on to. As our caravan bounced down the dirt road and around a few bends, passing a yoga retreat nestled in an emerald canyon and plunging hillsides covered in thick vines flowering fuschia and white, I was suffused, as always, with the magic and wonder of air travel: just yesterday I'd awakened in gritty old Brooklyn and now here I was, half naked in the jungle on my way to the beach.

"God, it's so pretty here," I said to Carolyn, sitting next to me.

"It is — and it's so great to be out of the cold," she said, a broad smile across her face.

We arrived at a thicket of palms and bamboo with a narrow, gravelly path leading to a clearing. We grabbed our boards and walked toward the beach as birds chirped and flitted overhead. As we picked our way gingerly across the rough surface, the dappled sunlight became steadier and brighter and the arched frame of tree branches and leaves opened like a camera shutter, turning what had been a patch of pale blue on the horizon into a broad expanse of sand, rock outcroppings, and ocean streaked with the soft marsh-mallow foam of gently rising and breaking waves. Flocks of pelicans bobbed in the water and skimmed its surface.

"Wow," Carolyn said. "This is amazing—I've never seen any-thing like it before."

"It's gorgeous."

After setting the boards on the sand and warming up, we split into two groups. Carolyn and I would be working inside in the whitewater with Kerianne and another instructor, a slight, aqua-eyed local woman named Tinis. The other four went "out the back," as they called it, past where the waves were breaking, with Harry and another coach. I was a little miffed at getting bumped to begin-ner status in the whitewater since I was already riding—riding!—unbroken waves back home. I felt like a kid being left back a grade, but it would soon become apparent that I was exactly where I be-longed.

Before we went into the water, Kerianne explained the resort's approach to paddling. We wanted to get as close as we could to where the waves were breaking—"That's where they have the most energy, and that speed will help give you stability as well as a longer ride," she said—and time it so that we could take five slow, smooth strokes as the water rushed toward us. Once it reached us, we would take three "power paddles," or fast, deep, hard strokes. Eventually that would be the point at which we'd start popping up, but for the moment, Kerianne said, she just wanted us to get the rhythm of the water and a feel for the mechanics of the board, so we'd stay on our bellies. I felt a flash of impatience. I wanted to get going on my feet as soon as possible so I could focus on the steering and turning and board-control issues I wanted to master.

As we started heading into the water, Tinis warned us to drag our feet in a shuffling motion over the sandy bottom instead of picking them up and setting them down. "We get a lot of stingrays here," she said.

My irritation quickly dissolved as I got into the warm turquoise water and found a groove of paddling, feeling the bump of the whitewater as it hit the tail of my board and the rush of the glide as I sped toward shore. It was different from being on the soft-tops I was used to—they now seemed sluggish in comparison, as if I'd gone from driving a car with a four-cylinder engine to a V-8 and could feel all the pent-up potential beneath me. The board was floaty and snappy and responsive, as if it wanted to go fast. I felt light and buoyant and happy, and like I was already progressing: at least now I knew how to catch whitewater on my own.

We came back out of the water to talk about our next drills, which would serve as an introduction to the trimming and carving turns I'd heard about the night before. Waves have particular spots that make for the best entry, Kerianne said, but once you're up and riding one, you need to be able to steer into different sections to make the most of it as the wave evolves. Water along the top line, near the lip, moves faster than water at the bottom (that's friction and gravity at work), while the ball of energy that churns just in front of where a wave is breaking (or about to), known as the pocket or the curl, has the most power—that's the wave rider's engine. The arcs and swivels and pivots you see skilled surfers performing are designed to tap into these areas of higher energy, whether racing to reach them or allowing them to catch up.

Surfers generally use two basic moves to accomplish this task: trimming and carving. Trimming, which involves digging a rail into the water to make the board bank in that direction, is a more subtle adjustment while traversing a wave face: a nudge toward or away from the shore to stay in the flow, or tipping up toward the lip or down toward the base to get the right speed. Carving turns are more dramatic, allowing for a complete change of direction, necessary for maneuvers like a cutback—a kind of roundhouse turn that takes you back to the pocket from a slow section—or a bottom turn, which lets you make a horizontal shift after a vertical drop into the wave. Those require surfers to position their weight toward the tail, which lifts up the nose and lets the board pivot, before moving their weight forward to speed up again.

On the sand Kerianne drew the outline of a surfboard, a line down the center, and four circles, two on each side. "Think of these as buttons," she said, "that you push with your weight. If you push either one in the front," she said, putting her hand on one and then the other, "you're going to accelerate in that direction. Push the ones in the back, and you'll slow down. You can even stall the board, make it stop completely, if you're right over the fins—it's like a brake."

We would try to replicate these dynamics prone on our boards. So we returned to the water—"Remember, shuffle feet, shuffle feet!" Tinis said, demonstrating as she went—and started out trying to trim. We would catch the wave and then, still lying on our bellies, gently lean to one side or the other, allowing the rail to dip slightly, which would make the board travel that way. Then we tried adding a version of the carving turn: trim in one direction, then slide to the back of the board, hold it as the nose comes up, lean to change direction, then slide back toward the front of the board to get it going again. The terms were still hard to keep straight—they both sounded like something you'd do to a rib roast—but my body was getting the hang of them, as if sensing the thread of energy oscillating from water to board to flesh and back again. It felt good just to be in the water, to feel it washing through my rash guard and over my skin, sunlight glinting on its rippled surface, but I also felt like a shade had lifted, giving me a better view on how—and why and when—to make the board move different ways.

Finally it was time to start popping up. Back on the beach, we drew crosses in the sand to help guide where to place our hands and feet when springing into position, lying on the long vertical line representing the board's center with our palms down on the horizontal mark where we'd aim with our front foot. When we came up, Kerianne said, we wanted to land in what the camp termed the functional stance: feet along the center line of the board, knees bent and tracking in toward one another, arms down with one over each rail. Beginners tend to end up in something known as the poo stance or stink bug, like a wide-legged squat with arms straight out to the sides and the butt sticking back. It can feel stable, but it's rigid and easy to get stuck in, without being able to move the feet or rotate the arms and hips to steer. The functional stance, she said, would make it much easier and quicker to shift our weight by moving our hips and even feet while staying balanced on the board.

I did a few pop-ups in the sand, noting that my front foot wasn't quite making it to the center line, landing just off to the left.

"Make sure you bring that foot over," Kerianne said, "or you won't be able to balance. It's fine if you need to move your feet around once you're up to get into a better position," she added.

"Okay, I'll try that."

Back in the water, I walked out to just inside where the waves were breaking, known as the impact zone. I waited for a good crash of whitewater and paddled in front of it, taking the five slow strokes and three hard, fast ones, pushed up with my arms, brought my feet under, stood for a second, and fell off. I got up, retrieved the board, found another rush of whitewater, and tried again, only to fall off again. More tries, more falls—mainly off to the left, where my insufficiently centered front foot was taking me. I tried to move it into position but found I couldn't, as if I had seized up and frozen onto the board. It was as if I were again in Montauk at my very first lesson, only it was more than a year later and I was right back where I'd started. By the end of our session, I was getting closer but felt I was nowhere near where I should be.

"That was fun!" Carolyn said as we walked up the beach toward our caravan.

"It was," I said hesitantly, "but I don't know why I was having such a hard time popping up. I can usually get to my feet at home."

"Maybe it just takes a little time to adjust to a new place?"

"Maybe—or maybe I need a bigger board," I said, brightening as we reached the shade of the bamboo grove. "This one's almost a foot shorter than what I usually ride at home."

Back at the rancho after a quick shower and snack, we gathered for our first theory class inside a wood-floored room that also served as a yoga studio. Harry had a map up on the wall and was explaining why Nosara was one of the world's most consistent places to surf. Most of its beaches, especially where we were, lie along an exposed stretch of the country's western coast that bumps out into the Pacific, bordering tens of thousands of square miles of open water with no large landmasses capable of shutting down swell traveling toward it in a near-180-degree arc.

"So when storms come *barreling* out of the South Pacific, bringing *monstrous* waves to Tahiti," he was saying, enthusiastically, "a few days later, *we get waves*. When storm activity picks up in the North Pacific in winter, which creates *enormous* swells in Hawaii, a few days after that, *we get waves*. And when hurricanes *spiral* off the coast of Mexico"—he paused for a moment, then dropped his voice to an insistent whisper—*"we get waves."* Apparently anything stormy happening anywhere in the Pacific could bring Nosara waves, unlike many renowned places in the world, which might have monsters bombing the coastline in one season and a flat lake in another. Hawaii's famed North Shore of Oahu, for instance, is a winter magnet for pros, who flood the area to surf combers that routinely reach thirty feet, while in summer it's a gentle playland for newbies and swimmers.

But while there are broad, knowable cycles and patterns of climate—or at least there used to be—waves, like the conditions that produce them, are flukey, with much about them remaining unpredictable, unimaginable, and unknown. That's at least part of what turns surfers into amateur weather forecasters and storm chasers, following the development of low-pressure systems and data readouts from a global network of buoys that transmit by satellite measurements of barometric pressure, wind direction and speed, air and water temperatures, and wave energy to figure out when and where they might find the next bitchin' ride.

The Hawaiians of old had rituals they hoped would make for good conditions, including beating the water with strands of morning glories while chanting exhortations for the great, "long-raging surf" to arise. But the modern system of forecasting has its roots in World War II, when Allied forces planning coastal assaults, including the D-Day attack in Normandy, took into account wave predictions from oceanographers at the Scripps Institution. Surfers and meteorologists continued over the decades to refine their divinations and distribute them. In the 1980s a flood of services offering easily digested forecasts emerged in Southern California, including Surfline, one of the leaders, which started out as a pay-per-call telephone report and grew into an online forecasting and multimedia site that boasts more than four million page views a month.

At surf camp we didn't need to worry about any of that. Harry and Kerianne would pore over weather predictions and the forecasts on Magicseaweed, another leading website, and tweak the daily schedule as they deemed fit. We just had to check the blackboard and show up.

After lunch Carolyn and I went back to our cottage and practiced our pop-ups on the concrete patio out front. When it came time for our next surf lesson, I took the ten-two. But I still couldn't get into position to stay upright for more than a few seconds. Kerianne and Tinis kept trying to help, calling me out of the water, showing me different approaches, including one that broke the pop-up into several steps — come to a tabletop position on all fours, slide the front leg through and drop the butt to half sitting, pull the back leg forward, stand up, shift weight to the front to accelerate by swinging the hip. I tried that, but it didn't seem to help much.

Before arriving I had been excited to improve over the week, fantasizing that I'd return to New York able to catch waves at will and ride down the line, impressing my instructors in Rockaway. I wanted it *so bad*, but it didn't seem to matter how much effort I put into it: I just wasn't any good, and I might never be. Carolyn was up on her feet every time, it seemed, while the other four were learning how to take off at an angle, ride the wave, stay up as it broke. They were all younger and fitter, and seemed to be having so much more fun and success, proof of which I saw in the video replays we'd go over in class as Harry deconstructed everybody's rides to reinforce the techniques we were learning. Everybody's rides but mine, that is —because there were so few, I almost never got caught on camera. I was the clear laggard of the group, always pulling up the rear as I struggled even to carry my board, the biggest of them all, always in need of remedial training—pop-up practice in the sand in the midst of a lesson; a few turns on a special soft-top as big as a barge; extra drills to practice between sessions in the water. And still I sucked, and sucked, and *sucked,* day in and day out. At night I'd fall asleep to a tape loop in my head: *Why is this going so badly? Why is it so much easier for everyone else? Will I ever be able to do this? Why did I wait so long to try?* Surfing was looking like so many other things in my life that hadn't gone as well as I wanted because I'd figured out I wanted them too late.

■　■　■

By Wednesday I was ready for a break. It was our scheduled day off, when the coaches would work on professional development and re-jiggering lesson plans while we would have time on our own. We'd been allowed to keep our surfboards in case we wanted to get in a session or two, but I was so sore in every part of my body—even my fingers and toes hurt—that the last thing I wanted to do was wrestle around in the water. As part of our resort package, we could pick an activity—ziplining, horseback riding, stand-up paddling, or a massage. I'd selected the massage, but Jennifer, the park ranger, had arranged for a boat ride down a canal to see local fauna, so I'd agreed to go with her in the morning.

"I'm a bit of a bird nerd," she said with a smile, binoculars in hand, as our guide steered the small boat into a narrow waterway that snaked for miles into the hills and jungle that swept away from the ocean. "So I'm really hoping to get to see a lot of different species."

"Oh, me, too — I'm not a birder, but I always love it when I get to see them. I actually saw a bald eagle once kayaking in Canada. Just took my breath away."

"Yeah, they're amazing. Well, I'm glad we're doing this," she said, taking up the binoculars.

We fell silent, hearing squawks and chirps interrupting the stillness as we slipped through water made gray by an overcast sky. Every so often I'd catch motion out of the corner of an eye and turn to see a spindle-legged heron with a fat middle of steel-blue plumage and a head streaked with yellow standing on the muddy riverbank, or an acid-green parrot with wings edged in red in a tree, or a compact creature of royal blue and black flapping overhead.

"Beautiful," Jennifer would murmur from time to time, looking steadily through the binoculars, her head rotating this way and that. "Just beautiful."

Suddenly I saw fuzzy, slim black arms swinging through lime-green foliage and a froth of lavender flowers. "There's a monkey," I said with a gasp.

"It's a howler monkey — *mono congo,* we call them," our guide said. I watched as it grasped leaves from the branches, stunned and enchanted to see a small primate eating breakfast just yards away. I wasn't isolated from civilization exactly, but I was definitely in the wild, and very far from home.

Later that afternoon a bunch of us hung out at the rancho. A DVD of a surf competition was playing on the TV while Jennifer paged through a book on surf technique. I was chatting with Evan about the lifeguarding course he'd taken the week before.

"It was tough," he said, "but just so great. And there was this cool older woman in our group. She comes around from time to time and she makes these awesome banana muffins for the last breakfast. She's, like, sixty or something, and was pretty much able to keep up."

"Wow, that's some kind of determination," I said. "She must be in great shape." I remembered learning to swim as a kid through the American Red Cross programs at the beach in Hyannis, which put a strong emphasis on water safety, survival, and rescue. I'd just made it to junior lifesaving, with its mastery of long stretches of the dead man's float and fashioning a pair of jeans into a flotation device while treading water, and ended my training there. I knew I'd hit my limit. I'd watched my sister take the senior lifeguard test, when she'd had to swim and swim and swim, seemingly forever, in rough, choppy gray surf, and didn't think I'd ever be able to do it.

"Yeah, she's amazing," Evan said. "She started surfing at forty-seven and still does it. She's riding a shortboard now." *There's hope for me yet,* I thought, getting up to grab us beers. I looked around the rancho, struck by how lucky I was to be in this place where we could all obsess about surfing and absorb its culture but where there were also beautiful birds and howler monkeys and warm, clear water, and a pursuit I could fashion, unhindered by obligations to a spouse or a child, in any way I chose.

I took a sip of the beer and felt the fizzy tingle fill my mouth. Maybe I'd end up like the woman in Evan's lifeguarding class, riding a shortboard in my sixties, and maybe I wouldn't. Maybe I'd just get to a middling level of competence with the longboard, be able to surf small and medium waves on my own. Or not. I couldn't know how far I would or wouldn't get, but for the moment I was here, with an opportunity to try to learn and grow and enjoy my surroundings. And that, for now, at least, was pretty damn good.

The next afternoon Carolyn and I joined Kerianne on our boards in the pool for a skills lesson: the mysterious turtle roll. The following day would be our last surf sessions, and it was time, she said, for us to have a go out the back. I was still struggling to get to my feet, and though I had managed a few tiny rides that morning in the whitewater, I was skeptical that I'd be ready for unbroken (known as green) waves on the outside.

"Well, we'll see how the morning goes," Kerianne said, "but it would be great for you to get out there before you leave. And either way, turtle rolling is a good skill to have."

The turtle roll, it turned out, was a way of paddling through breaking waves to get to the outside on a longboard. It hadn't been a big issue for me yet back in Rockaway, but generally, before you get to struggle even to catch a wave, you have to make it outside. If you're lucky, it's a smooth and easy swim atop your board, or even just a walk. But there are times, especially on big days at some of the better breaks, when you have to get through line after line of thundering spume whose force is uniquely suited to drive you back to the shore. To get through that mess, shortboarders can use a technique known as a duck dive—something Evan had been practicing in the pool before us—which looks a lot like simply diving under a breaking wave as you might do at any beach, though it involves holding the board near the nose and pushing down on the tail with a foot as you go under. But a longboard simply has too much volume and buoyancy to work that way; it's just too hard to sink it under the wave while you're on top of it. So instead, Kerianne explained, if the wave has already broken or is close to doing so, you speed straight at it and then roll over to the side so that you're dangling beneath the board, punch the nose through the water passing above you, roll the board right side up, and get back on and paddle forth.

"Sometimes you can use the momentum of the roll as you come back up and around to help you get back on the board," she said. "I'll show you." In one fluid motion, she spun to disappear under the board, pushed the nose forward, and came back up. The whole thing was graceful and strong and sure, as if she and the board were in an aquatic pas de deux. My attempts weren't nearly as smooth, but at last here was something in surfing I could pull off. It wasn't difficult so much as confusing: it took me a couple of turns to figure out that I needed to push the nose backward from my perspective to get it to go forward, and it was tough to remember which way to roll to take advantage of any momentum to get back on. But I felt pretty good about how it had gone, in the pool at least. The ocean, as always, would be a whole other story.

■   ■   ■

We were standing, Carolyn and Kerianne and Tinis and I, deep in the water, holding our boards, staring out at the horizon, waiting for the moment to start paddling out. It was late afternoon, our last session together, and the waves were coming one right after the other, rearing up just beyond an outcropping of rocks and crashing down. I'd stopped counting after twelve of them, wondering if we'd actually get to go and if my newfound turtle-rolling skills would be up to the task. "If we time it right, we might not even need to turtle —just paddle and get out with a dry head," Kerianne had said earlier, but looking at the onslaught of white foam rushing toward us, I wasn't so sure.

Four, maybe five or six waves later, Kerianne told us to go, swooping up onto her board and beginning to stroke. I took a breath and tried to spring into position but, stymied by the water's depth, got stuck midway, my arms locked straight over the board, my legs uselessly thrashing as I tried to hoist my lower half aloft. I tried again, failed again. "Come on," she said, looking back at me. "We need to go now." Finally I jumped up and wriggled and wrestled myself onto the board, askew, and, head down, began digging my arms into the water. I looked up and saw a translucent wall heaving not too far in front of me, so pretty and pale, like glassine, and yet full of menace, white flecks spitting off its ridge, which was starting to curl downward. As it crashed, I paddled hard toward the piles of foam churning toward me and rolled over, trying to hang on as the whitewater passing overhead shook the board like a washing machine with an imbalanced load and pulled me shoreward—I'd forgotten to push it through. I turned it over and surfaced, desperately kicking my legs against the current to get back on and start moving ahead, only to see another monster rising. Already drained, I windmilled my arms toward it as it unfurled in my path. Again I took a breath and again I rolled, this time remembering to ram the nose forward. I resurfaced, taking a shot of seawater up my nose and, clinging to the board, wondered if I could actually get back on it. Panting and coughing, I hung there for a second or two and then heaved myself up and started flailing forward again.

Kerianne appeared in front of me, paddling with one leg bent up behind her, the leash dangling from her ankle. "Grab onto my leash," she said. "I'll tow you the rest of the way." I fumbled for the leash, my hand grasping only air and water as she began moving ahead. At last I caught it and held on, paddling weakly with one arm as she pulled me to the outside. I dragged myself slowly to sitting and hunched over the board, feeling tendrils of something I hoped was strength returning to my body.

"Thanks. I was never going to make it without you," I said.

"You did fine. It just takes some practice to get that timing down."

Encouraged, I sat up a little straighter. I had made it out the back. My head was wet and I'd needed a tow, but I was finally sitting there with everyone else, watching the horizon, waiting for a wave.

"Does that look steep enough to catch?" Kerianne asked a few minutes later, as we watched a peak rise and roll toward us. I was flummoxed at the question—I had so little experience actually judging unbroken waves for myself that I couldn't tell. I looked at it, guessing that its sloped face and thick lip meant that it wasn't.

"Um, no?"

"Right, it's not," she said. We sat for a few seconds, staring out at the opalescent ripples rising like hope, at once turquoise and coral and cream. We went through a similar exchange on another wave, also not steep enough to catch.

"Turn around," she said, an unfamiliar sharpness in her voice. Something fluttered under my sternum as I realized there must be a wave coming. "Start paddling." I counted down the strokes as I had all week, trying to keep them smooth and rhythmic—*one, two, three, four, five*—before taking the three power paddles, reaching my arms deep into the water and pulling through it as hard as I could, and then suddenly I was at the top of the wave, the nose of the board tipping down toward a hollow of gold and blue, the tail lifting higher than I'd ever felt it. As I held on to the rails and slid down and down and *down* the face, the roar of water rearing and crashing somewhere around me, I took a deep breath and, aloud, talked my way through the positions to standing: "Tabletop, front foot through, stand up, hip forward, arm back." Immediately I was riding, whizzing toward the shore, first as if shot from a cannon but then as if I were floating inside a glass bubble like Glinda the Good Witch: time slowed down and space opened up and even the water went quiet, as if I were suddenly hearing it through earplugs. The sun was about to set and was bathing everything in amber and peach and pink. As I continued toward the shore and the thicket of palms and bamboo, I kept expecting the ride to end, but it didn't—it just went on and on and on, steady and smooth. I felt a slight shove as the wave broke, but I stayed upright and found myself slowing on the familiar, bumpier whitewater I'd been in all week. I coasted to the shore, stepped off the board, and bent down to pick it up, finally taking a breath as I stood and turned to see Kerianne racing toward me, paddling on her knees, Kerianne who had stuck with me, never losing patience or determination even when I had. She came off her board and ran toward me, yelling, "That was amazing! *I'm so proud of you!*" We hugged, jumped up and down together in the water. *I'm so proud of you*—I hadn't had much of anyone in my life who might say those words in so long, not my mother, not a partner, not even my father, who had been so stingy with praise. My chest seized up and my throat constricted as tears comingled with the ocean on my cheeks. And just like that, I was proud of me, too, proud for gutting it out in the face of so much failure and misery, for finding a way to focus on the experience rather than the result, for recapturing my faith in myself. My progress was hard-won—hard-won like that of the woman I'd met in Rockaway in the spring—and meant that I really could be a surfer someday, whatever it might cost to get there.

7

Dropping Anchor

JANUARY–SEPTEMBER 2012

THE ROYAL-BLUE WATERS OF JAMAICA BAY, BRIGHT AND metallic beneath a cloudless sky, stretched out below me, so sharp and vivid even through the row of cold-fogged windows inside the subway car that it looked like a colorized vintage film as the train chugged up and over the trestle from Broad Channel to the Rockaways. It was a Saturday afternoon near the end of January, and though I'd closed on the beach bungalow about a week earlier, I hadn't yet spent the night there. Since the place had no furniture, I'd brought along a sleeping bag and a pad, gear I'd bought during my fellowship year in California so I could go on a weekend field trip to Death Valley with a group of geology students and professors. I'd slept surprisingly soundly during my nights in the wilderness, as winds and coyotes howled outside my tent, so I figured the bedding would serve me just fine on the white vinyl tile floor in Rockaway Beach.

Standing with my back against the train doors, I noticed a man staring at me from across the way. Braced against an empty shopping cart, he was wearing a thick olive-and-red tartan wool jacket and worn black chinos that seemed too thin for the frigid temperature. He had thinning dark hair slicked back from his forehead, a chin and jawline dotted with patchy stubble, and bulging, bloodshot eyes as blue as the water below. He seemed neither threatening nor friendly, just maybe a little down, and whether he was swaying from the motion of the train or from booze or from both, I couldn't tell.

"What?" he called out, his voice gruff and gravelly. "Are you going camping out at the beach or something?" He gestured toward the sleeping gear I'd thrown in a tote bag along with an espresso pot, coffee, and a few tools. "It's frickin' cold out there."

I laughed. "No, I just bought a house, but it's not furnished yet, so I'm spending the night with these." *What are you doing, telling a stranger your business?* It caught me up short, those words, as if whispered in my ear by the paranoid ghost of my 1970s upbringing, back when it was a good bet that a stranger trying to talk to you on the subway was indeed out to get you. It seemed pretty clear that this guy wasn't, but I was still surprised that I was engaging rather than scanning the train car for a potential escape.

"Well, good luck to you," he said with a snort as the train began its descent toward the peninsula, passing a string of well-used bungalows perched on pilings in the bay. "I'm on my way out. Ever since they got rid of the movie theater, there's nothing to do but *drink*," he said, getting louder. "I can't *take* it anymore. I'm moving to Jersey tomorrow."

"Is there truly no place to see a movie?"

"Nah—not in the Rockaways. There's no place to do nothing out here, just *drink,* like I told you. That's why I'm leaving."

What sort of place is this? I thought as we slowed into my stop.

"Well, good luck to you, too," I said, gathering up my bag and heading toward the door. As it opened and an icy wind slapped me across the face, I realized that I knew almost nothing about the neighborhood, despite the many visits I'd made. All I'd really done was go to surf lessons and Bob's place, and I'd been so fixated on being there, I'd just jumped. I didn't think I'd ever live in Rockaway full-time, but now I was nervous that there wouldn't be enough to occupy me, even during short visits.

Those feelings faded away as I trudged through the cold and reached my street, the open sky over the beach and the steel railing of the boardwalk at the end of the block like a welcome mat beckoning me to come in. I hadn't picked up any groceries, but I knew there was a package of edamame in the freezer and a six-pack of Brooklyn Lager in the fridge—a housewarming gift the previous owner had given me when I came to pick up a set of keys he'd forgotten to bring to the closing.

I went into the house, set down my bag, and turned up the heat. I grabbed one of the beers and, still in my coat, sat in the middle of the living room in a black folding chair someone had left, eyeing the white fluff from the dogs that still clung to the bright-blue walls near the entry and the small painted shorefront images I hadn't noticed before—a surfer on a wave, a palm tree and sun, a beach ball, an umbrella, pail, and shovel, a pair of flip-flops—scattered between the windows next to the front door. I'd be starting from scratch with this house. I'd lived in seven different places since getting my first apartment away from my parents, that one a shared rickety railroad flat in downtown Brooklyn that scandalized my father more for being in an outer borough than for the small porn theater that stood with a fish market and dry cleaner across the street. "Diane," he'd said, exasperated, when I told him where I was moving, a place he would never visit. "When people come from all over the world to live in New York, they're coming to Manhattan, not Brooklyn." Over the decades my choices, for one reason or another, kept pushing me farther from the city center, and this one would be the farthest of all, almost twenty miles from my office, and the only one I'd found and decided to get on my own, with no boyfriend, husband, or family advising me. I wanted to furnish it differently from my Bed-Stuy place—make it open and beachy and just a little bit industrial and distressed, like its surroundings—and I thought about waiting a year to make any big changes. But I knew that I'd definitely want to knock down as many walls as possible and replace the vinyl tile with wood, so sitting there, I decided to go ahead with those renovations right away.

I sipped my beer, took off my coat, and pulled out a measuring tape and pad to start mapping out a floor plan, thinking I'd head over to the local pizzeria at some point for a slice, since I had nothing to cook with. I went through each room, measuring and mapping, imagining where I'd put a bed, how I'd improvise a closet, where I might stow a surfboard. I came downstairs, and, pulling a hammer and pry bar from my bag, walked over to one of the half-walls that stood where the front of the house had once been. I knew I wanted them gone, but before tackling the job I needed to figure out if they were load-bearing. I'd overseen several renovations, and although I didn't have a ton of direct experience in demolition or building, I'd done some work at the margins, creating a rental apartment in the Brooklyn townhouse after the divorce, staying up late into the night, tediously sanding and priming and painting cabinets shades of gray like Nimbus and Raccoon Fur and patching a two-by-three-foot hole in the bathroom drywall with the guidance of a DIY construction book.

So a few days before this trip to Rockaway, I had searched the Web for what load-bearing framing looks like, and with that image in my head I set to opening up a hole in the wall near a corner jutting into the living room, swinging the toothed end of the hammer into the aqua surface to make a horizontal line, then using the pry bar to pull out chunks of drywall. It wasn't easy going—a sledgehammer would probably have been a better tool—but after fifteen minutes or so I had worked up a sweat and a big enough opening to see the structure inside.

It was load-bearing—*fuck*. I'd been hopeful that I could take both walls down myself, partly to be able to see what the room would be like without them, but mainly because I was antsy to get moving, to start making the place my own. I'd been living in one sort of limbo or another for four years, moving from the larger to the smaller of the separate apartments I'd helped create in the townhouse in an effort to hold on to it, going to California, and landing in Bed-Stuy. I had come to feel as if I were in temporary quarantine from whatever my life was going to become, and I just wanted to *get it going.*

Tired from my efforts, I went upstairs and sat on the floor in one of the bedrooms. The walls were painted a soothing peach, and a stencil saying GOODNIGHT, MY LOVE, GOODNIGHT, MY EVERY-THING was above the window overlooking the community garden. *What will happen to me here?* I wondered, simultaneously melancholy and excited, the setting sun burnishing even the white floors a deep orange. Would I find a love to bid good night here, or end my days alone? Or would I become, as one of the younger male fellows at the journalism fellowship in California had suggested, "a cool older lady who takes a series of lovers and never settles down again"? *Whatever,* I thought with a mental eye roll, just as I had when he'd said it, pricked by the *older* in the equation. I had a home to make and a sport to keep wrestling with. I'd have to worry about the rest of it later.

■ ■ ■

"Hi, neighbor!" The voice boomed from behind the fence as I walked along the alley toward the house, masked by the tall, weathered wood pickets and Virginia creeper vines, which hadn't yet begun to bud. "I kept wondering if you were ever going to move in!" As I reached my steps, where the fencing stepped down to chest-high chain-link, the source of the voice, loud and deep and redolent of the neighborhood, became apparent: a tall, broad, middle-aged man with three dogs—a chunky black Lab, a lanky tan mutt, and a boxy white terrier who was obviously the boss.

"I'm Buddy," he said. "My sister used to own your house."

"Oh, really?"

"Yeah, but that was a long time ago. Now she's down in Florida."

"Good for her! Is this your place?" I asked, indicating the three-story white house looming behind him as the dogs roamed the concrete yard, sniffing around a big screened-in cage with a large, twisted tree branch rising from its center.

"Yeah, I grew up here. I own it with my mother."

"Wow, a Rockaway native. Well, I'm Diane. It's nice to meet you." I turned toward my stoop. "I'm sure I'll see you around."

It was the middle of April and I was moving into the bunga-low full-time—a decision I'd made suddenly, after only a few vis-its to camp on the vinyl tiles and rough out a floor plan with blue painters' tape. I'd quickly learned that while the neighborhood lacked many conveniences, it wasn't nearly as bereft as the guy I'd met on the train had made it out to be. There wasn't much in the way of cute little bistros or wine bars or specialty shops or coffee-houses, but there was a decent deli and a fish market on the corner, a perfectly adequate grocer a few blocks away, drugstores, discount shops, and a liquor store. So what if it didn't have the small-village charm I'd become accustomed to in Brooklyn? There wasn't a place to pick up an organic morning glory muffin and an extra-shot cor-tado on the way to work or to tuck into a bowl of meatballs and a glass of prosecco when I came home at night, but there was what I needed. I was back and forth to Manhattan every day anyway. My work commute from Bed-Stuy to midtown Manhattan was already a good hour door-to-door; another fifteen or twenty minutes surely couldn't be all that much worse. And in exchange I'd be responsible for one less monthly payment and get to live by the beach—maybe fit in a surf session before work in the morning—and close to Bob, so I had a built-in friend base. I hadn't thought I had all that much furniture: most of what I had kept after the divorce was stored at the family house on Cape Cod, and I'd given my living room set to a friend. But it still took the movers all day to bring everything in, including books, a mattress, assorted furniture and shelving units, cooking gear, clothing, linens, armoires, and my desk, a solid, heavy piece my mother had salvaged for me from a public school that was throwing it away.

I set up the shelving—open, industrial-style metal units—and hung some of my clothes on a rod the previous tenants had left in their bedroom, which I planned to make into an office and guest-room. The armoires couldn't make it up the stairs to what would be my bedroom, so I left them in the living room and added to the growing list of needs a dresser and a clothing rack to sub for a closet. By early evening I had things set up well enough for makeshift living while I shopped for the furniture I'd need and waited for the contractor to start renovating. My energy was flagging, so I picked up some slices from the pizzeria, stretched the sheets over the mattress on the floor, grabbed a pillow, and fell sound asleep.

I awakened the next morning to sun streaming through the bedroom window, momentarily confused about where I was. I rolled off the mattress, made my way through the remaining boxes piled in the bedroom and kitchen, unearthed the espresso and pot, and made a cup with a splash of cream. It was the first day of my beach life and I wanted to see what the ocean was up to, so I decided to walk to the boardwalk with my coffee barefoot just because I could, even though it wasn't warm enough to go shoeless. As I got to the end of the alley, the soles of my feet stinging from the cold, I ran into Buddy.

"What've you got there, a cappuccino?" he asked, peering into my cup.

"Sort of. It's espresso with just a tiny bit of cream in it."

"Oh, sounds good. I like a cappuccino sometimes, but there's no place around here to get one."

"Yeah, this is just about the only thing that gets me going in the morning. I was going to take a look at the water."

"I was down there earlier with the dogs. There's no waves."

"Oh, really? Do you surf?"

"Nah, not anymore—I stopped a few years ago. My knees couldn't take it. But when I was younger, man, I surfed everywhere—you name it, here, Hawaii, California, Puerto Rico. I even lived there for years, surfed all the big breaks—waves with twenty-, twenty-five-foot faces."

"Wow—that's a lot bigger than I'll ever be able to handle," I said, laughing. "I'm still learning. I'm not so bad when I can get into the right position, but even that's a struggle."

"You've just got to practice. Do a fast push-up and get your feet under you. None of that coming-to-your-knees crap."

The white terrier began barking and running around the far side of the house. "Enzo, cut it out," Buddy said, turning to go after him as the other two followed along.

"See you later," I said, heading toward the boardwalk. I passed a small skate park nestled below the beach entrance and then crested the steps up to the brick-and-concrete platform that connected the stretches of slatted wood walkway. *I can't believe I get to live here.* I breathed in the salty air, felt the warmth of the sun on my cheeks, watched the cormorants dive for fish and the gulls soar overhead. Then I noticed that there actually *were* some waves—not by Buddy's definition, maybe, but clean peelers about knee-high. It looked like a great surfing day.

A few weeks later I was at a group lesson in Arverne, lying on the board facing the shore like the other students, waiting for a wave to come and chatting with Kevin and another instructor, Vinny, telling them about the house.

"You actually bought a house out here? All right—way to go!" Vinny said. "Where is it?"

"It's one of the little bungalows on the community garden."

"By Buddy's place?" Kevin asked.

"Yeah, yeah, right there. Buddy's my neighbor."

"Man, that's awesome!" Vinny said, turning to Kevin. "This summer we'll be out there calling people off waves, letting Diane take them. 'Yo, yo, that's Diane's wave!'"

"Yeah, that'll be great," I said, laughing, "but that's the wave you have to make."

"Yup," Vinny said, nodding. "That's the wave you have to make. Speaking of that, there's one coming now. But I got a story for you when you get back."

I looked behind me, saw the peak rising, and began to stroke, trying to judge it for myself. I knew that to catch it I needed to match the wave's speed by the time it reached me, and I realized that I'd have to double my efforts to do so. I did, and even got to my feet to ride almost into the sand. I was feeling more and more confident but was losing my patience with not getting in the water by myself. I needed my own board.

"So back in the day," Vinny told me when I paddled over, "Buddy was king of the break. At the Jetty, any wave he wanted, everybody knew that was Buddy's wave and nobody went for it. That's just how it was. One day some guy's out there, and Buddy goes for a wave, and the guy drops in on him. Well, somehow Buddy got the next one, caught up to the guy, and clocked him while he was still on the surfboard. I don't know how he did it."

"That's crazy! I don't even understand how he could catch up to him on another wave, but also just the balance to punch somebody while you're surfing!"

"Yeah, he was something else."

The story felt emblematic of Rockaway and its rough-and-tumble surf culture, partly an outgrowth of the peninsula's overall isolation and economic decline, along with a sense of getting a raw deal from the city back in the sixties, seventies, and eighties. Early on, would-be surfers on the peninsula rode whatever was available, including ironing boards and wood planks, before a few locals began shaping boards like their counterparts on the West Coast. But the sport was technically illegal. A nineteenth-century state law barred even visiting a beach, much less getting in the water, when lifeguards weren't on duty, and when they were, they prohibited surfers from the waves because of the risks to swimmers. Still, you could often get away with it, and the constant threat of the authorities handing out tickets gave it a rebel edge. Plus, being on the East Coast, it required a certain constitution to handle waters that could hover near freezing in winter, especially before neoprene wetsuits became widely available, so surfers relied on insulation cobbled together from sweaters, thermal underwear, and diving gear. Rockaway simply wasn't your average beach town, and had none of the aloha spirit or good vibrations of Hawaii and California. "We weren't into the peace-and-love groovy," as Buddy put it in the 2010 documentary *Shadows of the Same Sun*. "We'd give you a quick beatdown for sure."

Surf spots all over are notorious for the presence of so-called regulators, who enforce general etiquette and the pecking order in the lineup. Depending on the place, that can mean any of a variety of intimidating tactics, including breaking boards, slashing tires, aggressively dropping in on rule-skirters, or beatings in the sand or the parking lot. And as surfing has become more popular and many of the better breaks overcrowded, the guardians in some places, like ritzy Lunada Bay in Palos Verdes, California, have become so committed to keeping outsiders from even attempting to surf what they see as their waves—known as localism—that they've pelted visitors with rocks before they've even made it to the water.

Over the centuries, surfing evolved in ways that reflect intensely local cultures; there's evidence of people riding waves using various craft—boats, boards, logs, bundles of reeds—in pre-Incan Peru and fifteenth-century West Africa. But the modern global sport derives from the *he'e nalu,* or wave sliding, practiced by the Polynesians who settled Hawaii, where it became a national pastime. Way back, it involved canoes or thick wood boards ranging from about five to twenty feet in length and weighing as much as 160 pounds. The longest type of board, known as *olo,* was mainly reserved for royalty, while regular folk rode the shorter kind, called *alaia.*

Western explorers and missionaries in the region were captivated by the apparent rapture he'e nalu produced in its practitioners. Watching a man paddle a canoe along breaking waves in Tahiti, the chief surgeon on one of Captain James Cook's ships wrote in 1777 that he "could not help concluding that this man felt the most supreme pleasure while he was driven on, so fast and so smoothly, by the sea." Almost one hundred years later, the Hawaiian historian Kepelino Keauokalani wrote that November was the month when high surf on the islands would lure wave riders to the coasts, with farmers simply abandoning their duties, picking up their boards, and heading to the ocean. "All thought of work is at an end, only that of sport is left," he wrote. "The wife may go hungry, the children, the whole family, but the head of the house does not care." He added, "All day there is nothing but surfing."

Contact with the West proved nearly fatal to the sport, as unfamiliar diseases like smallpox devastated the native population and missionary prurience discouraged surfing's practice during the 1800s. But as the twentieth century neared, westerners became fascinated with a novel attraction called surf bathing, then pursued in modest costume. A lengthy article in *Scribner's Magazine* in 1890 reported that the craze was sweeping Long Island and offered what passed for advice in those days, along with illustrations, on how men should play in the waves, on their own or with a female partner. "Never promise her, either expressly or by implication, that you will not let her hair get wet," Duffield Osborne wrote. "Above all, impress it upon her that she must do exactly as you say, that a moment's hesitation due to timidity or lack of confidence, or, worse than all, anything like panic or an attempt to break from you and escape by flight, is likely to precipitate a disaster which, unpleasant and humiliating when met alone, is trebly so in company." Around the same time, a new group of swashbuckling adventure writers, Mark Twain and Jack London among them, traveled to Hawaii and wrote about surfing, helping to spark a revival—largely centered on the Outrigger Canoe Club in Waikiki—and to popularize the sport on the mainland. Duke Kahanamoku, a Waikiki beach boy who became a three-time Olympic swimming champion, went on to become surfing's global ambassador, traveling the world, putting on demonstrations, and, along with a Hawaiian-Irish surfer named George Freeth, seeding the cultures that took especially strong root in Australia and California. Kahanamoku even visited Rockaway in 1912, the year before the completion of my house, where he swam and perhaps body-surfed for the crowds near Beach Thirty-Eighth Street. That was back when the peninsula was a mere thirty-five-minute ride on the commuter rail that ran from Penn Station and Wall Street, when grand-looking places like the Edgemere Club Hotel offered rooms and cottages for rent with a private bathing beach right on the ocean. It's not clear that Kahanamoku rode a board that day—local legend says he did, while some say he didn't—but there's evidence that he did ride the waves at Young's Million Dollar Pier in Atlantic City on that trip, using a seventy-five-pound, nine-foot-long, solid redwood board his brother had made and shipped over from Honolulu.

Either way, the sport developed slowly in the Rockaways and nearby towns on Long Island. In 1934, Tom Blake, a Wisconsin-born surfer who revolutionized the surfboard by inventing a hollow design (among other achievements), visited Jones Beach, where he rode waves with the lifeguards and introduced them to his shapes. Starting in the late 1940s, veterans returned from being stationed in California or Hawaii during World War II and the Korean War with the longboards they'd learned to ride there. By the 1960s the

peninsula was home to shapers and talented riders who drew spon-
sorships from coveted brands like Hobie, based in California, which
had become surfing's clear epicenter in this country.

There was no network of surf instructors on the peninsula then;
Buddy, for instance, learned practically by osmosis. "I was just always in the water as a kid," he told me. "I was always swimming,
and watching the older guys surf. I was just trying to figure out how
they did what they were doing. Eventually I got my own board, but
I always watched the best guys, tried to learn from them." The better waves were at a spot nearly two and a half miles away, he said,
so he'd walk down there every day with his heavy longboard. Later
he became a lifeguard, along with some of his surfer friends. "Guys
would mess around, not pay attention to what we told them about
the currents and rips, and then they'd get stuck out there, not be
able to get back in." He laughed, shook his head. "We'd just let
'em flail out there a little bit—you know, maybe next time they'd
be more careful. Then we'd go out and get them. But nobody ever
drowned on my beach."

Surfing continued to grow along the East Coast, especially on
Long Island and from the mid-Atlantic south through the Caroli-
nas to Florida, but also in Rockaway. In 1967 area representatives
went to City Hall along with a bathing-suit-clad contingent from
the Rockaway Beach Surfing Club—a crew of young enthusiasts
who broadcast their membership on blue satin jackets—to protest
the lack of safe surfing areas. In response, the Parks Department
designated three stretches of coastline for surfing, one in Arverne
and one in Rockaway Park essentially from dawn until dusk, and
another, a ten-block length of Belle Harbor, from six until nine in
the morning. The commissioner, August Heckscher, named after
his grandfather, the wealthy industrialist, real estate developer, and
financier, made the announcement after a summer weekend visit
to the peninsula to meet with members of the community. "It is
apparent that the surfers are well-mannered persons and include
among them a considerable number of charming youngsters," he

said at the time. "It is my job to find a place for this up-to-date, legitimate, and very beautiful sport."

But the rapprochement between surfers and the authorities proved temporary, and the breaks were at some point decommissioned, helping to stall the sport's momentum as the peninsula's fortunes waned. The postwar boom in cheap air travel, car ownership, and an improved network of highways had made a summer vacation or weekend place farther outside the city more accessible, driving down demand for Rockaway's seasonal housing and amusements. As many middle-class and wealthy visitors and residents settled in the suburbs, old bungalows and rooming houses in Rockaway became in essence welfare hotels, for which the city paid above-market rents for substandard living quarters to house poor residents who had been displaced by so-called slum clearance and urban renewal projects in other parts of the city. Slum clearance eventually demolished swaths of the bungalows and rooming houses that had fallen into disrepair, in some cases replacing them with public and subsidized housing towers or nursing homes and in others allowing vast tracts of land cleared for developments like Arverne by the Sea to lie fallow for decades. Both the Vietnam draft and the spread of drug addiction helped suppress interest in surfing. "A lot of people got into it," one of the Rockaway locals said of heroin in the 2010 documentary *Our Hawaii*, "and disappeared off the beach."

But in the late 1990s and early 2000s the peninsula began to see an influx of a new generation of surfers, many of them creative types from Brooklyn and downtown Manhattan, who started renting out some of the remaining bungalows, turning them into collective surf houses where people could store boards and wetsuits and have a place to shower and hang out after their sessions. Responding to the influx, in 2004 a Rockaway native named Steve, who had been one of the "charming youngsters" in the Rockaway Beach Surfing Club in the sixties, opened a shop on Ninety-Second Street called Boarders with his two sons. They and a handful of other surfers, and the

Surfrider Foundation, an advocacy group dedicated to protecting and encouraging the enjoyment of oceans and beaches, lobbied the city and state to establish an official break where it would again be legal to surf—and safer for everybody all around. In 2005 the Parks Department designated a surfing-only beach at Ninetieth Street, the Jetty, which proved so popular that it designated a second, at Sixty-Ninth Street, where I took lessons in Arverne, two years later. The rules reserved those areas for surfing when there were lifeguards on duty and swimmers in other sections of the water, but also made it legal to hit the waves anywhere you wanted at other times as long as you had a board, now considered an authorized flotation device. To some it all spelled doom: the end of what was once almost a secret spot and the beginning of being overrun by hordes of kooks, a term for those who show no understanding of or respect for the norms of surfing. But for me, as a newcomer, it was all good—I wouldn't have to sneak around the authorities or, I hoped, dodge aggressive guardians of the break.

■ ■ ■

A few weeks after I'd moved, I woke up one weekend morning to the sound of an animated conversation outside. I couldn't make out all the words, but the men involved obviously had deeply held opinions about whatever it was they were discussing.

"That's just the best on scrambled eggs," I heard, and "I don't know, it's just got a nice fruity kind of flavor." Then: "Now, *that'll* set your guts on fire."

Hot sauce! A bunch of the guys who lived in Buddy's house—a collection of apartments and single rooms for rent—were talking about hot sauce.

I made some coffee and went out back to the community garden, where one of my next-door neighbors, Mary Ann, was sitting with a few other women in the sun. I already felt like I'd lucked out with her and her husband, Dan, who lived on one side of me, and the couple who lived on the other. We were all packed in so tightly together, it could have been a disaster if they'd turned out to be loud or ill-tempered or bat-shit crazy, all of which I'd experienced in one form or another in the city. But instead they were a collection of sane and friendly, artistic, bookish people with kids who'd been quick to welcome me into the tiny colony.

I took a seat and said hello, introducing myself to the women I hadn't met. One was married to one of Dan's friends from college; the other, Kiva, was dating a guy named Tim who had been part of the effort to establish the surf break and had organized the community garden. They lived together in an apartment in a huge red Dutch Colonial across Ninety-First Street, where Tim helped the owner maintain and manage the building.

"Oh, I just emailed him the other day about trying to get a plot," I said. "I'd love to be able to garden back here, but I haven't heard from him yet."

"I'm sure he'll get back to you, but you can also just come to the first meeting," said Kiva, who was small with dark hair and eyes and an impish smile. "It's in a few weeks."

"Just so you know," Mary Ann said, "Kiva makes really cute surf bikinis. You should get some."

"Ooh, I'd love to check them out!" I said.

"Well, you can just come over sometime," Kiva said as a young piebald cat with brown spots I'd been seeing in the garden dashed along the fence behind her. "I've got tons of them in my studio at home, and I'm hoping Boarders will start stocking them later in the season."

"How did you get started making surf suits?" I asked her.

"I was out in the water one day and had to make a choice between going for a wave and keeping my bikini on," she said, "and I chose the bikini. I decided right then that I was going to find a way to make sure women—real-sized women, you know, with hips and boobs and curves—wouldn't have to make that choice again."

"I know," I said. "I was in Costa Rica last year—it was the first time I'd surfed without a wetsuit, and I wore these super high-waisted bottoms that I figured wouldn't come off. I mean, I thought they were cool in a kind of retro pinup way, but every once in a while I'd feel like maybe I was just wearing granny panties." I laughed. "But I look at some of these teensy suits girls wear and I don't understand how they stay on."

"Oh," Kiva said knowingly, with a smile, "there are ways to keep things in place. I know the tricks."

I hung out with them a little while longer, basking in the girl-chat and enchanted at the notion of buying a suit from my neighbor. What Rockaway lacked in fancy little bars and cheese shops, it maybe made up for in fun people making cool things.

Later that afternoon I walked over to the surf shop, intent on buying a board. I'd gone back and forth on make, shape, and size before I settled on a nine-foot-six epoxy model from NSP, the brand I'd used in Costa Rica. A midrange board that you'd see at a lot of surf schools and for rent, it seemed like it offered enough stability for my level but had features that would allow me to gain some skills and transition over time from flailing person to someone approaching intermediate status. I certainly wasn't ready for a premium or custom board, but since I'd probably need to store it somewhere prominent in the house, I wanted something that would look good, with colors that would coordinate with the urban-beach vibe I was trying to conjure, and a stripe along the midline to help me position myself on it.

I got to the shop, a small storefront with a trio of white-foam half-body mannequins dressed for the beach in the window. Inside, it was crammed with a rainbow of gear. Wetsuits, board shorts, bikinis, and T-shirts dangled from racks throughout the store; boards —boogie, surf-, and skate-—lined the walls; and leashes, skateboard trucks and wheels, cakes of surf wax, sticks of sunblock, and mysterious tubes and bottles covered the shelves beneath the glass counter. I told the young guy working there what I was after. "You should talk to Steve—he can help you out better than I can. I'll get him out back."

A few minutes later, Steve, a guy wearing jeans and a long-sleeved white crew-neck shirt who was younger-looking than his thick shock of white hair would suggest, came to the counter. I told him I was thinking about the nine-six but wanted to make sure he thought it would work in Rockaway.

"Those are good boards—floaty, durable—especially when you're starting out, and that model should be good for you for a while," he said. "But they don't make a nine-six. They go from nine-two to ten-two."

"I'm pretty sure they do make a nine-six," I said, despite the doubt suddenly gnawing my stomach lining. "I was looking at it on their website."

He reached under the counter and pulled out a catalogue and put on a pair of wire-rimmed reading glasses. He flipped through it, stopped, and scanned the pages. "Hmm," he said, looking up at me over the glasses, "you're right. Must be new this year." He looked back at the page, nodding, and began to read the description. "'Nicely filling the void between the nine-two and ten-two, the new nine-six is a modern performance longboard which will always deliver,'" he said, slowing down to draw out the words, "'from big bottom turns to long, cruising *nose rides.*'" He shut the booklet and looked up again over his glasses, still nodding. "Sounds like a great board. We'll get you set up to order one. Should take about ten days."

■   ■   ■

One balmy weekend in May, I was driving back from the mall where I'd gone to look at appliances and kitchen cabinets. The renovation had started and I'd need to order everything soon, and I'd reclaimed my SUV from my sister once I'd moved. The contractors had knocked down the half-walls, installed an enormous, expensive beam overhead and pillars down the sides to hold up the second floor, and ripped out the white vinyl flooring. Some of my new furniture had arrived: a fabulous, cushy white English roll-arm sofa; fiberglass Eames chairs in celery and cream; a tufted white armless chaise; and a reclaimed wood and steel coffee table fashioned from planks that appeared to have holes from a woodpecker. The place was beginning to feel more functional, if still transitional. The flooring I was after—pale, long, wide-plank white oak—was delayed, so I was living atop the islands and paths of corrugated cardboard I'd put over the sticky plywood subfloor.

Singing along to Gotye's "Somebody That I Used to Know" on the radio, I rounded the corner to my block to find every parking spot taken, even the illegal ones on my side of the street. I drove down the block in disbelief, watching the beachgoers flocking along, carrying folding chairs and umbrellas and hula hoops, a collection of gossamer coverups floating in the breeze and wide-brimmed straw hats bobbing above the crowds. I circled around, thinking I'd find a spot in the big lot outside Bob's house. No luck there. I came back down my block, hoping that someone had pulled out. No one had. *Jesus, where did all these people come from?* I thought as I wound through the streets, feeling a growing resentment as I saw spot after spot filled with car after car, gleaming in the midday sun. *It's like they just hatched this morning.* It was as if I had flaming daggers shooting from my eyeballs toward the day-trippers, known as DFDs—folks down for the day. *They just blithely show up, take our parking spaces, and then leave—they don't put in the work to live here, deal with the commute, the inconvenience of everything. Who do they think they are!*

Then I caught myself and burst out laughing. "Well, now *that* didn't take long," I said aloud. I hadn't even been in my place two months yet, didn't even have a legit floor, but I was already aggrieved, just like a longtime local. I finally remembered a place Josh from Bob's porch had told me he would go to when everything by the beach was taken, and I found a spot there. And later Steve let me know about a few others. But I was struck by the complicated set of emotions people who live by the shore, including me, tend to feel toward the summer visitors who inundate their neighborhoods, acting as both vital economic and cultural lifelines and competition for scarce resources.

"Shoobies," my friend Jonathan from *7 Days,* who'd grown up in a South Jersey beach town, told me when he drove out to visit one sunny afternoon. "We called them Shoobies, because they came down from Philly or wherever on the train with their lunch in a shoebox." Every region had its own name for them, its own particular brand of opprobrium. In California it could be "inlanders" or, for the ghostly untanned, "Caspers." In New England visitors were "from away," "cone-eaters," or simply "summer people."

In Rockaway it wasn't just the DFDs who came in for disdain but the subset of so-called hipsters—the young, the bearded, the tattooed, the waify—who generally hailed from Brooklyn, especially Williamsburg, and bore the blame among longtime residents for everything that was wrong with Rockaway. One day I passed by one of the guys who hung out outside the corner deli, often with a few other men who drank out of coffee cups and soda cans and talked about the prospects of local sports teams, or about how big the lottery had gotten and what numbers they'd played. "Look at 'em all," he said quietly into his cup. "Fuckin' hipstahs."

Many weeks later, my board, unexpectedly delayed, finally arrived. Excited, I practically ran over to the shop to get it. The guy behind the counter had unpacked it for me, made sure it hadn't been damaged in shipping, and laid it out on a rack like a padded sawhorse. It looked great, I thought: clean and white, with a thick stripe running lengthwise down either side of the midline in a gradient of orange fading to yellow and outlined in bright blue. He showed me how to put in the fins—it had what's known as a two-plus-one setup, with a large fin that slides into a central channel near the tail and two smaller ones fixed on either side, called side-bites—and how to adjust the big one toward the nose or the tail. "You'll have to play around with it to see what works for you," he said. "Toward the nose will give you a looser feel, with more maneuverability, while toward the tail will make it more stable."

"I think I'd want it all the way back, then."

"Okay, but it might not be so easy to turn."

Then he started to wax it for me, showing me how to lay down the beginning of a base coat and explaining how to make a bump pattern with wax suited for the water temperature to keep my feet from sliding off the deck. "Do you want me just to do it for you, or do you want to finish it yourself?" he asked.

"Oooh, I want to do it! It's my first board, after all."

"Okay, cool," he said, grabbing a box of cool-water wax from beneath the counter and handing it to me along with the base coat.

I carried the board and wax home, so excited that I didn't know what to do with myself. I had already bought a bikini from Kiva and a cute shortie wetsuit online, so I was all ready, I thought, to have a go at the Jetty.

As I brought the board inside, I realized precisely how big a nine-six was: too big to rest upright against a wall, as I'd planned, since my ceilings were only eight feet—something I hadn't considered. After bumping around the living room with the board, trying unsuccessfully to set it at a reasonable, stable angle, I gave up and put it on the landing in the stairwell to the basement.

Satisfied that it was secure, I practically skipped over to the water, anticipating my first surf session on my first board. When I got there, though, my heart sank: it was a mess. Tiny whitecaps fluttered over the surface, with barely a defined wave in sight. There was only one guy out there, and nothing much for him to catch. I watched for a while, hoping to conjure a decent wave out of the muck. Finally one took shape. He caught it and rode it in, then got out of the water and came up the steps from the beach.

"How was it out?" I asked him. "Looks sort of choppy."

"Yeah," he said with a chuckle, looking back at the roiling waters and kindly not pointing out that I'd stated the obvious. "It's really choppy."

"I just got my first surfboard, and I'm dying to try it out, but I'm not sure."

He looked back at the water, looked up at me, smiled, and said, "Wait for a better day. You'll have more fun with it."

Every morning for the next week I rose at dawn, made my morning brew, and walked barefoot to the boardwalk, looking for my opportunity, and each time I found a reason not to take it. One day the water was flat. Another it was messy. The next, too big. And another, too crowded.

One morning I came across a guy I'd seen a number of times doing the same thing I was: watching the surfers at sunrise, coffee cup in hand. He was dark-haired and barrel-chested and was probably in his fifties. His name was Tommy, he said, and he just liked to come watch the water and the surfers before heading into Manhattan for work. He'd grown up here and had surfed when he was younger but had stopped after moving away. Now he was back, living in one of the huge brick co-ops overlooking the ocean, near his mother, and he had started surfing again.

"Now look," he said as a wave started rising along the horizon and a few surfers turned to paddle for it. "Watch this guy over here —he's not going to make that wave." I watched where he was pointing and saw the same thing happen to the surfer that had happened to me a number of times: he missed it, and the wave just rolled on without him.

"How'd you know that was going to happen?" I asked.

"Because it's happened to him, like, three times, but he keeps trying, and missing, from the same spot. I try to tell people, especially if you're just starting out, that you have to adjust. If you keep missing the wave, move a little inside. If you keep pearling—you, know, nosediving—move a little outside. But people pick a spot and just sit there."

I was grateful that he let me in on his observations, but they were also, I realized, one of the many reasons I wasn't getting in the water: I felt too much on display. I lived with these people now, and I didn't want to be watched and judged and forever thought of as that girl who doesn't know what she's doing, that girl who can't get to her feet.

But I also didn't want to be like those nonsurfing surfers my friend Jay had told me about—people who claim the label but don't do the deed. So the next weekend I decided to drive down to Arverne. There were people who might be watching there, too, but not as many, in my experience, and they weren't my neighbors. My SUV, it turned out, wasn't quite long enough to fit the board comfortably, but I found that if I put the seats down and shimmied it in on a diagonal, with the nose on the passenger-side dashboard, I had just enough room to squeeze into the driver's seat and steer if I leaned up against the door and window. I was pretty sure what I was doing was ill-advised and possibly illegal—I could barely turn the wheel and was practically blind on the right—but I figured it was a short trip and I could take it slow.

I got there without incident, and even managed a pretty decent session, paddling around the break, trying to stay away from Frank's crew of instructors and students. The board, awkward to carry on land, was awesome once I got it in the water—buoyant and, after I got it up to speed, easy to paddle. I played around with it in the whitewater first, then took it outside to try to catch unbroken waves. I missed more than I caught, but that, it became clear, was my fault and not the board's. It was exactly what I'd wanted: easy and stable—a little too stable, even. The guy at the surf shop had been right about putting the fin all the way back; I'd need to adjust it if I wanted to turn.

I drove home, my neck, arm, and back cramping from my contorted position. *This is ridiculous.* It was simply no way to go about surfing. I had upended my life and now lived just steps from the peninsula's main break and yet here I was, twisted like a pretzel inside my car, putting myself and others in unnecessary danger. I'd have to get over my self-consciousness and try the Jetty.

I decided I'd try the next surfable day, which didn't present itself until the next weekend. That morning I brought the board out of the stairwell leading to the basement, topped up the wax, and headed down the alley, grappling to hold it, deck facing down, with a rail digging into my hip. Buddy was on the sidewalk, throwing the remains of a plate of rice onto the street, presumably for the birds. "Easiest way to carry it," he said, indicating the surfboard, "is under your arm, with the deck against your body and the fin in front. It's just the physics of the thing."

"Okay, I'll try it that way," I said, awkwardly turning it around. "It's just so wide in the middle, it's hard to get a good grip."

I made my way to the boardwalk, switching the board from one arm to the other and bumping the nose or the tail on the ground and steps a few times along the way. *Someday I'll have it all figured out.* But this would not be that day.

I looked out at the break, noticing the crowd of surfers clustered around the rock jetty that formed a wall and marked the eastern edge of the surfing area. It was the same kind of place as a lot of surf spots on the East Coast: a beach break, where waves form against the shoreline or over sandbars along the shallow bottom. Jetties like the ones we had in Rockaway, protective structures known as groins that jut out from the shoreline to help slow erosion, could collect a buildup of sand and help create peaks, and on big days even the hollow tubes known as barrels that you can slide into, though that was far from a sure bet. Beach breaks can seem more forgiving than the other main types—point and reef—because of their usually sandy bottoms. But they can also be unpredictable, since storms—or sand replenishment—can completely reshape the contours of the seabed and kill the wave or render the shoreline more treacherous. Waves there can also tend to close out, or break all at once along the face, making them difficult, if not impossible, to ride. A beach break's main advantage is that the waves usually peak close enough to shore that you don't have to paddle very far to get to them. The promise of the point break is a very long ride—a leg-busting mile-plus from the point to the pier at a spot near Chicama, Peru, on the South Pacific coast. That sort of wave forms by wrapping around a point or headland and then refracting off the coastline of the cove or bay next to it before breaking on the inside. Reef breaks, by contrast, form around underwater ridges, often coral set in deep water and far from shore, and require a long paddle or even a boat ride to get to them. The reward can be hollow, peeling waves on which surfers find the Holy Grail of getting barreled and an almost mechanized pattern of circulation, with a clear, defined takeoff spot and a calm, deep-water channel where you paddle back to the peak. The risk is paying dearly for missteps and gouging yourself on the banks of razor-sharp coral beneath the water's surface.

But whatever the type of spot, the underwater structures will dictate not only where and how a wave will form, peak, and spill over but also its primary direction, to the right or the left from the surfer's perspective facing the shore. In Rockaway the prevailing wave action, or longshore drift, moved from east to west, carrying and depositing rocks and sand and building up the jetty. That's why everyone wanted to catch waves there—the buildup created a larger, more defined, and predictable peak which then sloped down and away from the structure to the west, resulting in bigger, shapelier, longer, and more consistent waves, almost all of them lefts. But farther to the west, at intervals of a block or so apart, were sets of jagged wood pylons known as the sticks—skeletal remnants of old wood groins—that ran parallel to the jetty and had collected their own buildups of sand. That meant that there were other peaks to be found. They may not be as good, and certainly not as frequent, but at least they would be away from the pack.

I picked a spot where it seemed there was a peak far beyond where the jetty hangers would end their rides. I tried for a few waves but missed them, felt them roll underneath the board and continue toward the shore. Remembering what Tommy had said—*If you keep missing the wave, move a little inside. If you keep pearling, move a little outside*—I moved inside, but missed them again. Then I just sat for a while, watching the waves lift off the sandbars and roll toward me, trying to figure out where I'd want to be to catch them and how I'd stay out of everyone's way and not hurtle into the sticks. I paddled about midway toward them, thinking I could just go straight, at least for now. I was so focused on the horizon that I didn't notice I'd drifted near another surfer until I heard his voice.

"Hey," he said sharply. I turned around. It was a guy I had seen on the boardwalk one morning, telling another guy how he thought the break was overrun with outsiders who didn't respect the locals. "We gotta defend the break, whatever it takes," he'd said. "I mean, I'll stand up to them, I'll take the beating. I don't care about that." He'd paused. "I just gotta wait until my health insurance comes through."

Now he was sitting low in the water on a board much smaller than mine, wearing a white rash guard and dark trunks. "I'm gonna be nice to you," he said. "You seem to have a nice attitude."

"Oh, well, thanks."

"Listen. You need to sit farther outside, like I am, and paddle harder sooner. It looks like you need more time to get that big board going."

"Yeah, you're probably right."

"You also need to get closer to the peak, like where I am."

"Okay, I'll try that, but I don't want to get in your way."

"Don't worry about it—I'll find my way in. Why don't you try for this next one? Just paddle hard."

"Thanks," I said, thrashing to get the board around and flopping on the deck. I dug in but felt like I was at a standstill.

"Keep paddling," he yelled. I did, and suddenly I felt the tail lift and the board begin to slide forward. I scrambled to my feet and watched as I glided toward the shore with my block—my own block!—stretching away from the beach. I was full of glee.

I paddled back to the guy, thanked him for his help. "Think you got it now?" he asked.

"Well, not entirely, but I get it a little better."

"Okay, well, I'm gonna take this next one in. Have fun."

I stayed out for about an hour, catching some, missing some, letting a lot go by as I tried to divine their rhythms. Tommy was up on the boardwalk when I got out. "Hey, you finally got out there!" he said with a smile.

"Yeah, finally. It didn't go very well, though. I still have a lot of trouble figuring things out."

"You're doing fine," he said. "You just have to try for more waves."

The comment hit me like an uppercut to the jaw, spinning my head around. But instead of knocking me senseless, it shook me awake: I wasn't trying hard enough. I wasn't getting in the water enough in the first place, and then I wasn't trying to catch enough waves once I was there. Part of it was caution—I didn't want to squander my limited strength and energy on the wrong waves and then have nothing left for the right ones. But more of it was a lack of confidence and commitment. I was there in Rockaway, sure, but I wasn't following through, wasn't taking the many next steps needed to make the surfer's idyll I'd imagined a reality.

It didn't matter how early I got up to take a look at the water, there was always someone else—even someone who may have risen in darkness to travel from Manhattan or Brooklyn—already there. I'd leave for work in the morning and pass people coming down the street with boards under their arms and feel a surge of jealousy and irritation with myself for having yet again slept too late, dallied too long, or not finished my work early enough to have a session. I'd sit at the office, checking the forecast and tides, watching the waves on the live camera feed, eyeing the A train schedule, trying to figure out if I could make it home in time to pull on the wetsuit, wrestle the board out of the stairwell, and hit the water before the tide dropped too far or rose too high or the sun set. *What's it going to take to surf more?* I'd ask myself, frustrated, though I already knew the answer: reorganizing my life, getting up earlier, sticking to a schedule. In a word, discipline. No amount of passing the time on the long commute by practicing my surf stance on a moving train was going to substitute for trying over and over and over again on the board in the water. It was, as Frank said, *simple but not easy:* I had to try for more waves.

■　■　■

One morning I was standing outside my house, chatting with Buddy, who was telling me about Puerto Rico, where a lot of Rockaway folks went and where he'd lived for a time. He ran down all the spots he'd surfed there, along with all the injuries he'd seen. ("I saw a guy get his balls cut off—and I mean *cut*"—he paused, dropped his voice to a whisper—"*off.* He went over the falls and the board nailed him, just *nailed* him, right between the legs.") I was struck by the break names, some of them nondescript—Sandy Beach, Table Top, Indicators, Maria's—but others practically hostile, like Gas Chambers. Surf spots are often called after their locations (C Street), a defining physical marker (Tres Palmas), or a hint of who frequents them (Old Man's). But many of the scarier-sounding breaks around the globe have earned their creepy monikers, whether it be Cyclops in Australia, Ghost Tree in Northern California, Boneyards in Southern California, Dungeons in South Africa, Jaws in Maui, Teahupo'o in Tahiti, which means something like "place of skulls" or "to sever the head," or a body-surfing spot in Oahu known among locals as Broke Neck Beach, for the obvious reason.

Most of these places are home to singular, dangerous, even deadly giants that test every aspect of an elite surfer's skill and training: strength, agility, focus, wave knowledge, mental toughness, intuition, ocean sense. What a surfer can get in return is a rush that's been described as better than sex. Keala Kennelly, a leading big-wave specialist who helped lobby successfully for equal pay for women in pro league competition, described the sensation as being in sync with the raw power of nature, turning some senses practically superhuman. "Your sight has pinpoint precision focus, and your sense of touch is so amplified you can feel every drop of water on that wave and can anticipate how it's going to move," she said at a TEDx talk in Malibu. "In that moment I feel connected to everything in the world, and when I get spit out of the wave, for a few moments I feel like I'm the master of the universe." Susan Casey, who rode Jaws in Maui on the back of a Jet Ski piloted by the big-wave polymath Laird Hamilton, wrote in her book *The Wave,* "Nothing I had ever done or seen or been through had made me feel so alive."

I would never get to feel anything that intense in surfing, I knew: I had started far too late in life even to contemplate attempting waves that reached thirty or fifty or ninety feet high—waves with so much energy in them that the faces become something more like concrete than liquid. I'd seen videos of surfers falling from their boards and bouncing off the near-vertical surface before being engulfed. I didn't need to aim for anything with a height that could be expressed in terms of apartment buildings rather than body parts.

It was okay, though. I admired those giant-slayers, envied them a tiny bit, but didn't have the drive or personality for that end of the sport anyway. I had to try for more waves, but knee- to waist-high, maybe someday shoulder- or head-, would have to do.

■ ■ ■

Just after dusk on a hazy Sunday, I came home down the alley, passing under the lush tendrils of Virginia creeper illuminated by my neighbors' front lights, the sound of crickets reverberating around me, to find a party in front of Dan and Mary Ann's place—a dozen or so people standing around their front patio, sitting on their steps, and spilling onto the walkway.

"Hey, sorry about this. It just sort of happened," Dan said, getting up and coming my way. "You're welcome to join us."

"No worries, and thanks, but I think I'll just head inside," I said. "I've got to get up early for work in the morning."

"Okay, well, feel free to change your mind."

I turned to head up my stoop. "Diaaaaaane!" a guy named Kurt, one of Dan's friends, called out, holding a beer can high above his head. "You have to come join us!"

I thought about it for a few seconds and decided to take them up on the offer. *You can be tired tomorrow,* I thought. *You don't have anything complicated or important to deal with.* "Okay, I'll be back in a minute," I said. "Let me just drop off my stuff and grab a beer."

I came back out and chatted with Kurt, a stocky guy who was an enthusiastic surfer and sailor and quick to laugh. He'd helped me out in the water a few times. He'd lived in Hawaii, where he surfed and went spearfishing with friends at night and taught surfing to get by. "Whenever any of my students would get up on a wave," he said, "it was so much fun to see how excited they were. I'd just say, 'Isn't it great!'"

I noticed a woman sitting by the stairs who'd heard part of the conversation and smiled. "It *is* great, isn't it?" she said with a soft Australian accent. We introduced ourselves. A dreamy-looking beauty with wavy light-brown hair, high cheekbones, and big brown eyes, she said her name was Davina. She'd grown up in Melbourne and had lived in England and Brooklyn before moving to an apartment on my corner in Rockaway.

"So did you surf growing up?" I asked her.

"No," she said, laughing, "I didn't start surfing until I moved here. I was just always too afraid of the sharks."

"Huh, I thought it's practically required to surf in Australia!"

"I know, it can feel that way. I used to sail with my parents, but I didn't like being in the water too much. Every year someone would just get taken, you know. Here it doesn't seem so bad."

She asked me how I'd wound up in Rockaway, and when I mentioned the divorce, she reached out and put her hand on my arm and said, "Ooooh, you have a history," as if it were the most marvelous thing in the world.

I was glad Kurt had called me over. Summer life in Rockaway was beginning to feel a little like being in college again, with Bob's porch, the boardwalk, and the neighborhood side streets forming an extended quad. There was always something going on somewhere, and it was easy to meet people because we were all there for similar reasons: the call of surfing, the pull of the ocean, the weird, rough-edged peacefulness of the place.

Well into summer one weekend, I was walking up the boardwalk, marveling at the kaleidoscope of colorful and revealing beachwear on parade, an endless stream of bare chests and bottoms, straining boobs, tattoos, and piercings, improbable platform sandals, shorts cut like underwear, porkpie hats, and hair dyed pink or green or jet-black. I was headed to the concessions near Bob's house for a lobster roll and a beer. Under the curatorial hands of the foodie surfers behind Rockaway Taco, the three prewar brick bunkers built at intervals on the boardwalk between Rockaway Beach and Rockaway Park offered a livelier mix of food and drink than your average beach stand.

I passed by Simon, who was playing stand-up bass along with a jazz tune emanating from a boom box. I'd met him as one of Frank's surf instructors in Arverne, the guy who'd taught me *toes to the nose,* but had come to learn that he was a talented musician with quite a following; he'd led the rowdy punk-rockabilly downtown fixture Simon and the Bar Sinisters for decades and played around Rockaway in the occasional jazz trio or quartet and in a surf-rock band called the Supertones. He was like a lot of people in the neighborhood, who had any number of hustles to help pay the bills while preserving the flexibility to live here and surf. Far from fitting the clichéd image of being slackers and ne'er-do-wells, surfers were actually among the most hardworking, intense, ambitious people I'd ever come across. It's just that the root ambition wasn't necessarily to chase dollars but to chase waves.

Lobster roll and beer in hand, I went out to the open-air patio and saw Davina at one of the picnic tables. I'd been getting to know her a little—I'd run into her a few times when I'd opted to take the more costly express bus to midtown. One of those mornings we huddled together, talking softly so as not to run afoul of the unspoken agreement among the early riders to preserve the quiet. She was going to a wedding in San Diego in a few weeks and had found a used board on Craigslist that she was thinking about buying there and bringing back with her; she was flying an airline that would let you check a board for a relatively low fee. "I don't know if I'll get to surf there this time around," she said, scrolling through her phone to find the ad to show me. "I had so much fun the last time—such great waves. There aren't so many lefts, though."

"Oh, that's right, you're goofy."

"Yeah, so I always want the left."

The preference for left-breaking waves among goofy-footers, who ride with their right foot in front, and for right-breaking waves among regular surfers, who ride with the left in front, stems from a desire to travel facing the wave, known as frontside, rather than with it behind them, or backside. This is at least in part because it's easier to see the wave and divine where you want to go when you're facing it rather than looking over your shoulder.

But I always wanted the left, too, even though I was regular, I said, laughing. "I guess I'm just so used to going left because that's all there is in Rockaway. So did you find it?"

"Yeah, I asked these dudes in the parking lot. I was like, 'I need a left, where can I find a left?'" she said, laughing. "So they helped me out and I had a great time."

"I just don't know if I could do that. I'm still too shy!"

"Oh, I just love the adventure. You know, the hunt is so much fun."

Of course, I thought at the time, *it probably helps that you're gorgeous and charming. What guy wouldn't want to help you find your left?* I didn't have quite her adventurousness, but I liked her spirit — she was thoughtful and fun to be around — so I went over to where she was sitting near the concessions.

"Mind if I join you?" I asked.

"No, not at all! Please do," she said. I settled onto the bench across from her, lifted my cup of beer.

"Cheers," I said as she raised her cup of rosé.

"How's your day been going?" she asked. "Did you surf this morning?"

"I did!"

"How was the session?"

"Not bad. I caught two whole waves. Amazing."

"Dude, awesome," she said, bouncing her head like a stereotypical teen boy.

"Yeah, it was rad," I said, playing along as we both cracked up. "Actually, it was totally fun. Sometimes all I really need is one good ride and I'm happy. How about you? Did you get out?"

"I did — I went out with Greg and Brandon early this morning," she said, referring to her roommate and another local surfer. "They're both so good, it pushes me to be better. You should come out with us sometime."

"I'd probably be too intimidated at this point, but maybe once I get a little more confidence surfing by the Jetty."

"Well, whenever you're ready. But you know, at some point I want to try getting out of Rockaway — explore and find some great secret spot somewhere."

"Oooh, that would be fun. I wonder if such a thing even exists anymore."

"Maybe. You never know. How's your renovation coming?"

"Almost done! It doesn't look like it — I've got piles and piles of floorboards lying around. Apparently they have to acclimate to the environment before they get installed. But once that happens, probably in the next few weeks, the crew can put in the baseboards, paint, and that'll be it. I can't wait!"

I told her how much more open the place felt, as if it had doubled in size, with the half-walls at the entry gone. I hadn't been able to open up the floor entirely, but it had ended up working out anyway. As you walked into the living room, you could see straight through to the back window, the staircase, and the round four-seat table I'd finished in distressed white paint, but the rest of the kitchen was tucked behind a wall.

I noticed a guy wandering onto the patio. He looked to be in his forties or fifties and had sandy hair in a kind of short mullet—spiky on top, flowing to the base of his neck in back—and was wearing black jeans, a white button-down, and a skinny black tie.

"Oh my god," I said. "That guy over there—he looks just like Rod Stewart."

Davina turned to look and turned back, a broad smile making her eyes dance. "Oh, he just loves him," she said. "He always dresses like that."

"Really? Like in tribute?"

"Yes, exactly. He's just a huge, huge fan. Rockaway Rod—I don't even know his real name."

"This place," I said, grinning. "It's definitely got character."

■   ■   ■

About a month later I was back in Montauk for a long weekend; a friend from work and I had decided to have a quick beach getaway and were staying at the Beachcomber. We'd driven up on Thursday, and I'd booked a surf lesson for our first morning there. I found myself reflecting on how much my life had changed in the two years since I'd first driven the winding road to Ditch Plains by myself, completely unsure of what awaited me when I got to the break. Now I had a home, an obsession, a body that—despite my struggles on the board—functioned better than it had since I was a teenager, and a growing circle of new friends, among the first I'd made since I'd been in a couple. Rockaway offered up a fuller experience than I'd expected, and I was excited about what it might bring me next.

When I got to the beach, I felt intimidated at first: the waves seemed big and the tide was high, which meant a longer paddle out and negotiating the impact zone, where waves were breaking, to get outside. But just like my last time there, I flopped down on the board—an eleven-foot soft-top that was slimmer than the Big Green Monster—and followed my instructor, watching his blond, curly head as we charged on through. The lesson went well. The waves were indeed bigger than those I'd normally go for, almost chest-high, but they were different from the ones in Rockaway: thicker, shaped more like wedges, with faces that held up longer before beginning to break and peel nicely across the section. Back home, it seemed, half the time the waves just jacked up and dumped, closing out on the sand and taking me along with them.

With the instructor coaching me in—telling me when to paddle, helping me angle the board—I could catch the wave almost every time and get to my feet. *Maybe I'm not so terrible at this after all.* I got into a wave, sprang to my feet, and felt myself drop down the face and speed across it. Suddenly I was going farther into the break than I had, past the spot where the wave either crumbled or the momentum petered out and I'd fall off. I didn't know what I'd done differently or what was special about the wave, but it was as long a ride as I'd had since that spectacular beast in Costa Rica. As I whizzed along, I saw a guy paddling across my path, going for what remained of the wave. He looked toward me and I stared back at him, cocking my head to the side as if to say, *Don't do it.* We made eye contact for a second, and he pulled back, allowing me to fly on by to the next section. It was almost like catching a whole other wave.

A few days later I got an email from Kristin at CoreysWave saying that a local photographer had been out the day of my lesson and had gotten some shots of me. I took a look at the guy's website and couldn't believe what I saw: me on a surfboard, riding waves. Sure, I wasn't in the most elegant or graceful poses, but I was riding waves. It was proof! Proof that I didn't always completely suck, that every once in a while I could do something that looked like actual surfing. I bought a few images, posted them on Facebook, put them up on the refrigerator where I could see them all the time. *I can surf sometimes,* I'd think, looking at them. In Rockaway, I felt, I'd always need a reminder, a little spur to keep trying for more waves.

■ ■ ■

As the summer wound to a close, I was waddling home along the boardwalk, stuffed with the beef, black bean, and cheese arepa I'd gotten at one of the concessions uptown. I neared the Nineties and noticed a group of people holding their phones aloft and pointing to the ocean. My eyes followed but saw nothing out of the ordinary: just a vast expanse of shimmering water with some shadowy tankers on the horizon and the New Jersey shoreline off to the side. As I turned away, something tugged at the corner of my eye. I turned back to see a huge spray of water erupting from the sapphire sea and, moments later, an enormous, deep blue-gray ridge arching over the surface and then disappearing, like a submarine. Suddenly I gasped as a gargantuan creature emerged, rising out of the water —a zeppelin with a snout, its gaping maw scissoring open and its throat swelling like the bellows of eternity as seawater streamed out and around it, dwarfing the surroundings. I registered the din of the crowd—*ooh*s and *ahh*s and *wow*s and *holy shit*s—as it snapped its jaws shut and retreated to the depths, leaving only a black hole of a wake as proof it had ever been there. "A *whale*," I shrieked. "Oh my god, it was a *whale*." My whole body was quivering, and the words felt like they'd been torn from me by the force and size of the leviathan and my awe of it. I was simply amazed and giddy: right here, within the five boroughs, and on this strange buffer between some of the most built and unbuilt environments imaginable, I had seen a breaching humpback.

As I collected myself and continued walking home, keeping an eye on the water, I remembered a conversation I'd had with Kiva from the community garden, one of the many about how miraculous Rockaway was and how lucky we were to live there.

"It's just so great to live so close to nature and to feel like you're part of it," I'd said. "A place where you have to pay attention to it and its rhythms, you know, a place where—"

Kiva had finished my thought, saying, "—where weather really matters."

8

Hustle and Flow

OCTOBER 2012

BY THE SECOND WEEK OF OCTOBER, NINE MONTHS AFTER I'd closed on the house, my renovation was finally coming to an end. The pale oak floors were installed and gorgeous, and I'd had the baseboards and walls painted a soft, creamy white. All the furniture, cabinets, countertops, and appliances were in place, making a calm, pale, neutral background for my sea-glass-colored collection of frightfully expensive boho-chic pillows and throw blankets. It felt exactly as I'd wanted it to: open and clean and beachy, with places to sit in a damp wetsuit or curl up and read, watch television, or take a nap. All that remained were a few finishing touches, like the closet I wanted to install in the bedroom, so I called a contractor, who said he could come by the next week.

I didn't know it then, but more than 3,500 miles away, off the western coast of Africa, a few weather developments typical for the time of year were getting under way. It was still the Atlantic storm season, which runs from the beginning of June to the end of November and produces an average of six hurricanes a year. Fewer than two of them usually hit the United States, meaning that for the most part, East Coast American surfers get the hulking, powerful waves they yearn for without the worst of the physical destruction a tropical maelstrom can bring. The storms originate in an ongoing cycle: hot, dry air from the Sahara Desert collides with cooler, wetter air to the south in the forested regions surrounding the Gulf of Guinea, which creates an unstable band of winds that travel east to west known as the African easterly jet. These disturbances, which undulate as they travel, can form long north-south stretches of moist low-pressure air known as tropical waves, which in turn can foster collections of showers and thunderstorms and eventually cyclones distinguished by funnels of central air circulation. These can grow into tropical depressions or storms, or hurricanes, defined and ranked by wind speeds and the frightening, escalating damage they can cause. Near Cabo Verde, such waves—the typical origin of major hurricanes affecting the continental United States—form every few days throughout the year, but it's generally only from summer to fall that conditions are ripe for hurricane development, with vast stretches of deep water in the Atlantic and Caribbean reaching high enough temperatures to create the warm, wet air that fuels the tempests.

So far it had been a relatively active year, without a single major storm but with several deadly ones—Beryl, Debby, Ernesto, Helene, and Isaac among them—lashing the Caribbean and eastern North America. On that Thursday, October 11, a regular sort of tropical wave began heading out over the Atlantic Ocean from the coast of Western Sahara. In the next day or so it ran into what's known as an upper-level trough, an area of even lower pressure in the cold upper atmosphere, which drew it aloft, producing showers and thunderstorms. But the disturbance remained weak and disorganized as it floated about, buffeted by winds and other forces that kept it from growing into anything worth worrying over. For more than a week no one in the weather world paid it much attention.

Around four in the afternoon that Sunday, when the tropical wave was three days into its journey from Africa, I bounded into the Rockaway Beach Surf Club, a sprawling concrete yard set with benches and tables, with a large enclosure on one side that had an enormous multicolored Day of the Dead–style skull mural including a banner with the words LIVE SURF DIE. The enclosure housed a bar, along with studios for people who made skateboards and bags and pursued other creative endeavors. At the back of the yard was an outdoor shower and a row of board-storage lockers for rent.

It was a perfect, crisp, sunny fall day and the place was already packed with people attending the women's surfing workshop that Davina had organized. Over the months I'd become more a part of the scene—not quite a member, but comfortable enough to hang.

I'd made a friend in surf school, a pretty, petite, yet fierce woman with dark curly hair and sparkling green eyes named Riva. She was a journalist who'd lived overseas and had pursued dance and sailing growing up on the East Coast and yoga and martial arts as an adult. She'd always been interested in surfing but hadn't started learning until a few years earlier, on a trip to Panama, and she had been working at it ever since. She had recently gone through a breakup, so she was increasingly becoming my buddy in the waves and my partner in penetrating Rockaway and the surf scene in New York City. She lived in Brooklyn and had bought a board that she stored at Boarders, so we'd make surf dates for weekends and after work and often went for beers in the neighborhood together after a session or a class. She'd turned me on to a surfing meet-up in town, and a few weeks earlier we'd gotten together in Brooklyn for a surf-film festival. It had been a fun evening—one of our few times seeing each other outside Rockaway and dressed in work clothes—and I'd been surprised to see how big and vibrant the city scene was and how many movies there were that depicted more than just experts performing extreme maneuvers on titanic waves. We'd even seen a hilarious tongue-in-cheek documentary, *Kook Paradise,* that poked fun at the floods of summer visitors to Ditch Plains. Between films we'd met Brandon, a long- and curly-haired sprite originally from Long Island who was one of the club's cofounders. Riva and I had noticed Brandon out at the Jetty a few times. Once we'd seen him spin around and start paddling, seemingly for nothing. Then a peak appeared behind him as if out of nowhere, and in a flash he was up and sinuously making his way along the coastline in a graceful, relaxed crouch, arms close to his body and bent at the elbows, hands pointing forward like a sorcerer channeling the forces of the universe.

"Wow," I said. "That guy's so good. Did you see that pop-up?"
"Yeah—he's like a cat."

Now he and Davina were working together to build an educational and lifestyle company focused on women, Lava Girl Surf, and this workshop was their first big event. Presentation areas rimmed the space, with charts, graphs, and equipment for lectures on interpreting forecast data, fitness training, board and fin design, and surfboard repair. A stand in one corner offered soup, sandwiches, and veggie bowls, and inside the enclosure the bar was open. I'd meant to get there earlier, but I'd lost track of time while admiring and enjoying my house. I couldn't quite get over my glee at having designed the perfect cozy retreat, a place where I could unwind after a surf session, hang out with friends, make pictures, or just veg out on the couch—a spot in which I tended to doze off. I felt I was truly at the precipice of an exciting new phase, and one that I'd engineered by myself.

I signed in and paid my entry fee. "Here—you're in group three," Davina said, smiling as she handed me a slip of paper with a number on it and a raffle ticket. "This will get you a free drink," she said of the ticket, "and how it works is, you go to each presentation with your group. I'm not sure who's got three now," she said, looking around, "but, oh, just go join anything you want—Riva's already here somewhere—and don't worry about staying with your group. Talk to you later—I've got to get back to filming!"

I got my free beer and went back out to find Riva in the surf forecasting area. We waved hello at each other while Siobhan, who topped most people's list of the best female surfers in town, finished up her presentation on decoding multicolored maps and charts to understand how developing and approaching storms would affect Rockaway waves. Wearing a sheer navy sweater with white stars over a hot-pink bikini top and skinny black jeans, she walked along a display of printouts affixed to a long plywood board, explaining how the diagrams that looked like heat maps depicted in different colors the varying bands of wind speeds that spiral out, like a snail shell, from a central eye; the many different directions in which swell could travel from it; and how big, small, or messy it could be by the time it reached our shores.

"You want to be able to judge for yourself whether there will be good waves or not, especially if you're still a few days out," Siobhan said, her long, straight blond hair blowing in the breeze and her eyes hidden behind enormous black sunglasses. "You know, conditions can change. But if I check and can see that it's going to be really good during the week, I'll just tell them at work that I won't be in for a couple of days," she added, grinning. "I mean, they know not to look for me."

Brandon, speaking through the sort of megaphone you'd have seen at a 1950s pep rally, announced that it was time to head to the next session, which meant that Riva and I were due to learn about surfboard repair. As we walked across the yard, I caught a glimpse of Davina filming Brandon executing a soft-shoe, the kind of mini dance routine he frequently broke into, apropos of nothing, while walking up the street.

"I'm sorry I missed almost the whole forecasting session," I said to Riva. "Did you follow it all?"

"Well, not every bit of it," she said, "but some. I understand it a little from sailing, but a lot of it's new. Though we don't need to become experts—we can always just look at the forecast on Surf-line or Swellinfo."

"Yeah, that works. But I do wish I could figure out more on my own."

A few workshops later, the sun was setting and I was chatting with one of the presenters, an intense woman named Bridget who had sandy-brown shag-cut hair, fine features, and a wiry, athletic build. I asked her how she got her start in the sport, and she told me that she had always been an athlete but hadn't started surfing until she was an adult. She'd even met her husband through surfing, and they now lived together with four cats in a house on the bay side. "It's like I have always, *always* believed," she said, leaning in close and looking me straight in the eyes. "Do what you love and you will attract the right people into your life. Everything else will fall into place."

■ ■ ■

Over the next two weeks the tropical wave did a number of things, some unexpected, on its journey from Western Sahara. After languishing for several days in the middle Atlantic, it split into two systems, one of which headed north into the Azores while the other headed westward toward the Caribbean, where it found plenty of fuel to grow in the form of warm, deep water. By Sunday, October 21, or so, though the system had developed the defined, spiral air circulation patterns of a cyclone, some forecasters at the National Weather Service were dismissing a prediction from the European model that it would become humongous and continue inland toward the mid-Atlantic coast, even after hitting the colder Atlantic waters, which almost always weaken such systems before they're turned back out to sea. As the days wore on, however, the disturbance became tropical depression 18 and then tropical storm Sandy, which strengthened into a category 1 hurricane, rising to 2 and then 3 as it tore across Jamaica and Cuba before losing steam, stalling, expanding in fits and starts, bloating over the Bahamas, and then continuing on toward Florida. A number of anomalies helped it along. A semipermanent high-pressure system known as the Bermuda High, which normally repels storms approaching the East Coast, shifted position and effectively created a vacuum that would suck anything nearby up and toward the mid-Atlantic coast. The jet stream, the powerful but meandering bands of wind that circle the globe in the upper atmosphere and usually send anything that makes it past the Bermuda High away from the coast, was behaving differently, its forces pushing north rather than east. And in some areas surface ocean temperatures were running about five degrees higher than normal, which added to Sandy's ability to keep growing.

By Thursday, October 25, the storm had stranded thousands of Jamaicans in shelters and flooded Puerto Ricans and Dominicans out of their homes, killing several residents. In Haiti, still recovering from a 2010 earthquake and a series of tropical storms, hundreds of thousands were dead or displaced and the country was on the brink of a cholera resurgence. Sandy was now a slow-moving disaster and a big story, with headlines and broadcasts and tropical storm warnings and watches in Florida and the Bahamas and a consensus that it would near the Northeast and possibly collide with an Arctic blast traveling from the Midwest. In New York City, officials activated a coastal emergency plan but, seemingly stuck in a holding pattern of wait-and-see, didn't order any evacuations. "There will be a lot of rain along the whole East Coast, certainly in southern Florida, and then coming up," Mayor Bloomberg said at a press conference. "If this storm merges with another storm coming from the Ohio Valley, it has the potential to give you real weird weather, like snow, and a lot of rain and high winds. On the other hand, it might just go out to sea, and they just don't know." The same day a government forecaster gave Sandy a new name, which the media pounced upon: Frankenstorm; someone created the handle @TheFrankenstorm and tweeted, "I'm ALIVE."

Over the next day or so Sandy strengthened and weakened as it churned through the Bahamas, with the reach of the gale-force winds expanding as it went. The news was full of conflicting messages—something destructive was definitely coming, but exactly what and where remained an open question. In the end it seemed like it just might not be that bad.

So in Rockaway on Saturday, rather than searching for sandbags or moving prized possessions out of the basement or putting plywood over my windows, I was getting ready to meet up with Riva at the beach for the annual Halloween surf contest and after-party, dubbed the "Nightmare on 90th." The idea was to surf in a costume you could wear over or make part of your wetsuit, and since the one I'd bought for the fall was gray, I'd thought for a while about going as Bugs Bunny. I figured I could tape something approximating white fur to the chest and put some fuzzy white slippers over my boots, mittens over my gloves, and a carrot in my mouth. I'd even gotten a rubber rabbit's nose, but I'd chickened out in the end, afraid that I couldn't pull together something that I could actually surf in that would measure up.

As I walked over to the beach I ran into Brandon, who was standing on his porch wearing a crown, a white beard, and a turquoise blanket.

"Poseidon?" I asked.

"King Neptune! You going to surf in the contest? Everybody's out there already."

"No. I had an idea for a costume but couldn't get everything I needed in time."

"Dude, c'mon! It's not that serious—I mean, Davina pretty much just wrapped a blanket and a belt around me and said, 'There's your costume!' I can't even really surf in this getup, but it's fun out there."

"Next year," I told him. "This year I'm just going to watch."

"Okay, but definitely come to the after-party at the club."

"I will!"

I walked on and found Riva on the boardwalk near the Jetty, where the contestants were signing in. I noticed a Tin Man, a Jesus, a gorilla, and an Alex from *A Clockwork Orange*.

"Wow," I said, "this is amazing. These people go all out!"

"Yeah, it's great. Apparently there's more than one Jesus," Riva said, laughing.

We headed down to the beach to get a closer look at the water, which was taupe and choppy and sloppy, with about a dozen costumed surfers laughing and flailing in the mess, weighed down by the capes and tunics and jumpsuits they wore over their wetsuits. I suddenly felt a pang at missing out. Brandon was right — it wasn't at all serious, but it looked like serious fun.

Suddenly Jules, a tall, lean, dark-haired woman who'd moved into the rental at Bob's over the summer after John bought an oceanfront apartment a few blocks away, came bouncing over. "Isn't this great?" she said enthusiastically.

We stood together scanning the water, a riot of radical creativity and commitment to fun the likes of which I hadn't ever seen. There was Tommy, the guy I'd see on the boardwalk in the mornings, with the red helmet he often surfed in topping off a vampire costume, black cape flying behind him as he skimmed across a wave. Kurt, who'd welcomed me to the party on Dan's porch, was in the water, too, laughing as his tattered, wet Hulk shirt twisted and tangled and the green makeup he'd slathered over his legs washed away. And there was Bridget, with whom I'd ended the women's surfing workshop, riding a yellow-brick-patterned board in a Dorothy dress, uncannily seeming like she was indeed on the yellow brick road, off to see the wizard in the Jetty. And then there was a surfer in beard, top hat, and tails, cruising toward the rocks, unfurling a scroll as if to read the Gettysburg Address.

"Abe Lincoln!" Jules exclaimed.

"Wow," Riva said, "he can really surf." And he could. He'd somehow eased into a position of perfect equilibrium in which he could stay upright while holding the paper at top and bottom in front of him and ride smoothly down the line. I couldn't fathom what it would take to be so relaxed on a moving surfboard that I could do something more than just lock in and hold on, but I wanted it.

A few hours later Riva and I, still an overlapping chorus of that-was-so-great and I-can't-believe-how-much-fun-that-was, were at the Surf Club, known to some simply as the Spot, beers in hand. Standing outside in the yard, she asked if I was worried about the storm. "It seems like it could be bad," she said.

"I know, but then it might not be. I just don't know what to think. I guess I should be prepared for the basement to flood and to lose power, but it could just go out to sea, they say."

We had planned to meet in Brooklyn the next day to see *Chasing Mavericks,* based on the true story of a teenage boy's quest to surf Mavericks, the giant, cold, fickle wave up the coast from his home in Santa Cruz.

"Do you think you'll still want to come to Brooklyn tomorrow?" she asked. "You could at least get your car onto higher ground."

"Yeah, that's probably a good idea, but I don't think I'm going to be able to make it." By now I was thinking I should prepare for the storm instead.

Being at the Spot, you'd never have known that a growing menace was heading our way, literally just over the horizon. We were surrounded by festive, buzzing people—dozens of contestants and other surfers, some from Rockaway, others who lived in Brooklyn, all bathed in the peachy glow of the setting sun. We chatted with Mike, a nice and nice-looking guy wearing a Groucho mustache, nose, and glasses, who was part of the big surf-house rental on my block and was always willing to share a wave or encourage you into one, about how he liked to play ultimate Frisbee in Prospect Park. We saw Ryan, who grew hops at his house and in the community garden so he could brew beer along with a neighbor in their garages. I liked them all—didn't know them very well yet, but I liked what I knew, which didn't include, I realized, what many of them did for a living, that defining characteristic that had always carried so much social weight in Manhattan and Brooklyn. It was cool, I thought as I went to the bar, to connect through this singular passion and how people behaved rather than what they did to pay the rent.

The sky grew dark as the lights came up on the streets outside and the shuttle train lumbered overhead. An alt-blues-punk band called the Dead Exs was about to perform, and Brandon, now wearing jeans, a horned Viking helmet, and a furry green vest over his bare chest, climbed on top of the shed housing the bar to light a couple of jack-o'-lanterns. Soon one of them, carved in the angular, elongated style of a horror-movie typeface, glowed with a single word: SANDY.

■   ■   ■

Just hours after the party ended, the eye of the storm had made it to a few hundred miles southeast of Cape Hatteras in North Carolina, with heavy winds radiating for more than six hundred miles, pushing wave heights there to twenty-nine feet. By the time I got up on Sunday morning, it was no longer a question of if we'd get hit but of exactly where and whether it would be just garden-variety bad or catastrophic. Forecasters were now focused on an ominous concept: surge. Yes, there would be damaging wind gusts, and maybe some rain, but the real worry was all that seawater forced to far higher levels than normal and rushing ashore. Compounding the problem would be the full moon, which generally has the effect of pulling the tide level about 20 percent higher than usual, and the fact that it looked like Sandy could arrive at high tide on Monday night.

Speaking from the Office of Emergency Management command center in downtown Brooklyn on Sunday, the mayor announced a mandatory evacuation for low-lying areas like the Rockaways and warned that the bridges, tunnels, and transit system would shut down that night. That Mayor Bloomberg was even at the command center on a Sunday signaled that things might get dire—this was a guy who liked to fly out of town on his own plane on weekends—

but I was still planning to stay. I remembered Hurricane Irene the year before, when the authorities had closed down the transit system, issued evacuation orders for more than 350,000 residents, and warned that they might shut off electricity in Lower Manhattan to avoid damage from the anticipated high winds and floods. Alone in my apartment in Bed-Stuy, I was so worried that my windows would blow in that I spent an uncomfortable and near-sleepless night on my two loveseats arranged end-to-end in the hallway, the only place I could reasonably expect to avoid shattering glass. Though Irene did indeed cut a deadly and expensive swath of wreckage across several states, the city went largely unscathed, and officials looked like they'd overreacted.

"Irene, that wasn't nothing," Buddy said to me from his yard on Sunday morning as he moved trashcans into the basement and ferried the few plants remaining outside into the house. "Now, Donna, *that* was a storm — that was when the ocean met the bay. I think I was five, six years old when Donna hit. I can remember," he said with a smile, pantomiming a breaststroke, "swimming between these houses. No way am I gonna leave for Sandy."

Buddy wasn't the only who felt that way. Most of my neighbors were staying — Dan and Mary Ann next door, the family at the end of our alley, Tim and Kiva across the street, Bob around the corner, who'd marveled at the small size of the equipment he'd brought home from NY1 to broadcast coverage of the storm. "I feel like *Get Smart*," he'd said in wonder. "It's just a suitcase. A whole studio in a suitcase."

I hadn't yet prepared much for what might come, so I headed out in the car to drive to the strip mall to gather supplies, hoping I hadn't waited too long to get candles, a few gallons of water, and some food I wouldn't need to cook. But instead of turning so I could go to the shops, I found myself driving on along the waterfront, looking for places to pull over and stop, as though a tractor beam were guiding me to the sea.

You shouldn't be doing this — you're wasting time and you haven't done anything to get ready. It was my father's voice, or at least the version of it I'd internalized, the one that always scolded me for not being disciplined enough, for not following the rules, for not being exactly as he wanted me to be. It was speaking the truth, I knew, but I couldn't listen to it. I wanted—no, *needed*—to see what was happening out there in the ocean, as if I'd be able to actually watch the storm coming, divine from the sky, waves, and wind direction what it would do. I'd given over my life to the weather's whims already; I wasn't going to miss its drama now.

I stopped by Sixty-Ninth Street, where things looked much the same as they did uptown: colossal, beastly waves that dwarfed the jetties on an endless march to shore, dark-gray ridges and peaks so cold and hard they made the ocean seem like a mountainscape, more solid than liquid. One after another, nearly overlapping, they heaved up and crashed, thundering over the rocks, a sick, bilious green at their edges becoming foam and spray shooting up into the air, forming thick clouds that hovered over the boiling sea.

I drove downtown, winding through the pitted, rubble-strewn path bisecting dense fields of weeds where packs of wild dogs and small game had roamed back in the seventies and eighties; one old-timer in *Our Hawaii* told of seeing a guy with a shotgun hunting rabbits and pheasant back then. I parked alongside a few other cars in a decrepit asphalt clearing and made my way up to the boardwalk. This was the old-school spot, where Buddy and his friends had come to surf, where one guy always had to keep watch on the car while the others dodged broken glass and spent needles at the break.

A handful of surfers were out, their black wetsuits almost indistinguishable from water that looked even darker and more foreboding than it had uptown. Here the longer jetty and its sharper angle jutting out to the southwest seemed to form a kind of cove, compressing the waves into something taller, steeper, and more powerful, in turn creating a soupy mess near the shore as breakers crashed, rushed forward, and then sped back on themselves on the inside.

No one was even catching anything, just paddling and pivoting, trying to escape the pounding surf. As I left the boardwalk and walked through the makeshift parking lot, I came upon a guy in a wetsuit grabbing a towel out of his car, shortboard lying on the ground.

"Hey," I said as I approached him. "How was it?"

"All right, I guess," he said, looking at me sideways through an unfriendly squint.

"I just moved here, so it's my first storm," I said. "I'm not good enough to surf these kinds of waves, but I'm just trying to get a sense of the different breaks. I live near Ninetieth Street, so I usually surf there or in Arverne."

"Oh," he said, his whole face transforming as his blue eyes opened wide and his cheeks puffed up as he smiled, like the world was suddenly a new place because I was someone who'd committed enough to surfing to live here. He pulled back his hood to reveal spiky dark-blond hair. "Well, it usually doesn't work here unless you get a decent-sized swell and a north or northwest wind with an incoming tide. But the eastern swell is so big this time around that it's working. It's definitely messy—the wind's really on it—but I got some good rides. Generally, though, I'd just stay uptown, especially if you live there. It's not often going to be better down here."

"Oh, okay, cool. Well, thanks. I'll let you get going. I bet you want to get out of that damp wetsuit."

"Yeah, definitely. Take care, and good luck to you."

It was getting late—nearly two in the afternoon—and I figured I should get going, since the stores might close early. On my way back toward my neighborhood, I turned into the Stop & Shop in Arverne, listening to the predictions on news radio, anxiety beginning to flutter inside my chest. The peak of the storm would come the next afternoon or night, Dr. Joe Sobel was saying on 1010 WINS, with wind gusts between sixty and eighty miles per hour. That, along with the rain, would be enough to produce considerable tree damage, widespread power outages, and areas of flooding. But the cause of real concern was the strength and direction of the wind, which would pile up water from the Atlantic Ocean and Long Island Sound onto the coasts.

"We are concerned about considerable, widespread, serious coastal flooding," he said. "The south shore of Long Island, the Rockaways, Coney Island, the Jersey Shore, Staten Island, Lower Manhattan, and up the Hudson River as well—in many of those areas we think the flooding and the damage from this storm will be worse than it was from Hurricane Irene."

At the supermarket emergency supplies were running low, but I found a few gallons of water, cans of tuna, matches, and Shabbat candles, drove home, and took them inside. As I unpacked, I heard a knock at the door. It was Kiva.

"Hey," she said, standing on my steps, bundled in a hat and a heavy jacket. "I just want you to know you're welcome to come stay with us tomorrow if you want. We're on higher ground, and my daughter's going to her father's in Brooklyn, so you could sleep in her room."

"Oh, thanks so much, but I think I'll be all right."

"Okay, but you're welcome to change your mind," she said with a smile, turning and heading back down the alley.

I was touched by her offer, but also unnerved. *Are things really going to get that bad? Maybe it will be worse than Irene.*

I shook off the worry, finished unpacking my goods, and grabbed the camera for a quick walk around the neighborhood. At Ninetieth Street a few guys were sitting on surfboards far out from shore, tiny specks of black rising and falling from valley to peak and back again as the waves rumbled through, appearing and disappearing as if headed into the horizon on a roller coaster. Along with a few other people standing on the boardwalk, I watched as one guy tried to make it through the bubbling cauldron of mustard-tinged whitewater that covered most of the beach, paddling along the jetty, where there's usually a riptide to help motor you to the outside. But the walls of water kept coming, lifting off the sandbars, shivering like exhausted muscles unable to hold their own energy any longer, then releasing downward like slingshots, thundering as they hit and obscuring the surfer in mounds of foam. Each time he emerged, he was no farther out but farther from the jetty, having been pushed sideways by the strong littoral current that tended to emerge during and after storms.

"No way would I be out in this," a guy standing next to me said. "That current is no joke."

"Right," I said. "And everything's so disorganized. I mean, it doesn't even look like that much fun, unless you know what you're doing."

As the surfer turned around to head back toward the shore, giving up, at least for the moment, on the attempt, I noticed a small dark bump at the top of a wave many yards from shore. Someone had paddled into it. He popped up, a stick man made tiny by what had to be a fifteen-foot wave. For a moment everything went still, as if the universe had hit the pause button, as the wave hovered in the eerie nanosecond when it reaches its highest plane before breaking, the surfer suspended at the top. I held my breath. Suddenly the action resumed. The wave started rolling onto itself and the guy shot down the face, finding a path between and around the fields of churning, breaking water to blaze all the way across to the set of sticks two blocks away.

As he finished the ride and headed into shore — no doubt to walk back to the jetty and paddle out again — a collective whoop tore out of the small group of us watching, releasing all the pent-up tension and excitement of that ride. It was a spectacular sight, that guy moving *so fast* across that monstrous wedge. It held precisely zero attraction for me — I would never belong out there in those kinds of conditions, no matter how good I might become. But now that I had a notion about what that sort of surfing required, I was in awe of it.

I walked up a few blocks to the beach's main entrance. There were TV remote trucks already in the parking lot, reporters broadcasting in front of the ocean, police cars on the boardwalk, with officers trying to corral surfers out of the water. The sun had just set, backlighting the cloudy sky an eerie blue, as if we were suddenly under a giant LED-illuminated computer screen. Rows of city buses stretched along the streets in front of Bob's house, maybe ten or fifteen in all. He was on the porch as I walked by, taking it all in amid his preparations to house the camera operators and reporters he'd be managing.

"I don't know who's going to be in all those buses," I said. "I hardly know anyone who plans to leave."

"Maybe they're going to evacuate the adult homes or something. But I don't know where they plan to take them."

I walked over to the beer store for a six-pack. "Hey, how's it going?" the owner, Phil, asked. "Ready for the storm?"

"I don't know. I hope so." I walked to the back, found an IPA I liked, and took it to the counter, where Phil was talking with a burly customer.

"Yeah, I don't know, it's hard to tell how bad it's going to get here," Phil said.

"Here? Well, you never really know," the guy said. "It might not be so bad. But I'll tell you one thing. Broad Channel?" he said as he hoisted a case of Bud Lite under his arm, referring to the low-lying island between Rockaway and the mainland. "Broad Channel's gonna be underwater."

■ ■ ■

Overnight and into the morning, the storm, at that point a category 1 hurricane, traced a path over the warm waters of the Gulf Stream, the strong Atlantic current that feeds out of the Gulf of Mexico and Caribbean and runs up the east coast of North America before heading toward Europe. After tracking parallel to the coast roughly five hundred miles out to sea, Sandy approached Virginia, and, while strengthening to a category 2 hurricane, with roughly one-hundred-mile-an-hour winds at the center and forty- to fifty-mile-an-hour gales stretching for a thousand miles, began to turn left and head in toward New Jersey and New York. The nightmare scenario was coming true: Sandy, now interacting with the bands of frigid air that had swept across the Midwest, was morphing from a weakening tropical storm system into something meteorologists call posttropical or extratropical and, like a northeaster, was drawing new strength from the cold.

I woke up thinking I should put the car in an obscure parking lot Steve at the surf shop had told me about for when DFDs took all the spaces during the summer, but by the time I got there it was full, so I parked outside Tim and Kiva's, allegedly the highest spot on the block.

When I returned, I found my neighbor Dan out on his front patio with a roller suitcase, looking sheepish. He had been planning to stay, he told me, but had decided to evacuate with his wife and their infant daughter. "I so want to be here," he said. "But I have to try to do the responsible thing."

I wished him good luck and went inside. Feeling antsy, I grabbed the camera and headed to the boardwalk. Nothing seemed particularly doomful. The wind was picking up, slicing through my sweater and rain jacket and blowing my hair in spirals above my head. It was drizzly and gray, with thick, pregnant clouds overhead, but that wasn't so unusual for a northeastern autumn. When I reached the boardwalk and looked over the beach, though, I felt a squeeze in my gut. The Army Corps of Engineers had only recently replenished the sand lost in Irene the year before, and it was almost entirely gone. The waves, still a menacing charcoal, were heaving up, exploding toward the shore, and rushing all the way under the boardwalk. It was midtide, going toward low. What would happen when Sandy hit that evening, during the second high? I turned around and noticed Whalemina, the pottery-adorned whale statue that welcomed visitors to Rockaway Beach, now sitting in a pool of water. *The leading edge of flooding. At least she's in her natural habitat.*

I crossed the parking lot, passing by Bob, who was standing on the porch in front of a camera, reporting on the storm. I walked back home and contemplated the meager emergency kit I'd managed to cobble together. *Will I be all right?* I'd snagged the last half-dozen battery-operated LED candles at one of the discount shops and dug up the expensive flashlight and intimidating shortwave radio I'd gotten in anticipation of an outage from Irene. Along with the water, beer, tuna, and candles, I had peanut butter, crackers, coffee, cream, and whiskey—ingredients that struck me as the makings for an all-night rent-week party I might have hosted in some other lifetime. Having gotten through the enormous East Coast power outage in 2003, which blacked out tens of millions of customers across several states and Ontario, I figured that if I didn't open the fridge too often I could keep things cold enough for a day, after which I could just put everything outside.

I watched a little bit of the news. Neighborhoods around JFK Airport, just across the bay, were already flooding, parts of Atlantic City were under eight feet of water, and Mayor Bloomberg was describing conditions as "deteriorating very rapidly." Forecasters were expecting surges reaching eleven feet that evening—much higher than what Irene had brought. Even if I wanted to leave now, I couldn't, with the bridges shutting down. "You're sort of caught between a rock and a hard place," Bloomberg had said of flood-zone residents like me at a press conference. "You should have left, but it's getting too dangerous to do so."

There wasn't much for me to do, so I turned off the television and busied myself straightening up the house and posting pictures on the Facebook album I'd started, "Hurricane Sandy: First Storm in the Bungalow." By early evening it was already dark despite the much-worried-over full moon, hidden behind the clouds. High tide was due in a few hours, just about when Sandy would be making landfall.

I was sitting upstairs in the office, shopping for four-by-five film for the large-format view camera, an old-fashioned contraption involving bellows and sheets of film and a hood under which to focus, which I hoped to get back to using, wanting to reclaim the hobby that had been the first thing to bring me a taste of joy after the divorce. Surveying the contents of the basement earlier that day, I'd put the camera and its lenses, along with some of my favorite boots—sexy, expensive, designer heels with the bad-bitch edge I'd thought was appropriate for my single status—on the lip of the waist-high cement retaining wall that held back the sand under half the house that no one had ever bothered to dig out. As I completed my order, I began hearing a dull rumble, along with shouting and the clank of the chain on the fence of the community garden. I looked out the window and in the jaundiced light of the streetlamps saw that water had begun rushing down the block and that someone was trying to move a car into the garden.

I looked across the street to where I'd parked to see water lapping at the hubcaps of my SUV. "Oh my god, it's happening," I said aloud, suddenly jittery. I grabbed my digital camera off a shelf and leaned against the window to snap a few pictures. I thought I could see the water actually rising: it was now just kissing the midline of my tires, and its rumble was getting louder. I heard a loud crack and the distinct sound of trickling, then gushing water.

And that would be the basement flooding, I thought as I put down the camera and raced all the way to the torrent. Water cascaded down a wall toward the boiler and from some part of the foundation, sluicing through the sand in the crawlspace and gushing over the retaining wall to bounce, hard and loud, on the concrete floor. I hopped up and down a few times on the step, turned, and ran upstairs for the camera, seized by a compunction to document the moment. By the time I got back the water was twice as high and undulating higher. I felt queasy and lightheaded as images of flood victims on the news saying, "The water just came up so fast," flashed through my head. Now I knew exactly what they meant.

I stood there, frozen, as the water kept rising, the roar of its march filling my ears. "What's going to happen here?" I said. High tide was still hours away. *How high will it go? Will it fill my house?* The dizziness passed, leaving my mouth tasting tinny with fear. I envisioned victims of Katrina trapped on their roofs. Could I even get up there? Katrina had happened in August, and this was the end of October. Would I die of exposure?

I have to get out of here. I would go to Bob's—his house was taller and on high ground, there would be other people there, and they would have food, water, and a generator. Alone in the dark with a maelstrom threatening to escape from my basement was no way to get through the night. I took a couple of pictures and thought maybe I should cut off the gas and electricity—surely those things don't mix well with water—but I needed to pack some stuff to take with me first. I ran upstairs, frantic, found my purse. I stuffed in my laptop, the LED candles, cell phone, toothbrush, flashlight. It hadn't occurred to me to buy any waterproof gear, so I pulled on the most rugged-seeming things I had: a pair of flat-soled, shin-high black leather boots and a lightweight hooded down coat. I put my bag near the door, looked around to see if there was anything else I should take. My eyes landed on a pile of DVDs. *Surf movies!* I threw a couple into my purse. We could watch them on my laptop while we waited for it all to unfold.

Flashlight in hand, I clomped back to the basement, where water was now kissing the bottom few steps. The ceiling suddenly seemed like a cat's cradle of pipes and levers and strapping and I had no time to figure out which ran to the gas, so I decided to leave it alone and just cut the electricity, flipping the switch on the main power breaker. I turned on the flashlight, made my way upstairs and to the front door.

When I opened it, I realized how much worse things were than I'd thought. Howling winds whipped through the trees and swirling waters lapped up my steps. *Should I even do this?* I thought as I went outside, locked my door, and contemplated the cold, the dark, the wet. Maybe not, but I couldn't go backward, couldn't bear the thought of being trapped alone. I lifted one foot, looked around, saw no downed or detached power lines, took a deep breath, squeezed my eyes shut, and let my foot sink. My eyes snapped open and air filled my lungs at the shock of cold water quickly filling my boot and soaking my jeans, but at least I wasn't frying to death. I descended to the alley and trudged toward the street, water up to my knees and then to my thighs as I reached the sidewalk, the chaotic, overflowing ocean getting louder as I went. Maybe it was the sheer energy fueling and released by the storm that made everything feel electric, but I was as alert as I'd ever been: sounds crackled and popped; the outlines of objects flashed and sparkled; observations and thoughts shot through my head like flaming arrows.

Eyeing the foam-capped eddies near the telephone poles, current sweeping down the block and around the corner toward Bob's, and the wind buckling the NO PARKING signs and white PVC fencing along my neighbors' yards, I thought I'd be safer in the middle of the street. But as I stepped off the curb, a force hit me so hard that I could barely stand, stunning me into a moment of clarity: *I could die out here.* I was in a current that could sweep me off my feet and smack me headfirst into a telephone pole or toss me around like a rag doll until I drowned. I stepped back and, sheltered by a parked car, just stood there, trapped and afraid and dumbfounded. I felt paralyzed, and rooted to my spot. I didn't want to go back to my house, soaked and defeated, to wait it out alone, but I didn't think I could make it to Bob's. *I don't know what to do.*

I heard the thin strains of a woman's voice calling my name, almost ghostly as they floated through the howling storm. It was Kiva, calling to me from her porch. "Diane, *Diane, hold on,*" she called, her voice barely audible over the tumult.

She walked to the back of the porch and bent over, rummaging around. When she stood up, she had a long pole in her hands. She came down a few steps, braced herself against the railing, and leaned out, stretching the pole toward me.

I took a few steps from between the cars, almost losing my balance as the current lashed at my thighs. I stopped about midway across, trying to stabilize myself and marshal my strength. Two or three steps were all it would take to reach the pole. *Use your core,* my trainer Rob's frequent exhortation, went through my head, so I sucked in some air, tightened my abdominals, and pushed myself toward her again. Out of the corner of my eye I saw a garbage can hurtling toward me, its industrial brown plastic almost indistinguishable from the frenzied water. "Watch out," Kiva shouted as I barely swiveled away from it. I took another step, and another, and then reached out and grasped the end of the pole, and made it to the steps and up to the house.

"Oh my god, thank you," I whispered in relief as I hugged Kiva, almost collapsing into her.

Twenty minutes later I was sitting on the living room couch wearing a pair of Kiva's yoga pants and socks, with a bowl of warm pasta and broccoli in my lap.

"I don't know what I would have done if you hadn't been out there," I told her. "I've never been rescued before."

"I'm just so happy it worked," she said with a grin. "I saw something about how you're supposed to do it on the news, and I knew we had a pole out there somewhere."

Her boyfriend, Tim, emerged from the basement, his blue eyes even rounder and brighter than usual. "There's only about three inches of water down there," he said, shaking his head. "I can't believe it." Then the power went out.

We lit a few candles and continued chatting, wondering how bad it would get. Tim and Kiva seemed unafraid of the storm and well prepared for the potential disaster, with kerosene heaters and flashlights and candles. These were sturdy people who made things for a living and camped and surfed and seemed capable of handling whatever came their way, I thought, hoping some of their can-do pixie dust would rub off on me.

I had no way of knowing what would happen next, much less how I would respond. But I realized that we were facing one of the starkest consequences of life at the ocean's edge. The water that could bring such profound exhilaration, peace, and joy had cracked open the foundation of my house and then almost knocked me off my feet. I wondered if everything would be left standing.

With the amber light of the candles bouncing off the cherry-red walls, I shook off dire visions of my house filled with water, or collapsed, or floating away—the new floors and furniture and old things I'd obsessed over and loved saturated beyond repair; power, heat, and hot water gone; and no money to restore them. But before I could get too far into dwelling on whether I'd made a tremendous, rash mistake in throwing over the comforts of Brooklyn for this vulnerable spit of land and spending all my extra cash to turn that funny little bungalow into a home, lights started flashing outside, metal scraped on asphalt, and car alarms honked. We ran out to the porch, along with one of the instructors from surf school, known as Mike the Beard, who lived in an apartment upstairs. I could just barely make out the whitecaps on the river that used to be our street and the mass of sedans and SUVs, including mine, that were now crumpled into a blinking, beeping heap.

"Man, I think that's Buddy's car," someone said behind me.

"Yup," I said, feeling oddly calm. "It's crashed into mine."

"Oh, no, is that your car?" Tim asked.

"Yeah. Don't think there's much damage, though." Somehow the car still seemed largely intact—and maybe it would be okay in the morning. But I couldn't worry about that now. There were clearly bigger problems at hand.

We stood in silence for a minute. Then I heard Mike the Beard behind me. "Duuuuuuude," he said softly. "That's the boardwalk."

I looked back at him and then followed his gaze up the block toward the beach. It took a minute for my eyes to adjust and see what he was talking about, and when they did I couldn't stifle a gasp. A half-block-long section of the boardwalk—several tons of the neighborhood's physical and social spine of wood, concrete, and steel, which connected us all along the peninsula—had broken free and javelined onto the block, its lampposts, benches, and street signs twisted but still intact.

"Brandon says they're holding the surfboards up against the doors," said Mike, the blue light of his still-working cell phone glinting off his cheekbones and black beard. Brandon's apartment, just on the corner, had big plate-glass sliders overlooking the ocean, by then a fury with thirty-foot seas that were ripping apart houses just two miles away. Mike shook his head. "This is something."

We went back inside, spooked by what we'd seen. "How close is it to high tide?" I asked.

"Not long now. Actually, I think we're right on it," Tim said.

"Okay, then. It shouldn't get much worse, right?"

"No, we should be okay," Kiva said. "I think we should probably head to bed soon. There's nothing we can do, and we're going to need our strength tomorrow."

"That's for sure," I said. I grabbed my bag.

"Let me show you my daughter's room," Kiva said, referring to the teenager I'd seen Tim take into the water for the occasional surf lesson over the summer.

I followed her to the room, suddenly exhausted. Water was still streaming from the ocean into the streets, and I could feel how heavy and damp the air had become as I pulled my phone from my bag and got into bed. We had made it through the worst of it, I thought, and though we wouldn't know the extent of the damage until we got up in the morning, we would get up and we would be together. I was safe and tended to, nestled among my people, all so attached to living in this faraway peninsula at the mercy of the ocean that we had stayed in the face of a fury so destructive it threatened our very existence. With the last gasps of my dying cell signal I tried to send my sister, who was safely ensconced on the Upper West Side, a message that I was all right, and then I put the phone on a chair next to a bottle of purple glitter nail polish, the final thing I saw as I drifted off, fitfully, to sleep.

||||||||||||||||||||||||||||||||||||||||||||||||||||||||||||||||||||||||||||||

PART III

UNDER THE DOME

All I need are some tasty waves,
a cool buzz, and I'm fine.

—"JEFF SPICOLI,"
FAST TIMES AT RIDGEMONT HIGH

9

Unmoored

OCTOBER 30, 2012

IT WAS MORNING. MY EYES WERE CLOSED BUT I SENSED it from the light, even as I swam across the gummy molasses border between asleep and awake. I didn't know where I was or why my body felt so heavy, as if I were beneath a sheet of cold metal. I opened my eyes, looked around the unfamiliar room as it came into focus: the half-fogged windows, the silvery clouds streaking the sky outside. *That really happened last night,* I thought as I pushed myself to sitting through the dense, moist air and damp bedding. *It wasn't a dream.*

I saw my phone on the chair, the glittery nail polish an incongruous sparkle. I picked up the phone, noted that it had no signal. I dropped it in my purse and made my way to the living room, which was bathed in the soft glow of a new day filtered through gauzy red curtains. Everything was silent and still, as if the earth had finally expelled all its fury and now lay spent.

I went to the bathroom to retrieve my not-yet-dry jeans and soggy boots from the tub. No one seemed to be around — whether they were all gone or asleep, I couldn't divine — but I wanted to go see about my house. Kiva had lent me a pair of sneakers, so I put them on, found my coat, and walked into the hallway, my stomach aflutter with nerves and fear and adrenaline as I opened the front door and stepped out onto the porch. It was an oddly beautiful morning, hazy and softly lit. I looked across the way and felt relief flush through my body: the house, along with its neighbors, still stood. I closed my eyes and breathed out, a long funnel of air that took some of the tension with it as my shoulders relaxed down from my ears. Then I opened my eyes and noticed everything else. The water had mostly retreated, leaving behind a blanket of sand covering the street and sidewalks, forming lopsided hills and plateaus with pools and rivulets around and between and through them. A haphazard tangle of cars stretched out into the middle of the street, some crushed into each other, with one jammed beneath the long section of boardwalk, which reached almost to the end of the block. I took it all in without truly taking it in — it was too enormous to grasp, the amount of damage and what it might take to fix it. I went down the steps and glanced at my car, the rear end pushed onto the sandy sidewalk. It didn't seem all that banged up, except that it had flooded and drained: the front-seat cup holder was full of water.

Navigating the dunes, I crossed the street to the alley leading to my house. As I approached, everything seemed the same, except for all the sand and leaves and branches littering the walkway and the absence of the huge, heavy, half-wine-barrel planters I'd stowed outside. I stood in front of the house and stared at the horizontal line of dirt that ran across it, above the stoop, only dimly comprehending that it was a water line, marking the point to which the flood had risen. Whether it had seeped inside I couldn't tell.

I climbed the steps and turned the key in the lock, held my breath, and pushed. The door didn't open at first, seemingly stuck on something inside. *Jesus, did all the furniture get pushed against the door?* I steadied myself, leaned my weight in, shoved, and felt it yield. I peeked inside and again felt relief. Everything was as I had left it, and with the exception of a dark patch on the floor in the entry, there was no sign of water. I went in, put the purse down gingerly so as not to break the magic spell that had spared me more damage, and walked to the basement door. I opened it and peered down the steps.

And there it is, I thought, seeing that brackish water covered the bottom few steps leading down from the first floor and had soaked a few feet of drywall above them. *How am I going to get that out of there?* I felt a shiver of panic rising into my throat, so I swallowed hard, pushing it back down. I would have to find a way, but not right now. I took a few steps down, breathing in the mineral, metallic smell as I crouched to look around the basement. The dark pond was almost to the ceiling, just below where it had soaked the insulation. Everything else was submerged—the sand in the crawlspace, electrical box, boiler, hot water heater, rugs, lamps, clothing, bedding, view camera, and god knows what else I had down there—except for the surfboard, which was floating near the stairs, having been swept from its perch. *At least the surfboard will be all right—it's meant to get wet,* I thought. Then I realized that I could see better than I should have been able to: light was coming in from one side of the basement. *Could that be a hole?* I wondered as I turned and went back upstairs. I walked outside and around to the side of the house, and there it was: a three-foot hole in the foundation, with chunks of broken concrete piled just inside. That was the crack I'd heard as the house began flooding, leaving the basement open to the elements and whatever critters might want to get in.

I went back inside, wondering where I'd find anything to cover it up, worrying that I'd soon have feral cats, raccoons, or rodents living there with me. I checked the faucets. The water was running, which meant the toilet would flush. *Well, at least there's that.*

I changed into my own clothes and walked around the house a few times, examining the living room and kitchen as well as the bedroom and office upstairs, pinching myself to make sure I wasn't imagining things, that I wasn't sleepwalking or in some sort of fugue-state hallucination that my house seemed largely okay. Finally satisfied that what I was seeing was real, I grabbed the digital camera and went outside. I wanted to get over to Bob's to see how he and his place had fared in the storm, but I also needed to see what the ocean looked like and what it had done to the neighborhood.

I made my way slowly down the street toward the water, unable to stop staring at the sloping boardwalk as I passed, the jagged border of the broken boards, the hand-stenciled PLEASE DON'T TRASH YOUR BEACHES sign, a toppled lamppost, the twisted street sign that had named our beach entrance for Richie Allen, the surfing firefighter who'd died on 9/11. At the corner another section of boardwalk lay along the crosswalk, one edge jutting up into the air. I doubled back, walked around the dislocated boardwalk, and realized why it was angled upward: a fire-engine-red Mini was wedged beneath.

It wasn't very cold but it was still windy, with clouds starting to break up and expose a pretty blue sky. I took a few steps onto the parkway and stopped, looking around, my brain dulled by the scope of the destruction. The whole boardwalk, as far as I could see, was gone. The ocean, surging forward, had ripped the entire walkway off its supports, leaving behind a Stonehenge of concrete pillars lining the shore. Portions of it had slammed into the sides of houses along the road; a lamppost jutted out of the foundation of a house on the parkway. Mountains of sand rose before me, while traffic lights hung at odd angles, swaying in the wind. The skate park was a pile of rubble. "Wow," I said. "This is crazy." I walked over to the beach, where the ocean was still a boiling froth, with waves rising and crashing and receding in any number of directions. It wasn't far off high tide, but the beach felt more exposed, as if the storm had hollowed it out, leaving vast swaths littered with gnarled branches, warped metal mesh fencing, plastic bags, chunks of concrete, and crooked fingers of rebar. I walked over to our entrance, where the steps and concrete platform remained standing, like a ruined ziggurat. Someone had taken a ragged American flag on a pole and squeezed it into the wreckage, where it fluttered more or less upright. It was as good a symbol as any, I hoped, of Rockaway in that moment: tattered but not defeated. I climbed up the steps and looked out over the peninsula, and could see that the boardwalk had snapped off near Eighty-Seventh Street but that beyond that— beyond the stone jetty—it remained intact and relatively undamaged. *Maybe the rest of it isn't so bad.*

I went down the steps and walked toward Bob's, thinking, *Thank god I wasn't out in this,* imagining myself crushed by the concrete behemoths propelled by Sandy's seas. Even the ground beneath my feet was unrecognizable, with vast stretches of sand interrupted by concrete walkways that had cracked and heaved up as if something monstrous had tried to escape from beneath. As I approached Bob's street and the big parking lot, I realized that something was missing, but it took me a few seconds to figure out what: Whalemina, whose open mouth generations of children, myself included, had run into and explored when it was at the Central Park Zoo and which had become, in its pottery-encrusted incarnation, a beacon of welcome to the beach. All that remained was its encircling ring of rust-colored log fence posts, pushed sideways by the water's force.

The parking lot was a ruin, too—more lengths of boardwalk and metal railing heaped atop one another, cars sandwiched between them. It looked exactly like what it was: a disaster.

Bob's house, though, wasn't. Broken windows in the basement suggested a flood, but the rest of it stood tall and proud as it always had, and the porch appeared unbreached. I knocked on the door, but no one answered, so I went inside and up the stairs.

"Hey, how are you?" Bob greeted me, giving me a hug as I got to the top. "Did your house make it through okay?"

"Yeah. The basement's full of water and there's a hole in the foundation, but otherwise nothing. I feel really, really lucky. How about here? Looks pretty good inside."

"Yeah, the same—basement flooded but nothing else. It was so freaky last night. We have tape of the whole parking lot flooding and water lapping up the steps. I'm so proud of the house—it did really well. But we *were* really lucky here. Have you heard about Breezy?"

"No, I haven't heard about anything yet."

"There was a huge fire that burned down a lot of houses—we don't know how many yet. And a couple of others in Rockaway Park."

"Are you serious? Fire? How do you have a fire with all that water?"

"No one knows yet, but it was awful. Firefighters couldn't get to the houses because of the flood."

"Oh my god, that's terrible."

"I know—I can hardly imagine. Are you hungry? We've got a ton of food."

"No, I'm okay for now, thanks. Sort of running on fumes."

He laughed. "I know what you mean. Everyone's out reporting, but they'll be back later. I've got to get back to work, but you're welcome to spend the night here if you want. We've got the generator, so at least we'll have a few lights on."

"That would be great, thanks. I'll get my sleeping bag and come back later."

I wandered around the neighborhood for a while, needing to take stock of just how bad things were. The boulevard and parking lot at the strip mall looked like a lake studded with uprooted trees and crooked utility poles; a block over from my house, a pole, half broken in the middle, dangled precariously from the wires overhead. Electricity, I realized, wouldn't be restored anytime soon.

A few hours later I was back on my street, where Tim and Kiva had set up a fire pit at the entrance to the community garden and were talking about making a supply station on their porch and rigging a camp stove so that we could have a communal cooking area. "I'm sure everyone's got food that's still good. We can make chili and soups and stews," Kiva said. "Keep the fire going so everyone can stay warm."

"That's a great idea," I said. I didn't have much to contribute—some canned tuna and tomatoes, maybe, but no fresh meat or vegetables. "I'll see what I've got that'll keep and put it on your porch."

I noticed a dark-haired young woman who lived in one of the street-level bungalows down the block from me staring off into the middle distance. I went over and asked how she was doing.

"Not good. Not good."

"How badly are you flooded?"

"Completely," she said, looking down, shaking her head. "Just everything." She looked up, shrugged. "I mean, this is all I have left," she said, gesturing to the gray sweatshirt and sweatpants she was wearing with thin white canvas sneakers.

"Oh, no, I'm so sorry. Do you need anything—some warmer clothes?"

"No, thanks, I'm okay. I'm going to my dad's tonight. After that . . ." She stopped, looked down again, shook her head. It seemed clear that she wasn't coming back.

Conversations went on around me. Tim had a line on getting some cleaning supplies; the sewage treatment plant a few blocks away on the bay side had flooded, so who knew what was in the water that soaked us? Someone knew somebody with a generator and pump, so we could start clearing out basements soon. I sat on a tree stump, feeling the warmth of the fire and looking blindly at the street. *This is an actual disaster,* I thought, the sand and rubble coming back into focus. *Shouldn't the Red Cross be here, handing out water and blankets?*

Maybe tomorrow. I stood up and walked back to my house. It would be dark soon, so I needed to get going. I grabbed the sleeping bag, a knapsack, and a flashlight and left.

"Stay safe," someone called out as I walked past the fire.

"Thanks—you, too," I said, somehow knowing without knowing that I would.

10

Treading Water

A FEW DAYS AFTER THE STORM, I WAS IN MY KITCHEN when I noticed a man in a neon-green vest and hardhat walking behind the house. I went out back and saw that he was undoing a latch that had appeared on my gas meter at some point during the aftermath. He told me that he was from out west, one of the many utility workers who had arrived from all over the country to help the local gas and electric companies get their systems functioning again. Though the distribution network was fine, he said, they'd been going house to house to make sure that none of our supply lines had been damaged. "You're all set here," he said. "You'll have your gas back in a few minutes."

"That's awesome," I said, suppressing the urge to hug him. "Thank you—that's going to make a big difference."

Espresso. I can make my own espresso, I thought, so excited and grateful that tears welled up in my eyes. I went back into the house, filled the pot with water and coffee grounds. When I tried the stove, I almost jumped with delight at the ring of blue flames springing to life. Here was a filament of my normal life, a thin tether linking me to how things used to be. I put the pot on the fire, went outside to the crate where I'd stowed a few things from the fridge, pulled out the cream, and sniffed it to find it smelled fresh. It hardly mattered that the basement still held several feet of water and I still had no power, heat, or hot water. What I was about to have was a steaming cup of my usual morning brew, and a familiar ritual and taste and smell that might make things feel right for a second.

Coffee in hand, I went outside and joined the group of neighbors sitting around the fire, a morning habit we'd all gotten into of checking with each other on how the previous day and night had gone and trading information about the prospects for getting help. Buddy was saying that he planned to make dinner for the block that night. "I got all this stuff I need to cook before it goes bad," he said. "I got pork chops, I got sausages, hamburger—all kinds of stuff. I got the last of my tomatoes from the garden—I'm gonna use them, too."

"Well, I put some canned tomatoes on Tim and Kiva's porch if you need them."

"Nah, I think I'm okay. I had so many tomatoes I almost didn't know what to do with them all."

I had plans to go into the city that afternoon, so I'd miss Buddy's dinner. There wasn't much public transportation—the flood had knocked out the rail connection to the peninsula, and the buses were sporadic at best—but some neighbors had offered me a lift to the Upper West Side, where I planned to stay for a few days with my sister. I had a list of things I wanted to buy, rain boots, batteries, and some warm layers chief among them. It hadn't been particularly cold yet, but there were rumblings of dropping temperatures and the possibility of a northeaster blanketing us with snow the next week, and I wanted to be prepared to get through it with no heat. I saw Brandon coming up the block on his way to the Surf Club, which he, Davina, and a few others had turned into a relief center, collecting and distributing emergency supplies. Jules had been volunteering there and had confirmed that Brandon and Davina were dating, as she, Bob, and I had begun to suspect. "I saw a butt-pat," Jules had told us.

I stood up to say hello to Brandon and to ask if there was anything in particular I could bring back from Manhattan.

"Warm clothes or blankets," he said, "like maybe fleeces or something like that. It's going to get cold soon."

"Okay, I'll see what I can find. Anything else? Anything *you* might need?"

He thought for a minute. Then his eyes widened. "Socks!" he said. "Dry socks."

"That I can do!"

"Thanks." He turned to leave, looked back at me, and cocked his head. "Still smiling," he said with a grin. "You're still smiling."

And I was. I now had a clearer sense of the scope and toll of the disaster and felt even luckier knowing how much worse it could have been. More than one hundred homes had burned to the ground in Breezy, as had more than a dozen in Belle Harbor, though miraculously no one had died in them. At that end of the peninsula, where there's no boardwalk and houses sit along the shore, the storm had ripped off whole facades and swept away supports and walls, collapsing rooms or leaving them exposed and askew. In the multistory public housing projects there was also no heat or hot water, but the power outage meant that the elevators were at a standstill and there was no running water, so that disabled and elderly residents were imprisoned in their apartments, unable to flush their toilets and with no access to fresh food or basic necessities.

The devastation wasn't confined to Rockaway. Other parts of New York City and the region had been similarly inundated, trapping people in their homes or carrying them away in the flooded streets. The drowned bodies of a father and son were found clinging to one another in a house on Staten Island. On the street, surging floodwaters swept two young boys, aged two and four, from their mother; searchers found their bodies a few days later. I heard about a man down the street from me who'd died after a heart attack, but otherwise almost everyone in my immediate area, it seemed, had survived. And though the Red Cross still hadn't made an appearance—at least not that I had seen—other entities, such as Occupy Sandy and Team Rubicon, had begun organizing to help out, establishing supply and food stations throughout the peninsula. Groups of Sikh men had found their way to various street corners, where they set up folding tables loaded with piles of sandwiches. Klaus Biesenbach, then the director of MoMA PS1, the contemporary art museum in Long Island City, who had a weekend house on the bay side of the peninsula, had sprung into action after seeing how little attention Rockaway seemed to be getting as much of the rest of the city recovered and more or less moved on. He'd offered up the museum as a shelter for anyone Sandy had displaced, fired up a tweet storm to his sizable following, wrangled his art-world connections into the effort, and organized volunteers, including celebrities like Michael Stipe and Madonna, to come out to the neighborhood. Riva was pitching in, sometimes renting a car and driving out, sometimes coming with a group. Over at the Surf Club, Brandon told me, they were overwhelmed with trying to coordinate all the people who were showing up to help: "It's everybody I saw in the water and at the club all summer—all those surfers from Brooklyn and Manhattan." Those people were no longer being dissed as hipsters, apparently. Now they were "helpsters."

I had every reason to keep smiling, I thought. I was spending my nights at Bob's, where there was an endless parade of neighbors, friends, reporters, and camera operators, so I had food, shelter, and people trying to make sure I was okay. And now I even had espresso.

A few days later I was standing on the street staring at my car. It was a bright morning and I felt restored, if not exactly rested or relaxed. I'd had a brief, glorious respite on the Upper West Side with my sister, who had understood and supported my sudden love of surfing and my move to Rockaway, even if she hid any worries she might have had over my pursuing a sometimes dangerous sport. We lived very different lives, but she, too, felt the pull of the beach, having reveled in our Cape Cod summers. During my escape to Manhattan I'd indulged in the luxuries of her kindness and concern, hot showers, dinner at a restaurant, and home-cooked meals. And with distance from the disaster, and in the company of a caring relative, I'd begun to understand how foolish my decision to stay through the maelstrom had been. Yes, I'd managed to survive, but I hadn't needed to be there to see precisely where the house might be breached to guide future repairs, and once the flooding started, there wasn't a thing I could have done to make matters any better. It had been reckless and selfish, I realized. I'd just ended up worrying the people who cared about me.

At the same time, as much as I'd been grateful for the taste of civilization, I'd felt unnerved after a night or two on an air mattress in my childhood bedroom and some time at the office. Like someone out of *The Matrix,* I had the sense that the blinders were off and I'd seen the real world and no longer belonged among the sleepwalkers, who were supportive and sympathetic but had no idea what was going on out there. I'd taken advantage of the uninterrupted Internet access to file an application for disaster aid with FEMA; the agency was taking a more preemptive approach with Sandy than with some past disasters and preapproving grants without the customary home inspections, which meant that I might have government cash deposited directly into my checking account before an inspector came to determine that I needed it. But after that, I felt I couldn't linger in areas that showed no signs of the storm. I needed to be in Rockaway, where there was wreckage to handle.

So I'd gotten a lift back, in an emotionally obverse journey, riding from the intact sector—the canyons of skyscrapers and the little villages of the boroughs as grand and charming and romantic as ever—into the rubble. Yet I felt my heart rise and swell, as always, as the car crested the bridge out of Howard Beach and continued into the Jamaica Bay Wildlife Refuge, with the smell of salt, the sight of water, and the sheer breadth of air around me signaling that I was getting closer to home. I kept that feeling even as we came through the refuge and across Broad Channel, where handwritten signs threatening to shoot or crucify looters hung on porches, boats sprung loose from their moorings in the storm still rested along the median, and a collection of officials tried to guide traffic with emergency vehicles, flares, and flashlights.

When I got back to the neighborhood in Rockaway, it still looked like a disaster zone, though the Sanitation Department and the Army Corps of Engineers had made obvious progress: the street was largely clear of sand, which was now heaped in an ever-growing mountain at the end of the block, and the cars were in a more or less orderly line at the curb. My insurance company had declared my car totaled—they said that once a car is flooded, it's too dangerous to try to repair, and I should just clear out anything I wanted to keep and someone would come take it away. I didn't think there was much in it, save a box of books I'd been meaning to donate but hadn't. I crossed over to take a look and saw that the back windshield was shattered. I didn't think it had been that way before, but maybe I just hadn't noticed.

Inside, the box of books was indeed sodden and unsalvageable. I walked around to the front door and peered inside, checked the front and back seats, door pockets, and finally the glove compartment, where I found the collection of CDs some of my music-loving friends had made to help me through the long drive home from the fellowship in California—a rite of passage in trying to take charge of myself as a single woman. They were an eclectic bunch of songs that spanned genres, including R & B, disco, rock, and country— disks you could just put in and let play for hours.

As I looked at them, I remembered a particularly strange and solitary part of my journey. I'd come across a ghost town in the Nevada desert and spent hours there with the view camera, trying to capture the bizarre mixture of aspiration and disappointment embodied in the abandoned mining equipment, half-collapsed houses, and rusted school buses scattered throughout the dry wilderness. As winds blew dust and weeds around me, I set the legs of my tripod into the scrub brush, startling a scorpion. I realized, watching the tiny, irritated creature scuttle across the dirt, flexing its barbed tail as it went, how easily I could have been stung had my hand been closer, and how completely vulnerable I was while invading an environment I didn't fully understand. I was as defenseless against that scorpion and the red ants that soon massed around my open-mesh shoes as I would have been against a drifter coming my way, up to no good.

And yet I wasn't scared. There was something about the meaningfulness of my pursuit, the feeling that there, in that place, I was finally ignoring all the little voices that said, "Stop! Don't! You are not made for this sort of thing," the voices that I now knew had been plaguing me all my life. In that ghost town I'd felt like I had a creative force field around me, a protective shell keeping me safe as I chased after something that consumed my imagination and brought me pleasure. Out there in the middle of nowhere, I realized, I was pretty sure no one was interested in harming me. It reminded me of what my father used to say, dismissively, when I was too frightened of a spider suspended across the threshold to leave the house at the Cape: "That spider's not even thinking about you."

As I looked at the CDs, covered in a gritty film of brown gunk, deposits of whatever might have been in the floodwaters—untreated sewage, oil, gasoline, chemicals, and other poisons I didn't know how to clean—I realized that I had the same feeling of protection in Rockaway. Maybe it was my upbringing—I'd survived the chaos of my childhood mainly by waiting for the storms to pass —or maybe it was something else making me feel that things were going to work out for me here. Either way, I left the CDs in the car.

One of my neighbors, an older man whose family had lived there for decades, came over as I crossed the street.

"You see the back of your car?"

"Yeah. I was trying to remember if that window was broken the morning after the storm."

"Nah," he said. "The army did that—backed a Humvee right into it."

"A Humvee? Are you serious?"

"Yeah. They came through here with Humvees doing some kind of work, and one of them busted your window."

"Ah, okay. Makes me wonder if we're going to survive the cleanup," I said, laughing. "Doesn't matter, though. I'll be fine with the insurance."

"Well, that's good."

"Yeah, it's definitely a help. But I'm going to miss that car. We've been through a lot together."

I went back inside to start getting ready to clean out the basement, which had almost entirely drained in the few days I'd been gone, leaving everything sheathed in mud. I still needed to have the foundation hole patched, but I'd been told it was cold enough that I didn't have to worry about mold yet: the temperature was too low for it to grow. Even with the sunlight streaming through the hole and down the stairs, it was too dark to distinguish one heap of muddy things from another. The flashlight wouldn't be enough, so I unearthed the five or six clip-on bike lights I'd used during the year in California, put in new batteries, and set them around the basement. It wasn't perfect, but it would work. Looking around, I suddenly felt overwhelmed. There was just so much stuff. I couldn't figure out where to start, or how to decide whether to keep any of it. I'd gotten an industrial-sized drum of eco-friendly cleaner, Tyvek coveralls, and rubber gloves off Tim and Kiva's porch, but I was otherwise daunted and unprepared.

I went back upstairs and outside, hoping the fresh air would help me focus and gather energy for the task ahead. About a dozen young people, looking entirely too clean and bright-eyed to be locals, were coming down the block. Two of them, guys with short hair, one pale, the other dark, came over.

"Do you need any help?" one of them asked.

"I was planning to try to muck out my basement," I said. "There's a lot of things like furniture, clothes, rugs, some leftover construction materials down there. The water finally drained, but now it's pretty muddy."

"Well, we can help you out," one of them said, smiling.

"Really? I don't have any cleaning equipment or a shovel or anything."

"We can probably just carry stuff upstairs," one explained. "We're here with the group from MoMA and we just want to help."

"Wow, thanks — that's so kind of you. Come on in," I said, leading them down the alley. "You're sure? It's really gross."

"Yup, we'll be fine," one said cheerfully.

"Okay, then," I said, turning to take them into my underground mire. "I don't think I'm going to want to keep much of the stuff, so we can just put it all out on the street, I guess."

"Fine," one of them said. "We'll just start here and work our way in."

One after another, we carried muddy, soggy pile after muddy, soggy pile up the stairs and out to the street: lamps and towels and blankets I didn't need; jackets I hadn't worn in years; extra floorboards I'd kept in case something needed replacing; a pile of rugs the previous tenants had thrown over the cement floor; my grandmother's mahogany magazine rack, which I'd never found a way to use. I stumbled, felt my foot crush something inside a plastic bag. I looked down and saw that it was a container of white paint, which had splashed up my legs and onto the floor: the remains of what the painters had used just a few weeks before. It was hardly the worst of what might be coating the basement, I thought, picking the bag up and carrying it, dripping, to the growing pile on the street. I looked around and saw that everyone else was doing the same thing, making mountains of dark, stained mattresses, wet insulation and wallboard, pipes and coats and chairs and broken china.

I went back downstairs to find one of my helpers holding up

my two favorite pairs of boots, both with high, chunky heels that brought me up to about six foot two, long leather sheaths that skimmed just below the knee. "What about these—are you *sure* you want to throw them away?" he asked.

I had to think about it for a minute. One pair was smooth, shiny taupe leather with a refined western edge. The other was black and butch, with a thick, tubular sheath that wrapped over the foot and heavy silver zippers running up the sides, and had seemed to demand a peaked leather biker hat and a studded collar around my neck. I loved those boots—had paid a fortune for them and imbued them with all the badassery I imagined I'd need in my postdivorce life. I'd built outfits around them, stridden around the house in them, even used one of them as my first social media profile picture. But I'd never gotten up the nerve to wear either pair out of the house. I'd just never been able to drum up all the moxie in my quotidian existence that I saw reflected in my bedroom mirror. I certainly didn't need them now.

By the end, all I'd saved was the surfboard and the view camera, and I was feeling good about having cleared so much from my past life and achieved a kind of surrender-to-the-storm weightlessness. Beaming and muddy, my two helpers joined me outside. It was pretty clear that they'd done what they could, though they asked me if there was anything else I needed.

"Oh my god, no. You guys have been great. I can't believe how much you got done."

I went back inside to take stock of where things stood. We'd tracked a good deal of mud across the living room floor; I'd have to try to clean that up and then get a drop cloth or something to protect it from whatever the next phase of basement remediation would be. Suddenly I heard a child's excited voice out back: "Look, Lenny, it's still here!"

I peered out the kitchen window: it was Vivian, the nine-year-old daughter of my next-door neighbors. She was with her brother, seven years older, running from tree to tree and shrub to shrub, cataloguing each plant that remained. It had taken some doing, her mother, Susan, had told me, to convince her that the house hadn't blown away, and this was her first time back to see it for herself. "Look, Lenny! It's still here," I heard over and over again. "And this one, too!" Look! Look! Look!

■   ■   ■

A few days later I was out in the parking lot in front of Bob's, which had become a hub for relief efforts and service restoration. Someone had set up a charging station on the boulevard, which was constantly ringed with people jostling and maneuvering to get at an open port, and a few of the utility companies had trailers for customers to get information about restoring their services. There was a stage under a tent where officials could make announcements, and long folding tables covered with messy heaps of sweatshirts and blankets, bags of bread, and cans of food—the haphazard detritus of well-meaning donations.

My job by then was to write about alternative energy for the business section of the *New York Times,* and I had a story in the works about how solar power was (and wasn't) helpful in the disaster, for which I'd trudged two or three miles into Belle Harbor for interviews with homeowners who had solar panels on their roofs. Some days I'd run what felt like reconnaissance missions into Manhattan, spending the day at the office and loading up with supplies and groceries before heading home on long, grinding trips on crowded trains and buses and special shuttles that ran on mysterious schedules. More than once I found myself shivering at night in the cold for what felt like an hour at some weird airport parking lot or under an elevated train trestle, with a crowd equally desperate to get home. But I was also trying to help out on the Metro desk, so I'd agreed to cover a press conference some of the utilities were holding in the parking lot to provide updates on how residents could go about getting assistance.

A spokesman was outlining how storm victims could start registering for restoration either online or by fax when suddenly I snapped. "With what *electricity?*" I shouted out, nearly spitting with rage as others in the crowd began yelling, too. I was exhausted and rattled and exhausted from being rattled and I had had just about *enough.* I'd lost any sense of the professionalism and decorum I'd tried to demonstrate over the years as a representative of the *Times.* "I mean, really — *what are you talking about?* How are people supposed to *fax* and get on the *Internet* with *no fucking electricity?*" I knew the guy was only trying to do his job, but I couldn't stop myself, couldn't keep in check the anger that made my head feel hot and tight, as if it might burst. No one seemed to be in charge; no one seemed to be coordinating anything. The crisis had got the better of them.

Spent and raw from my outburst, I went back to Bob's, sequestered myself upstairs, and, still fuming, typed up my notes and sent them off to an editor. I went downstairs to find Jules back from volunteering at the Surf Club, with a stack of Uniqlo long underwear, both tops and leggings. "They had a bunch of these, so I grabbed some. Thought we could all use them, so I got different sizes." She'd also gotten us packs of hand and foot warmers, strange little pellets we could put inside gloves or shoes that would provide heat for hours.

I felt all the anger drain from my body, as if her thoughtfulness had reached in and pulled out a stopper. Yet again I was the beneficiary of someone's generosity. I needed to keep reminding myself: I was one of the lucky ones.

■   ■   ■

Some time later I was on my way home from the office on the ferry that had started running between Wall Street and a makeshift pier about ten blocks from Bob's house. It wasn't super-convenient, but it was a pretty ride and a decent substitute for the A train, which was still disconnected from the peninsula. In the mornings I'd walk to it with Bob or Davina or whoever else I ran into, and I usually returned at night on the still shaky combination of subway and buses so I could avoid making the walk from the pier in Rockaway alone; the area remained a dystopian no man's land after dark. This time, though, it was early and still light as I sipped a beer and watched as the ferry slid away from the city and down past Brooklyn and the amusements of Coney Island, noticing how the number of buildings with lights diminished as we went.

It was dusk when I got to Rockaway, and enough people were trudging downtown with me that I figured it would be safe to walk. About fifteen minutes later I started crossing the parking lot, nearing Bob's house, where I was still spending my nights, along with the rotating NY1 crew. I looked up and what I saw stopped me in my path. The house loomed above, its white fish-scale shingles turned rose-petal pink by the setting sun and the sky a shade of periwinkle, all its windows glowing creamy yellow. *Lights!* Bob's house had *lights* in *every room!* I stood, rooted to my spot and full of emotion. It felt like the most beautiful thing I'd ever seen. And at the very top, something was flickering around a room in a circle, like the shadow of a ceiling fan.

I went into the house and met Bob upstairs. "You got your lights back!" I said, hugging him, exuberant. "Congratulations."

"I know, it's awesome," he said with a grin that lit up his whole face. "I'm so excited. And you know, I'd forgotten—there's an electric thermostat in your room, so you have heat!"

"Oh my god, that's great. But don't you want to sleep there? It's your house!"

"No, no, it's fine. You stay there."

"Are you sure?"

"Yes, I am. Be warm."

"Well, thank you. By the way, do you have a ceiling fan in your bedroom? I saw a shadow from the street."

He laughed. "No," he said, shaking his head. "That was me, jumping around."

"You're kidding me," I said, cracking up. "Well, it's an exciting moment. I think I may be able to get my power back soon, too. I've finally gotten in touch with an electrician who can come before next month. They're all full up."

"I know. And they all want to be paid in cash."

"Right. At the bank in midtown, I feel like they're starting to think I'm a gambler or drug addict or dealer or something—I'm taking out thousands of dollars at a time, always in big bills, so it's not so bulky, and it always seems to be the same teller. He actually said the other day that I might want to give them a few days' notice, because they don't always have enough hundreds on hand."

"That's hilarious."

"Yeah, and then of course I'm terrified all the time that I'm going to get mugged or robbed at home. I mean, people know we're all here with piles of FEMA money in our houses."

The recovery had by then become a major operation, and the parking lot outside Bob's was like an eternal, incongruous tailgate party. There was a warming tent where a revolving cast of people from relief agencies and nonprofit organizations and university kids from all over the country would serve food—sometimes sandwiches, sometimes full-on hot meals. You couldn't walk more than a few blocks without coming across someone offering you something —food, warm clothes, blankets, water, and batteries. The utilities had moved their trailers uptown, near 116th Street, so I walked there to get a form from the power company. Once a licensed electrician rewired my circuits and replaced the box, he'd sign it, I'd walk it back to the trailer, and I'd have my power back that day or the next.

The system ultimately worked, and finally, the day after Thanksgiving, my lights came on. The house had been without power for nearly a month, and I was thrilled—not just because things would function again, but because now, I felt, I could move forward with everything else I needed, like running a dehumidifier and getting a cleaning company to treat the basement for mold. I'd signed up for Rapid Repairs, the city program that could replace my damaged boiler and hot water heater, but in the meantime I could now get an electric heater for my bedroom so I wouldn't have to sleep in my coat under every last blanket I owned.

A few evenings later I was sitting by the glowing embers of the fire in the garden when I heard a man's voice. "Hey," the voice said, a disembodied, insistent whisper whose source I couldn't see. "Hey, *hey*—you want a surfboard?"

I stood up and peered around, finally realizing that the voice belonged to one of my neighbors across the street, a tall, lanky guy with jet-black hair who had grown up on the block with Buddy. I crossed over to him, unsure of what he had in mind.

"Thanks," I said, "but I've got a board already."

"Well, if you want another one, there's a bunch of them lying on the beach. They tore down the lifeguard station today, and they must have been in there. Somebody's going to grab them."

"Yeah, that's for sure—or they'll just end up at the dump. Maybe I'll take a look."

A while later I headed over to the beach, and after trudging around the dunes in darkness for a while, I came across the boards, strewn in a heap with other trash and rubble. There were a couple of shortboards that seemed pretty beat up, but there was also a light-colored longboard that seemed shorter, narrower, and slimmer, and therefore more maneuverable, than mine—exactly the sort of thing I might be able to grow into. I took it home and set it on the living room floor. It was a creamy off-white with the thin tan line of the stringer, a central plank traditionally made from wood that adds strength and rigidity, running down the front, and a blue-and-black logo of five overlapping dolphins in a semicircle near the nose. I turned it over and looked at the back. Written in pencil under the clear coating was a serial number, the dimensions—nine feet long, twenty-two and one-quarter inches wide, two and three-quarters inches thick—and the name of the shaper, Jesse Fernandez. The rails at the nose and tail were cracked open with gouges in the exposed foam, which meant that I wouldn't be able to take it out until it was closed up, as water seeping into a board makes it heavier and can corrupt the inner core, slowly eating it away.

I can fix this, I thought as I stared at the dings, as surfboard injuries are known. I'd learned how to do a down-and-dirty repair using putty from one of the presentations at the women's workshop at the club shortly before the storm. It wouldn't look great—the guy who had given the presentation had described it as an effective but "half-assed" method compared to the more involved and permanent approach using flammable, brain-cell-killing fillers and coatings and sheets of fiberglass—but it would do the job. I'd just need to know what the board was made of in order to get the right stuff for it. The chemistry of the materials used in polyester (sometimes called fiberglass) and polystyrene (sometimes called epoxy) models were incompatible. Put the wrong fixer in a ding and it could dissolve the board's guts.

The board turned out to be polyester, made by a company called Wave Riding Vehicles, or WRV, a well-known Virginia Beach–based brand that got its start in the 1960s. So after finding a tube of the right kind of putty at a hardware store one evening, I cleaned the crumbled bits of foam, splintered fiberglass, and sand from the wounds, broke off piece after piece of putty, kneading each one until it reached the consistency of bubblegum, and then plugged the holes, removing the excess and smoothing things out as best I could. In the end my repairs looked terrible—like someone had smeared lumps of plaster over the tail and nose—but I was excited anyway. Someday I could learn the real way to fix a ding and do the shaper's work a little more justice, but for now I was pretty sure the board was watertight and ready to ride.

On the morning of my birthday, in early December, I pulled on a neoprene one-piece bathing suit Kiva had made that she called a core-warmer, a sleeveless vest with a hood, a wetsuit, boots, and gloves and took the board down to the beach. It would be my first time in the water since the storm—it just hadn't seemed right to go in while everyone was in the early throes of the disaster—and I felt a little bit like a kid bundled into a stiff snowsuit. It was a surprisingly warm, sunny day, in the upper fifties, but the water was colder, hovering around fifty degrees, and my new fall-to-winter wetsuit wouldn't be warm enough on its own.

I walked in and felt the chilled water seep in around my feet, ankles, and calves, then my knees and thighs, but I knew I'd warm up soon enough. I hopped onto the board and started paddling, looking down at the dolphin logo and the chunk of putty at the nose, feeling lighter and more mobile as I went. Still, I was conscious of how much more effort it took for me to stay balanced and to propel the thing forward because of the reduced volume in comparison to my regular board, which was six inches longer, a little bit wider, and more than a half-inch thicker at the middle—arithmetic subtleties that make an enormous difference in performance. This was going to take some getting used to.

I sat for a while, struggling to stay upright, just like when I'd started surfing, as I gazed out at an ocean glittering with sunlight, unable to remember another birthday with such balmy weather. I watched a few thigh-high waves rise, crest, and roll toward the shore, then spun around and tried to catch some. That part turned out to be not so difficult—I had to paddle harder than usual, but the board seemed like a magnet for waves. Getting to my feet was another story, as this piece of equipment left me far less room for error and tossed me into the water over and over again. When I finally landed in the right spot, though, it was almost a revelation: the board wanted to fly. I managed a few more rides and then, hungry and happy and exhausted, went back home.

I stripped off the wetsuit, rinsed it in the shower, and shivered through what I hoped would be my last cold-water sponge bath. The folks from Rapid Repairs were due to deliver and install a new boiler and hot water heater that day, so I set myself up to work at the kitchen table so I wouldn't miss their arrival. The crews, from a number of different contractors, were only loosely coordinated and operated like roving bands of freelance operators. You might get a call and an appointment for whatever work you needed, or a team might just show up and knock on the door and move on to the next needy household if you weren't around. One crew that I'd met a week or so earlier, which was supposed to handle the job, hadn't come back after getting reassigned to another area; the day before, another group of guys had shown up out of the blue and gotten to work removing the old equipment, and had promised to return the next afternoon.

I'd had plans to celebrate my birthday with a group over drinks in Brooklyn that evening—a joint gathering for me and another friend—but as the sun began to set, it became clear that I wouldn't be able to make it. At dusk the Rapid Repairs guys arrived and completed the installation, allowing me to take the first hot shower in my own place since the end of October. I missed seeing my friends, but that was all right: forty-eight, I felt, was off to a grand start.

By early in the New Year, Rockaway, though still far from normal, had made great strides forward. The Sanitation Department, along with the Army Corps of Engineers and FEMA, had moved several hundred thousand tons of rubble through Jacob Riis Park and Fresh Kills on Staten Island. Most people in the area had basic utilities back, and even though our supermarket hadn't reopened, there was now a shuttle train, the H, running up and down the peninsula so we could get to the Stop & Shop in Arverne. The Surf Club was shutting down the emergency operations, and Brandon and his partners were turning their attention to gutting the enclosure—I helped rip out the remaining drywall and insulation that, three months after the storm, was still wet—and reimagining the club. It would remain part community center and hangout, but it would no longer house the maker businesses, instead becoming more of a bar and event space, with expanded surfboard storage and a permanent food offering.

Around that time Bob, John, Jules, and I decided to reconstitute movie night, a casual gathering we used to have at Bob's before the storm, to counteract the stress we were all still feeling. Movie nights would start out with an episode or two of *Johnny Staccato*, the moody, stylized show that ran from 1959 to 1960 starring John Cassavetes as a Greenwich Village jazz pianist who moonlights as a detective, and then we'd watch a film. Sometimes it would be something with a Rockaway theme or setting, like *The Bungalows of Rockaway*, a documentary, or *The Detective*, in which Frank Sinatra chases down and tackles a suspect on the sands of Arverne. But others it was just something one of us had on hand, like the three-part Ken Burns documentary about Prohibition. We watched only the first installment together, though: the images of all that contraband liquor spurred us to drink so much that we all ended up drunk.

This time it was just me, Bob, and John in the den, watching *No Looking Back*, an Edward Burns production set in a blue-collar seaside town and filmed around the area, including on my block. These seemed to be the most gorgeous images ever recorded of Rockaway before the storm: unpeopled shots of the neighborhood after a rain or at dawn, the streets glossy and bathed in tones of carbon and pewter, the herringbone-patterned wood slats of the boardwalk turned blush-pink. I could feel my chest grow full and tears building under my eyelids when Bob said precisely what I was thinking.

"Oh my god, Rockaway looks so beautiful."

"I know," I said, my voice cracking. I was barely able to get out the words.

"It just looks so beautiful," he said again. Then we all sat in silence, taking in shot after shot of homes along rain-slicked streets and the ocean, none of us able or willing to speak the obvious question: would it ever look that way again?

11

In the Curl

IT WAS A BRIGHT AND COOL SATURDAY MORNING, AND emerald-green grass seemed to stretch around us for miles. I was in Sonoma, having breakfast with Eric, my ex, at an outdoor picnic table at a roadside diner where, as at seemingly every place in California, the food was several notches above what the ramshackle surroundings, artful though they were, might suggest. I'd flown out the night before and was due to spend the week in the Bay Area reporting a few alternative energy stories, and I planned to drive up the coast to surf the next day. Eric, after a few years in Vancouver, had taken a job at a nonprofit in San Francisco and had bought a weekend house in Sonoma. After the breakup I had taken a six-month hiatus from communicating with him—I'd needed a quiet period, I'd told him, some time without being in touch at all to fully absorb that we weren't together anymore. After that, though, we'd stayed connected through email, quasi-regular phone catch-ups, and the occasional meeting when he came through New York. Over the years we had managed to salvage and maintain—enjoy, even—a real friendship.

He'd picked me up at my hotel that morning and driven us to the diner, nestled on a road just outside of town near the vineyards and spas and resorts that wind up through the verdant hills. Eric was, he said, closer than he'd ever been to living the life he wanted, surrounded by great locally grown and produced food and wine and stunning natural vistas, bike paths, and hiking trails. He seemed happy—less tense, more present, more able to let the iPhone be, than when we'd been together—and had gone full-on NorCal: flip-flops, jeans, featherweight down shell, and a beard.

"Well, you always did want to be closer to nature," I said. "It's funny that you and almost all of your guy friends from Buffalo ended up out west."

"I know. It kind of makes sense to me, but it's a little weird," he said, his big round eyes as bright and green as the grass around us. "How are things in Rockaway?"

"Sort of nuts," I said. "My house is fine." I told him how I'd had the hole in the foundation patched and a cleaning company in to treat the place for mold. "But they're trying to get enough of the boardwalk fixed by Memorial Day for the concessions to operate, so there's construction all day and night, with, like, klieg lights and backhoes and pile drivers." I looked over at the traffic whizzing by and the spring-green hills beyond.

"Well, that sounds awful," he said.

"Yeah, it is. I mean, I'll be glad for the concessions, but I'm literally rattled all night. Pretty much every morning when I get up all the pictures on the walls are crooked."

Later that week I was winding in and out of fog along the Pacific Coast Highway, catching feathery glimpses of the steely waters and jagged cliffs below me. I was on my way from San Francisco to Pacifica, a surf spot right next to another Rockaway Beach, about a half hour south of the city, where I was due for a surf lesson. I'd already had one good session a few days before at Bolinas, nestled between the Muir Woods and the Point Reyes National Seashore, about an hour northwest of the city. I didn't know the town but I knew the area: Eric's step-aunt, a wealthy bon vivant who'd been generous in sharing her love of fine food and wine, had a house we'd visited in Stinson Beach, just a few miles along the bay from Bolinas. I'd always been impressed by her ability to navigate the terrifying, twisty stretch of two-lane highway that unspooled between the house and her apartment in San Francisco, full of hairpin turns and blind ascents high above the ravines that plunged toward the ocean. I was a nervous wreck on those trips, taking in the gorgeous, perilous setting through a squint, while she remained steady and sure, hands quiet on the wheel, chatting about whatever she was up to, from tending the feral cats near her house to mentoring young singers at the opera.

I'd had to drive that road on my own to get to Bolinas and back, swallowing my fear and telling myself that I was a perfectly competent driver—I'd made it across the country in one piece, after all —and that I couldn't live forever cutting myself off from things I wanted to do. I'd had to use the pullouts a few times, frankly grateful for the break from steering, when I noticed a line of traffic piling up behind me. But I'd done it, and it was something I probably wouldn't have dared while I was married.

I'd had a lovely day with Eric in Sonoma—gotten a glimpse of his life, met his girlfriend, who I'd liked, and enjoyed their easy affection with each other. I was actually over us, I'd realized, even as I felt how much I missed having intimacy and companionship. But I was also conscious of how much I had changed, and how much surfing was a part of that. It wasn't that I was suddenly some brave badass charging through the world and grabbing hold of my destiny or some such bullshit. I was still plagued by the same shyness, reticence, and insecurities I'd always been plagued by. The difference was that my drive to surf—to continue to work toward getting better while trying not to beat myself up if I didn't—was giving me a way to just do it: to get out there and explore and experience places and people on my own. Photography had been the first thing to give me a way to do that, too, but taking pictures, recording from the periphery, I found, didn't help me be *part* of a place, share something with other people—a good ride, a pod of dolphins on the horizon, a sneaker set of huge waves suddenly appearing out of nowhere.

I was finally becoming a surfer, I felt—traveling to places I wouldn't have gone otherwise, driving frightening, sometimes deeply pitted and pocked unpaved roads in my quest for a wave I could handle. I was getting out there, wrestling with my fears, trying to find the right balance for me between being adventurous and being rash.

Just the month before I'd found myself on the wrong side of that line a few times in Puerto Rico, where I'd escaped with friends I'd made in Rockaway, including Brandon, Davina, and Riva. I'd been sitting in the water with Brandon one morning when he suddenly turned and started paddling outside. A few seconds later I saw why: a shiny turquoise wall was growing quickly on the horizon, its peak far higher than anything that had come before. I hit the deck of my board and aimed for it, but I wasn't sure I could make it over the top. As I got closer, I couldn't figure out what to do. Turtle? Turn around, try to get ahead of it, and catch the whitewater? Turn around, sit on the tail of the board, and hope it would wash over me? Keep going? Pulled in so many different directions, I did the worst thing possible: I froze. I looked up as the wall continued to build above and arch over me, white flecks flicking off the top like spittle, and then hover, weightless, over my head. Brandon appeared at the crest, about to drop down the face. He saw me and pulled back, his mouth forming a silent "Oh" as he went, his expression saying, *Watch out.* He disappeared over the back, the lip began to fold in on itself, and I started paddling again, hoping I could somehow get through. I rolled under the board, found myself in a swirling cauldron that tossed me around but then let me go. I got myself righted, still holding the board and coming to a crouch, realizing that I was in only about three feet of water surrounded by humps of brain coral with another glassy blue wall coming at me. *You need to get outside,* I thought, but my leash had wrapped itself around something underwater that I couldn't see and I was stuck. Frantic, I looked out at the wave, down at the leash, and back again. It was almost upon me, but I couldn't get free. So I took a deep breath, held the board with one hand, and hunched, covering my head with the other arm. The wave crashed all around me, yanking away the board and spinning me around. I opened my eyes underwater, sensing that the board was floating nearby, but I wasn't sure where. I could see sunlight and the bubbles and foam from the turbulence and felt a firm pressure on my chest. It was nothing I couldn't get through, I thought, and I had no real fear that I would drown, but I recognized the dynamic of a hold-down, when the power of a wave pushes and holds you under the water, a potentially deadly force of big surf.

Suddenly the pressure released and I came up to see the board bobbing on the surface and yet another wave on its way. This time I managed to get the leash out in time to paddle ahead of the monster. It broke thunderously behind me, the force of the whitewater slamming me toward the shore.

I still had so much to learn about how to handle myself in the ocean, I realized. Crouching under a wave as it broke, as I had done many times in Rockaway, might result in just a wet smack on the back of my neck when the surf was small, but a wave could easily turn into a bone-crunching force when it was larger. All things being equal, power in ocean waves, it turns out, increases exponentially as they grow, essentially as the square of the height. That means that a six-foot wave, the biggest I could ever see myself attempting, is not twice but four times as powerful as a three-foot wave, and a nine-foot wave would pack not three times the force but nine.

That's how people riding—or in the wrong spot on—big waves end up with broken limbs, embedded coral, paralyzed, or dead: that force crashes on them, heaves them into the reef, or drills them down into the darkness, holding them there for too many seconds at a time. Even though I had no plans to surf anything above my head, ever, the hydraulics were at root the same, and I'd need to work on managing them better.

Unlike during my time in Puerto Rico, surfing in California had thus far gone without incident, and I'd felt rewarded for making the scary drive to Bolinas, where the locals guard the town so fiercely that they religiously take down road signs marking crucial turnoffs whenever the authorities put them up. It was a beautiful break set along a bay rimmed in craggy hills, with long, mellow, rolling waves that I found easier to negotiate than those in Rockaway. In Bolinas, I actually had time to get up, adjust my feet, fine-tune my stance, and still have a long ride. That's partly on account of the coast's southern orientation and location within a crook on the shoreline, which helps shelter it from wind and big swells. But in general, the Pacific coast of North America gets more consistent, bigger waves than the Atlantic, whether at a beginner-friendly break like Bolinas or a newbie-to-expert place like Trestles in San Onofre.

The reasons for this start with the fact that most non-tropical weather systems travel from west to east, bringing the Pacific coast more consistent swell. In addition, that swell tends to travel over longer distances from its origin before reaching the continental shelf on the West Coast, which is narrower than on the East. That means that the western waves generally have more energy and come out of deep water more abruptly, creating more size and power. Then too, they often have a better shape and quality because there are so many permanent physical structures like points—landmasses that jut out into the sea—which create longer and more consistent rides.

I'd gotten to enjoy enough of those rides that toward the end of my trip I decided to go for one last session in Pacifica, closer to where I was staying in San Francisco. By contrast to Bolinas, Pacifica was easy to get to and easy to find, with the south end of the break sitting just below a Taco Bell that might well have the nicest view in the franchise. A mile-long, northwest-facing, crescent-shaped cove whose cliffs on either end offer some protection from the wind, it was another beach break with clusters of rocks and boulders in its shallows. It was known for waves that can be small and mushy or long and glassy, suitable for beginners and beyond. I pulled into the parking lot near the strip mall with the Taco Bell, a grocery store, and a coffee bar in addition to a surf shop and wove my way around the clusters of men, women, and teenagers pulling off wetsuits and strapping equipment to the tops of their cars or running onto the sand with their boards under their arms.

About twenty minutes later I met my instructor, a young, dark-haired guy who'd arrived late because he'd had to take the bus from a few towns over. We chatted about my surfing, went through the obligatory pop-up practice in the sand, and then headed into the cold, deep-teal water with a silvery sky overhead.

I looked to the left, where a tree-covered promontory with houses set at the base formed a steep wall to the cove and functioned almost like a point. Clusters of surfers were sitting out at the tip and a little bit inside, catching waves that would crest and allow them to ride far across the bay. But there were also waves rising and breaking across the horizon, as well as along underwater formations closer to shore. That's where we were headed.

"Let's stay here on the inside for now and see how it goes," my instructor said, guiding us over the rocky bottom. "I'm not going to be pushing you unless I think you need it, but just be sure to be careful getting off the board when you're over the rocks. A buddy of mine stepped off his board yesterday and broke his ankle. He'll be out of the water for, like, two months."

"Okay. I'm pretty good at falling flat, since it's the only way I know how to stop at this point," I said.

"Cool. Make sure it's really flat, though."

We tried a couple of waves, most of them messy and more white-water than wedge, but I wasn't quite getting to my feet. "This is the thing," I said as I carefully walked the board back to him. "I do fine on the sand, and then in the water my pop-up's still inconsistent."

"Well, it's always different in the water," he said with a laugh. "But what I always say is just think about kneeing yourself in the chin."

That was an approach I'd never heard, so I tried it on the next wave and it worked: I was up and riding, seeing the Taco Bell, various wetsuit-clad surfers resting on the beach, and a few people walking their dogs getting closer as I went. Approaching the black ankle-breakers near the shore, I fell back and flat, pulled the board to me by the leash, and walked it back out.

"That was awesome. Thank you!"

"I don't know, but it tends to help people get their feet under them."

And so it did, for the rest of our session. *Toes to the nose, knee to the chin,* I thought, chuckling as I climbed into the car, damp and sandy and carefree and already a little sore. There were so many ways to think about the pop-up—even so many ways to approach it: push up and spring off the toes in one motion; push up, lunge the front foot through, and slide the back foot forward; or push up, plant the back foot first, and then step the front through. I hoped I'd be able to settle on one and no longer have to think about it so much anymore—and get solid and quick enough to attempt bigger, faster waves—but the words of Kevin, one of the instructors back in Rockaway, came to me. He'd told me about an older man who had the most complicated and awkward pop-up of anyone he'd ever seen, involving several stages and including his knees, but it worked for him. "How you get up," Kevin had said, "is how you get up."

A month later I was back in San Francisco on another work trip. Luckily for me, California was more or less the nerve center for alternative energy, home to much of the innovation and enterprises driving the industries forward. I'd finished reporting a story the day before about an effort to fly a featherweight plane powered entirely with solar energy across the country and was due to head home on the red-eye that night, so after I checked out of my hotel I went back to Pacifica to rent a board and try to surf on my own.

"Cute top," a woman in the parking lot said of my bikini as I pulled up the wetsuit. "Does it stay on?"

"I'm not sure—I've only ever worn it under a wetsuit. But it's made for surfing, so I'm guessing it will. It's a Calavera."

"Oh, cool. I've seen their suits online but not in the shops, and thought they looked great. Maybe I'll give it a try. See you out there," she said, turning to head toward the beach.

When I got into the water, I saw her sitting with another woman all the way over near the promontory and pretty far outside, almost at the corner where the cliff met the ocean. I stayed on the inside, close to where I'd been during my lesson, figuring I would have a better chance of finding my way into the waves. I caught a couple of small bumps, felt the thrill not just of the rides but also of having read them right. Then I saw a bigger wave gathering itself on the outside, a steep peak forming off the cliff with a long, gentler slope called the shoulder running from it in my direction. From the way it was standing up and angling toward the shore, I thought I could catch it where I was and still have some wave to ride. I paddled for it and felt the tail of my board lift—it was going to work! But taking a quick look to the right, I saw that my friend from the parking lot was on it already and closing in on me fast. I'd have to pull out. I caught a few more inside nuggets, then went for the shoulder of another big wave, only to have to yield again. On the third try, though, as she came barreling along, before I could pull off she gestured for me to go ahead and take it as she pivoted over the crest toward the back of the wave. I caught it, scrambled to my feet, and rode, managing to turn just enough to fly along parallel to the coastline. Even though I wasn't in the fastest part of that wave, it still had more power and speed than the little nuggets that had been peaking on the inside.

I ended the ride by falling off the board. I pulled it to me, turned around, and paddled back out. The woman and her friend were in that same spot. I kept looking over, hoping she'd look back so I could somehow signal my gratitude, thinking maybe I should just paddle over and say thank you. But it was enough for me that day to be out there by myself, finding my own way into a rhythm with the ocean.

As I drove back toward the city, I kicked myself for not taking advantage of the opening. That woman and her friend would probably have given me some advice about where to sit, at least, and maybe even have helped me into a wave or two, rooted me on when I did something right. Women tended to be that way, I'd found, supportive of each other, with a generosity in the water that approached some of the deeper meanings of aloha—a spirit of kindness and giving, the word itself made from roots that can mean sharing and in the present (*alo*), joyous affection or joy (*oha*), and life energy, life, or breath (*ha*). There are other ways to look at the word and its components, but a literal translation could be "the joyful sharing of life energy in the present" or "joyfully sharing life." It wasn't only women who could be this way. Many men back in Rockaway had let me take waves that were rightfully theirs or given me advice on where to sit, when to go, how hard to paddle. But in my limited experience, that wasn't the norm or the vibe when there were a lot of dudes in the water, fighting for position and dominance, while it was when there were women around. The whole experience was just more welcoming, nurturing, playful, and fun. "When you say a spot's localized, it's always localized by the men," Rachel Harris, a teenager from Santa Barbara said, smiling, in the 2009 documentary *The Women and the Waves*. "There's no women, like, telling you to go home."

A few hours later I was sitting at an outdoor table at a bistro in the Mission, feeling happily drained, with sand still between my toes, having a late lunch with a friend, Murat, who worked in clean energy finance. He asked me how the surfing was going, and I gave him my usual spiel—better, but my improvement was slow and sketchy. "I just feel like I do so much better in lessons or outside of Rockaway," I said. "I can halfway decently ride waves from time to time, but I've got no consistency."

"Well, how often do you get into the water?"

"Twice a week or so. Three if I'm lucky."

"So you're really only surfing less than half the time you could, at best."

I could feel where he was going with this. As a finance guy, he was looking at the percentages, but he was also getting at the same thing as Jay had at the Carlyle Hotel almost two years earlier: *You're never going to get good until you buy a board and surf every day.*

True, I thought, taking a sip of prosecco and looking out at the small apartment buildings and attached row houses that lined the street, a collection of red-brick, limestone, and gaily painted Victorians, and back at him.

He started telling me about a friend he'd met through a meditative dance session he did once a month in Marin. She lived in Bolinas and had decided to surf every day for a year, "to see if she could do it and how it might change her practice and her relationship to it." He paused, took a bite of bread and olive oil, sipped some red wine. "Then at the end of the year she decided to go for another year, and then another. I think she's somewhere in the middle of the third year. She has a blog about it. I'll send you the link."

"Wow, that's incredible! But I don't know if I could take on that kind of commitment."

"Well, what if you decided to surf every day for a month?"

"Huh," I said. "That's something I could maybe do."

"Maybe I could help—or we could help each other. I'd have to think about something I want to do every day, but we could make a deal to report to each other when or if we'd done the thing each day. It wouldn't need to be like a full-on report, just a 'Hey—surfed this morning,' or something like that."

"I gotta think about whether I can do this, but I like the idea of it. Is there anything you've been wanting to do that you've been pushing aside?"

We sat in silence for a while as he looked out to the street. Then he turned back to me. "Write! I've been wanting to write. Not necessarily a particular project, just some thoughts, stories I want to get down on paper. But the day always seems to get away from me."

"Okay! That's something. Let me chew on it a little bit and get back to you, and maybe we can figure out when to get started."

Several hours later I was waiting to board the red-eye home, getting closer to deciding to go ahead with the monthlong experiment in May, starting in a few weeks. I'd gone to dinner at an oversubscribed little restaurant near the Fillmore District that Eric had recommended, which specialized in small plates, and I'd been told I'd have to wait forty minutes just to get a berth standing at the bar in front of the open kitchen. It was the sort of thing I'd never have agreed to in New York, but somehow here I didn't mind. They'd sent me to a homey bar around the corner for my wait, and called me when my space was open. I squeezed in with a few other diners—young couples on dates and, judging from the frequency of photographing and note-taking and Instagram-posting, food bloggers—with whom I ended up chatting and even sharing a dish or two, like we were old friends at a cocktail party. It was not my usual M.O., interacting so intensely with strangers, but I'd had a great time. It would be all to the good, trying a different approach to my surfing, I thought, and at least one thing was for sure: I wouldn't come out of the end of the month any worse as a surfer.

■   ■   ■

I was nearly finished with my month in the water, and other than on a few weekends out of town and a stormy day or two when lightning struck, I had been getting in with a surfboard every day. Having to report to Murat certainly added to my diligence. I didn't want to back down or weasel out of the deal. Sometimes it was a quick email exchange — "Surfed!" "Wrote!" — and sometimes more, whether an appreciation of how a simple, clean commitment to regular effort brought a surprisingly deep reward or an admission that we hadn't been able to surf or write, in which case we'd make a new commitment to get to it the next day. There was something in the act of making the promise to another person that made me feel accountable — to him, yes, but more to myself. It was forcing me to live up to what I said I'd do and be more honest when I didn't, to stop telling myself stories and rationalizing about why I should wait for another day. My schedule, work and social, was now organized around *when* I could get into the water rather than *if,* a small yet profound switch that had the effect of making the rest of my life more structured, almost disciplined.

Some days the waves were perfect for me — clean and easy and about thigh-high — and I was able to catch them at an angle, get to my feet, and ride down the line. Others it was messy and choppy and steep, so I worked on trying to distinguish surfable waves from the disorganized mush. Other times it was flat, so I did paddling drills and practiced my sit-spins, since I still missed waves from time to time because I was too slow getting into position. On a few occasions I went out when the waves were beyond my abilities, so I tried to find patches of whitewater that wouldn't be in anyone else's way where I could practice my pop-up.

One time I sat at a near-empty break staring toward the horizon as dark lines of shadow appeared in the deep blue surface and gathered into humps that weren't hollowing out into peaks I felt I could catch. Then I saw two of them forming way out at sea, a few yards apart. I watched them, intent, trying to decide which would be better and where each would peak first. They got closer, and I kept looking from one to the other — *Maybe this one, no, that one, but I'm closer to this peak, but that one looks better, wait, it's going to peak over there* — when suddenly there was a perfectly good wave with a nicely formed peak right in front of me that I hadn't even noticed. I spun around with a start and paddled frantically, hearing Frank's exhortation — *Give it all you got* — in my head as I went. But I was too late and missed it, along with the other two, which never turned into much of anything anyway. I had focused so hard on how I thought those faraway waves would develop, overthinking and trying to ensure perfection, that I'd ignored my immediate surroundings and botched the whole thing.

As the month wore on, I felt myself getting better. But one weekend afternoon I was out with Riva, Brandon, and Davina and they were all catching waves and gliding along, chatting and laughing with each other between rides, but I couldn't catch a damn thing. Frustrated, I got out and sat stewing on the beach, feeling a mix of resentment and shame. *Why does this have to be so much harder for me than for everyone else?* I grumbled to myself. *I know I can do this. Why can't I do it now?* It was like I was back in second grade, having a tantrum fueled by performance anxiety, as I had every night before our weekly creative writing session at school. "But what if I don't feel like being creative on *Thursday?*" I'd wail at my mother, stomping around my room and flinging my dolls, balking at the idea of creativity on demand. "What if I feel like being creative on *Tuesday?*"

"You're such a worrywart," she'd say gently. "Just sit quietly, be patient with yourself, and something will come to you."

She was right, as usual, and something always came. But I continued to worry that it wouldn't, every damn time.

But that day I thought about her advice and sat quietly on the beach, trying to summon some patience for myself. I looked out at the water and started to notice that the waves were doing something strange. They were peaking outside, somewhere along a line near the tip of the jetty, rolling in and breaking midway, and then re-forming into new peaks before breaking again near the shore. Whitewater was so easy to catch — I thought maybe I'd be able to get a wave just as it broke and stay on as it formed a whole new wave inside. The approach worked, and soon I was cruising along the soft shoreline breakers, even turning this way and that, swiveling toward the sand.

"Mama, you got *style*," Brandon said as he passed me on his way out of the water.

Another morning, when it was flat, I went in with no surfing expectations, thinking I'd stick with my drills: one hundred paddles; sit, spin, lie down, sit, spin the other way, lie down; lather, rinse, repeat. I'd gotten through only a few rounds when I noticed a navy shadow forming in the royal-blue expanse just below the horizon. I watched it come toward me and morph into a wedge and then a hollow: it was a *wave*. I scanned it for a peak, paddled toward it, sat up, spun, hit the deck, and with just a few strokes slipped in and sped toward the beach. I was elated. I had the break to myself, and suddenly I was able to get a handful of easy rides.

I was learning how sometimes, in a pursuit, an attitude adjustment—looking for what you *can* do rather than getting stuck in what you can't—is the first step to changing the outcome. Being in the water so much had forced me to focus on what I could get out of each session, since I was there anyway, and *voilà!* I was improving. And now apparently I had style.

By the end of the month I'd made it twenty-one of thirty-one days—more than I normally would have, but not as many as I'd wanted. So I reupped with Murat for June and got in each day, sometimes getting in more than once. I was stronger than I'd ever been, leaner than I'd been in decades, and thoroughly pleased with myself. In the water I was getting my feet beneath me more often than not and shuffling into position when I didn't land on the board in quite the right spot. It maybe didn't look so pretty, but it felt fucking great.

Rockaway was getting better, too. The A train was finally running all the way out to the peninsula again, ending the meandering, packed commutes on shuttle buses, and the rushed, 24-7 construction that had shaken my house and set my teeth on edge for so many months was finally over. We didn't have the boardwalk, but we had the concessions, concrete islands of food and drink overlooking the line of high-tech sandbags running along the beach, infrastructure that eventually would undergird a new, higher dune. It was only the first phase in a multiyear plan to rebuild the boardwalk and beach into something that could better withstand future storms, even as scientists, advocates, and some lawmakers questioned the wisdom of rebuilding coastal areas that could be wiped out by rising sea levels and ever more destructive weather.

My spirits were running high anyway. In addition to the makeshift setup on the beach, we had a white geodesic dome at the head of the parking lot outside Bob's house that Klaus from MoMA PS1 had worked with Volkswagen to install as a temporary community center and art and performance space. And there was even a new wine-and-tapas bar on the boulevard, Sayra's, co-owned by a woman who had grown up in Rockaway Beach and had put bubbly and meatballs on the menu.

One Saturday evening around that time I met up with Bob and Jules on the porch and headed over to the dome for a dance party. It was a perfect Rockaway day, sunny but not too hot, and I'd had two surf sessions, one at sunrise, known as dawn patrol, and one after a lunch of fish tacos at the stand. I'd hung out after that on Bob's porch, where I'd met some friends of Jules's, Italians who shared an apartment a few blocks away. One of them, a good-looking, flirtatious surfer with wavy blondish red hair and brown eyes named Giorgio, seemed to take an interest in me and had said he'd be at the party, too.

It was about an hour before sunset when we got there, and it was already crowded, both inside the dome and outside at the picnic tables on the patio. Giorgio, wearing jeans, a white T-shirt, and a white blazer, walked toward me. He had a small black camera, an old-school 35-millimeter Leica type that he'd secured around his neck with a piece of white cotton string.

He smiled as we came together. "Nice camera," I said.

"Thanks. It is the camera of my grandfather."

"It's really cool. Are you a photographer?"

"No, but I like to take pictures. I've been talking to the guys at Veggie Island," he said, mentioning the small grocery and café that was near Rockaway Taco. "They were maybe going to put up some of the pictures I took after the storm. Maybe you want to see them sometime."

"Sure, I'd love to. I only took a few pictures in the days right after the storm. Then I just couldn't, you know. It was all just too much. Better now, though. Isn't this place great?"

We chatted for a while, then broke off as people came over to say hello and he went to take pictures. I flitted about, hanging with Davina and her roommate, Greg, Bob and Jules, and the many other people I'd gotten to know. It felt like a high school reunion. Everyone looked great in the pink and purple lights and sparkles thrown off by a spinning disco ball, all smiles and laughs and "Hey, great to see you" as if the hangover fog of the storm had finally lifted. Eventually I found myself back with Giorgio, swaying gently to a reggae song. He was from a small town in northern Italy, he told me, and had been a snowboarder in Europe before moving to New York a number of years before. He'd lived on the Lower East Side and fallen in with a group of surfers, who had introduced him to the sport. He still snowboarded from time to time upstate, but he had fallen in love with surfing enough to move out to Rockaway.

"Which one do you like better?" I asked.

"It's funny, because I think I am still a better snowboarder than surfer, but I maybe like surfing better. Means more to me somehow."

"I've never snowboarded, but I've skied a little bit—not well, of course," I said, laughing. "But then, I don't surf so well either."

"You should try snowboarding. It's fun, and it will be easier for you now that you surf. So tell me, are you seeing anyone?"

"No, I'm single."

"But how is this even possible?" he said, backing away, eyes going wide, almost aghast.

I laughed. "It just happened that way."

He moved closer, ran his hand lightly up and down my arm. And then, in the middle of the dome, under the spinning disco ball, he kissed me. I felt like a teenager all over again, giddy and excited and full of anticipation.

An hour or so later Davina and I were chatting outside on the patio about how much fun the party was but how much more fun it would be if there were alcohol. "Maybe we should go get some," she said.

I spotted the bar across the parking lot. "Frozens," I said. "We should go get as many frozens as we can carry and bring them back for everyone."

"Oooh, that's a great idea. Let's go!"

We squeezed ourselves through the crowd that packed the front patio and the throng inside the bar. "How many should we get, do you think?" I shouted at her over the din.

"I don't know—maybe eight? We can probably handle two in each hand."

We got the drinks and, holding the small Styrofoam cups precariously by the lips, bumped and jostled our way to the front of the barroom, screaming "Excuse me!" as we went.

We got to the front patio and took a breath, eyeing the crowd, which seemed even more densely packed than before. "I don't know about this," Davina said, laughing. "We may just have to drink them ourselves."

A surfer with an uncanny resemblance to Mick Jagger who sometimes tended bar around town and rode a skateboard with an enormous, beefy brown dog pulling him along looked over at us and smiled. "You want me to clear you a path?" he said.

"Oh, that would be great," Davina said.

He turned around, cupped his hands around his mouth, and shouted, "Make way for two gorgeous girls bearing frozens. *Make way!*" Miraculously, the crowd on the patio began to part. A path opened, and suddenly I was a gorgeous girl carrying frozens. It didn't matter whether I was or wasn't gorgeous—though Davina obviously was. I *felt* that way.

He turned back to us, grinning. "There you go." We thanked him and made our way back to the dome, sloshing the drinks and giggling as we went. "I'm going to look for Bob," I said as we headed inside, "and see if I can dance my way to him without completely spilling these!" Drinks distributed, we met up on the dance floor, raised our cups at each other, and then moved together to the music. I was about to take a break when Daft Punk's "Get Lucky," my favorite of that summer's anthems, came on. There was no way I could leave. Soon a throng packed in, and it felt like I was dancing with everyone I'd ever met in Rockaway, all circulating around one another, forming into groups and partners that broke and reformulated into new configurations, all part of the communal release of the dance floor.

The song ended, and, sweating and drained, I went out to the patio, where I ran into Giorgio. Bob and Jules were headed back home to the porch, so we went along with them. I went inside the house for a beer, and as I turned from the fridge, Giorgio slid his arms around my back, kissed me, and then suddenly yanked up my shirt, pulled down my bra, and ran his tongue around a nipple. I felt a current sizzle through my body—it had been *so long*—and I was stunned by the speed and directness of the move, but excited by it, too.

"So wait a minute," I said, pulling his head up to face me and putting myself back together. "Are *you* seeing anybody right now?"

"I have a girlfriend, but don't worry about her," he said. "I'm breaking up with her tomorrow."

"Okay," I said, "but let's not take things too far until you do."

Nearly two months later I was in the water as the sun set, surfing with Giorgio. We'd been out for almost an hour already, but the waves were so much fun we couldn't convince ourselves to leave. He had indeed broken up with his girlfriend, and we'd slept together a couple of times but had settled into a flirty friendship. We'd get together for dawn patrols in the morning, sometimes ride the A train into Manhattan together, cook dinner at my place after an evening session, or hang out at his with packs of his high-spirited, food-obsessed European friends. He was fun and adorable and living a full life—and he made me feel good—but he was at least fifteen years younger than I was, so we both knew from the beginning that it wasn't ever going to be a real romance.

The sun set, turning the water from pale jade to pinkish blue to steel gray and now jet black, the wave crests illuminated by a near-full moon. I caught a few, fascinated by the mystery of riding in darkness. But soon it was time to go. I was tired and getting hungry, and Giorgio was flying to Mexico the next day and needed to start packing. We got out of the water together and walked up to the boardwalk, the glow of the streetlights turning everything grainy and amber, like an old sepia photograph. We hugged goodbye, touched damp cheek to cheek, then turned in different directions and walked away.

■　■　■

Near summer's end, on a bright and sunny day, I was back in Montauk at Ditch Plains, sitting in the midst of the packed break, unable to find a clear spot to even go for a wave. I'd never seen it so crowded—it was even worse than Rockaway, where the deluge of attention following the storm had attracted ever more DFDs—so I decided to try at the edge of the surfing area, close to where it seemed a lifeguard would be preserving the waters for swimming.

I stroked across the break, eyes on my destination, chest up high above the five-dolphin logo, feeling strong and secure and noting the other surfers watching as I went. As I neared the edge of the crowd, I saw the suggestion of a shadow out of the corner of one eye. I looked, and *holy shit*—it was a wave. I sped up, angled toward the shore, charged forward just in time to catch it: a nice aquamarine wedge that took me all the way across that section before petering out where the water suddenly got deep. Finally *I* was the one surfing a wave while everybody else sat dumbly on their boards, watching.

By the time I got back to that spot, at least ten other surfers had come over, and I didn't get as clear a path to a wave again. But knowing that I could identify and ride them, could actually *compete* head-to-head with other surfers — paddle-battle them and *win* — gave me the confidence to try for more.

I like this life, I thought as I came off the beach and crossed the road to the yellow cottage where I'd begun my surfing adventure and was staying again. Maybe I'd drive over to a grocer and lobster pound on another side of town to pick up the makings for dinner, see if I could find a farm stand to get some late-season corn. It occurred to me then, dimly at first but with a rapidly brightening intensity, that maybe I wanted to keep things as they were and not upend them by having a child on my own. I'd spent so many years chafing under a hair shirt of unfulfilled promise, plagued by the scratchy notion that I was somehow unrealized, that I hadn't accomplished what I should have — and could have, if I'd just started out sooner. But I wasn't feeling that way so much anymore, and had even worked through the inadequacy I'd felt when the three rounds of IVF I'd undertaken with donor sperm after the divorce had come to naught. I'd had to abandon the idea of a pregnancy with my own eggs, and I'd put my maternal ponderings on hold after that, and then again after the storm, when I was too focused on just getting through the day to contemplate anything long-term.

Now that I was firmly in recovery mode and stable enough to confront my future, I had jettisoned the idea of donor eggs and had been thinking about adoption. I'd been convinced at some point that motherhood was what I wanted, that it was the missing piece of the puzzle that would give me a baseline of happiness, a reason to get up in the morning, a sense of purpose and fulfillment.

But I was coming to see that, unwittingly perhaps, haphazardly for sure, I had created something I wanted to preserve. I knew I'd be giving up on an aspiration, deciding to let it go, and could come to regret that I'd never get to have that fierce love and connection parents experience with their children — never get to nurture someone in the way my mother had nurtured me. But maybe I could find some of what I craved another way, and maybe that would be enough.

12

Reeled In

SEPTEMBER 2013–APRIL 2015

I WATCHED, BOBBING ON A SURFBOARD IN THE MIDST of a lesson, as the chilly sapphire waters off the coast of Cape Cod undulated and rolled, forming waist-high wedges that gently tipped over and peeled toward the shore. One of my mentors in publishing, who'd hired me for my job at *7 Days* and then been instrumental in bringing me to the *New York Times* in the mid-1990s, was marrying his longtime boyfriend at their summer house in Provincetown that weekend, and I had of course found a way to go surfing while I was there. I'd never spent much time at that end of the Cape growing up and was struck by its untamed beauty and the wild, California-style beaches with vertical bluffs plunging down to the sea. I'd asked my instructor, a tall, slim man with short brown hair sometimes known as Gus, if we could start the lesson by looking at waves together: I was trying to get better at reading peaks and entry points and distinguishing rights from lefts.

But at the moment I was distracted from the lesson by the little hound heads with big brown eyes and long whiskers that kept popping out of the water just a few yards away. They belonged to seals, some of them pups.

"You see them a lot this time of year," Gus, from an outfit called Funseekers, told me. "Some of the breeds have their young around now, so they're all over the place."

The whales had been breaching like crazy in Rockaway, and I'd seen the occasional seal sunning itself on the beach, but it was nothing like this wonderland. "Labradors of the sea" was how a friend who'd grown up in Silicon Valley said he'd always thought of them back when he was surfing. "You'd just see them hanging out with you while you were waiting for a wave," he'd told me.

He'd found their presence comforting, and I understood what he meant: those puppy-dog eyes, the curiosity, the benign aura, and a seeming desire to play made it feel good and safe to be around them. Of course, that wasn't entirely the case, for wherever there are seals there's the risk that sharks, their main predator, stalk the same territory. Just a few weeks earlier I'd read an article in *The New Yorker*, "Cape Fear," by Alec Wilkinson, about efforts to track sharks off the coast of Truro, which is next to Provincetown and not far from where I was surfing. Researchers had embedded tags in about thirty great whites since 2009, and one of them, named Julia, was a solitary beast whose signal had been picked up more than 750 times off Truro in 2012, a third of them close to shore. She had apparently returned to the area in the spring of the next year and had been detected regularly since July. Sharks, "like all big, fierce creatures," Wilkinson had written, "exemplify the mysterious and ungovernable parts of our lives. White sharks roam the ocean the way unspecified urges and figures roam the psyche—liable to appear abruptly, often destructively, and whenever they decide to, on their terms, not ours." He'd added, "Once you enter the ocean deeper than your knees, you become part of the food chain."

We were definitely out deeper than our knees that day, and so

I was hoping that Julia and whoever else might be trawling these waters were far, far out to sea and already well fed. Since my recent trips to California, a juvenile great white had attacked a man fishing in a kayak at Pacifica in June (he escaped unharmed) and Stinson Beach had temporarily closed after a shark sighting in August. I didn't say anything just then to Gus—didn't want to somehow conjure something up by expressing my fear—but I couldn't stop scanning the horizon for that stubby dorsal fin whose shape had haunted me since the summer of *Jaws,* when the mere sensation of being in water, even in a swimming pool, could frighten me enough to get out.

Part of my aim in learning to read the waves was to be able to better divine which way to go on them. Almost everything in Rockaway was by default a left, but I'd seen people go right sometimes and get good rides, and I still found it tricky to distinguish our peaks.

"Some places, especially beach breaks, have waves without a real defined peak," Gus said, "and you can go either way. But even then it's usually the case that one direction is going to give you a better ride than the other."

We looked at the waves for a while, and I began to see that though there were slopes on either side of the peaks as they formed, one was often longer or seemed more substantial than the other, meaning that that was the way to go.

"Okay," I said, "I'm going to try to read them myself, but if you see a good right, let me know. I'm also trying to learn to turn that way."

We looked for a while but didn't see any rights. I tried a couple of lefts, but they felt too steep as I started to catch them, so I froze up and pulled back.

"I thought you had that one," he said after I'd done it a second time.

"They just feel too steep to me, like I'm going to pearl."

"Ah, I see. Well, I think you're getting into a pretty good position on the board, and you're in the right spot on the wave. Just keep the board on an angle and try looking out when you're popping up, rather than down. It'll take some of that steepness out."

I tried that on the next few waves and it worked. When I didn't look down, I found them easy to catch and fun to ride, standing up for longer than they often did in Rockaway. Feeling good, I decided to wait for a right. I saw what I thought might be one, and when Gus confirmed that it was, I angled the board to the right and started to paddle. I looked back, checked that it was still peaking, paddled a little harder, and caught it. As I felt the board hydroplane, I jumped to my feet, turned a little more, and rode down the line . . . *to the left.*

I started laughing even before I finished the ride. Gus was chuckling and shaking his head when I came back. "I know, I know," I said. "I went left."

"You really are programmed to go that way."

"Yeah, it's like my body doesn't think it's surfing unless it's going left. I'll just have to keep at it, maybe talk my way through it."

It took me several more tries before I finally went right on a right, and when I did, it was awesome. Now I knew what all the goofy-footers in Rockaway were talking about. It wasn't that going left felt bad, but going right felt so, well, *right,* like riding frontside made me even more of a part of the wave.

■   ■   ■

One night in late fall I was at home, sitting at the computer in the office upstairs, checking boxes about things I liked to do and what level of relationship commitment I was seeking and uploading some pictures of myself looking happy and active—at an art gallery opening, smiling in a cute dress and sunglasses in Bob's yard one summer day, on the wave in Montauk. I felt at peace, with the relaxed sensation of being in the kind of cosmic flow that comes after a good long surf session and a hot shower.

I had decided to follow a friend's advice in creating an online dating profile, see if I could make something happen for myself. "I'm taking a new approach," she'd said over dinner with another single female friend. "Just post pictures, and don't even bother with writing long answers or an intro. The pictures are all that guys are going to pay attention to anyway. If they like what they see, they'll find you."

Many of the people around me had a romance or its prospects, and I was missing the attention and companionship and sex of my recent fling. Bob was migrating into a relationship that seemed to have real potential with a smart, pretty, fun woman who was a journalist. John, Bob's former tenant who had introduced me to the joys of rum floaters, appeared to have found love, too. Brandon and Davina were still together and seemed ever more committed. Even Gus, my surf instructor on Cape Cod, had been heading off to a date after our session. I wasn't focused on finding a serious relationship; I just wanted things to change. So without any particular expectations, I posted my profile—pictures, mainly—and waited to see what would happen.

I didn't have to wait long. I got a lot of responses, a few of which seemed promising at first but ended up going nowhere. There was one, though, from a guy about my age, that I kept going back to. I couldn't tell if we'd be a good match, but he had already gotten under my skin. "That picture!" had been his first message to me, referring to the Montauk wave. His name was Todd. He was a jock— he liked to play basketball—with a creative streak; he spent his free time taking pictures, so we had a few things in common. Though he was a farm boy from Iowa, he had lived in the Bay Area and was now in Brooklyn. And he had an interest in helping people, which appealed to me.

So on the last day of January I raced down the metal-edged steps to the A train at Times Square, hoping I wouldn't trip and go tumbling headlong into the station: no one wants to show up bruised and battered to a first date. I'd gotten stuck at work and was running late and worrying about it—I didn't want Todd to think I was a workaholic who wouldn't be any fun to go out with. At least I was able to get a cell signal on the train and let him know.

When I got to the restaurant, I saw from the street that he was waiting right inside the door. *He actually looks like his pictures—but cuter,* I thought. He had short brownish blond hair and was about my height. He was wearing jeans, sneakers, a purple sweatshirt, and a string of multicolored pony beads. I wasn't entirely sure what his style was, but I could see that he had one.

I opened the door and leaned in toward him. "Hi, sorry I'm so late," I said, extending my hand. "I'm Diane."

He had warm chestnut-colored eyes that went wide as he looked at me. "Oh my god, you're even prettier than your picture," he blurted, then added, "but I'll get over it."

Not a bad opening, not bad at all.

There would be a wait for a table, so I said I'd go grab a beer, as he already had one. I could feel him checking me out as I stood at the crowded bar, hoping it didn't take too long. I finally got my drink, but in minutes our table was ready.

We took a look at the menus. "Well," he said almost immediately, "I know what I'm having."

"What?"

"Fish tacos. I started eating them when I lived in Oakland for a year and just really liked them, so I pretty much order them whenever I see them on a menu."

"Huh, that's funny—I'm the same way. I started eating them when I lived in Palo Alto for a year. There was a Wahoo's near my apartment and it's practically all I ever wanted to have. I think I'll get them, too, if you don't mind."

"No, go ahead!"

"We have good ones in Rockaway. You should come out and try them sometime."

The rest of the date went well, I thought. He told me about farming for his stepfather during the summers, learning to maneuver a twelve-row cultivator *just so;* about his love for Foucault, Derrida, and Marx; about his twenty-seven months in the Peace Corps, when he learned the Philippine dialect of the small town where he was stationed well enough to get work as a translator; and about his activist days in the 1990s trying to save community gardens with a leftist group on the Lower East Side. I could see that he was funny and smart, and he seemed kind. It also turned out that we had probably crossed paths without knowing it, maybe been at some of the same parties over the years. He knew a lot of people in my circle through basketball, since he'd played in New York City leagues that had included a lot of publishing folk.

"I learned how to pronounce a lot of words from those guys," he said at one point over dinner. "There were words I'd never heard spoken before—just read them. Like *respite.* For the longest time I thought it was res-*pyte,*" he said, laughing. "You know, 'I need a respite from feeding these hogs.' No one really says that in my little town."

After a few more dates, including one when I practically mauled him at a Fort Greene bar, he came out to Rockaway for a night. "I brought condoms!" he said in greeting, cheerfully. We fell onto the couch, kissing and caressing and pressing against one another. We went upstairs, and I was surprised by how easy and comfortable I felt being naked with him and how good the ridges and firm peaks and troughs of his athlete's body felt against mine. *I could get used to this,* I thought as I drifted off to sleep. I woke up in the morning thinking about a story he'd told me in which he remembered Mike Tyson once saying, "Everybody has a plan until they get hit." Well, I'd been hit.

■ ■ ■

On a workday morning toward the end of the summer, Davina rousted me out of the house and into the water. We'd both been talking about not surfing enough lately, so she'd determined to get us both back in the habit. I was sitting on a new used surfboard from Stewart, the company started in Laguna Beach in 1979 by Bill Stewart, who helped bring shortboard performance characteristics to longboard design. I'd bought it from a guy on Craigslist while on one of my West Coast work trips, but I had no board bag or any sort of case in which to bring it back, so I'd gone to a Home Depot and bought pipe insulation, packing tape, and a mess of bubble wrap to pad the thing. But one of my reporting sessions had gone long and I'd gotten stuck in traffic on my way to the airport in Long Beach. I ended up trying to wrap it at the gas station where I'd stopped to fill up the tank before returning the rental car. It was near sunset as I lay the board on the ground and struggled to swaddle all its nine feet and four inches with yards upon yards of bubble wrap as they fluttered in the breeze and threatened to roll away like tumbleweeds. As I worked, I noticed two sketchy-looking guys, one of them holding a bike by the handlebars, arguing on a ramp that led toward me from the housing complex overlooking the gas station.

"I didn't cut your fucking chain!" one of them said.

"You better not have, bro. I find out you did, I'll fucking cut *you!*"

"Don't you fucking accuse me, motherfucker!" the other guy said, moving chest-first toward his adversary.

"You didn't cut my chain, you got no worries. You did, you do."

As they argued and menaced each other, chests puffing and jutting, they edged closer and were now standing right over me. One guy shoved; the other shoved back.

I looked up at them. "Excuse me, fellas. Could you take your fight somewhere else, please? I'm trying to get this board wrapped here."

They stopped and looked down at me as the world seemed to go silent and all motion seemed to cease. *Uh-oh,* I thought. *Did I say that out loud?* I held my breath.

"Oh, sorry," the guy with the bike said. "We'll get out of your way." They backed off, started yelling at each other again, and I returned to my task, beginning to breathe and shake with adrenaline, relief, and disbelief that I'd been so intent on my project that I'd risked antagonizing two guys, already riled up, who seemed a little strung out. As I was finishing with the board, one of them came down the ramp. "Need any help with that?" he asked.

"No, thanks," I said. "I got it."

I now laughed over the whole thing with Davina in the water. "I don't know what I was thinking," I said. "Surfing makes you crazy. Not brave—crazy."

"Yeah, but it's a beautiful board. I completely get it."

"Well, I'm glad I got it, and me, home in one piece."

We traded off a few waves. I told her about how things were going with Todd. Soon after our first overnight date, we'd progressed to spending every night together. He'd even shown up at my place after work one day with a small portable stereo so that we could listen to the tapes he had made of Hal Jackson's *Sunday Classics* radio show on WBLS, which showcased black music of the ages. He'd set up the stereo, slid a tape into the deck, pulled me into his arms, and swayed with me in the kitchen to Johnny Mathis singing, "Wonderful, Wonderful."

"Now, *this* is what I had in mind," he'd whispered into my ear. I hadn't gone looking for a real romance, but one seemed to have found me, despite some of my doubts about our long-term prospects.

"We have a lot in common," I said to Davina in the water, "but we also have different worldviews. And I just don't know that I'm ready for a commitment."

"But sometimes things are just right, even though you might not think it's the right time, you know?" She turned, paddled for a wave, and whizzed toward the shore. I took the next one, rode it in, fell off, went back out. When I got there, she had a big smile across her face. "Nice wave," she said.

"It was fun. Yours looked good, too."

"It was. But you know, the thing about Todd? I think he's perfect for you."

"Maybe. I just really like the guy."

I looked toward the beach and saw Riva, her dark curls tousled by the breeze, about to get in. She had moved to a bungalow up the street, so I was getting to see her more frequently.

"Good morning, ladies," she said as she paddled up to us. "It looks so nice. How's it been?"

"Good," I said. "Easy, but with a little bit of punch. One's coming your way now."

"Ooh, thanks," she said, turning to catch the wave.

She paddled back over to Davina and me after her ride. "There's a good farm dinner coming up at Edgemere," she said. "Jerk chicken!" One of the impresarios behind the boardwalk concessions had started a farm on an empty lot down in the forties, where there weren't a lot of supermarkets. The idea was that people in the community would rent plots and sell their produce at the farm and to area restaurants in the hope of becoming self-sustaining. The place had also started having dinners at picnic-style tables with a different local chef each time.

"It sounds so cool, but I'm not sure I'll be able to make it," I said. "But I'd love to go sometime."

"I'll send you the calendar," Riva said. "Maybe we can make a plan."

"Definitely," I said, turning to get another wave.

I came back, told them I'd need to head in soon. "But maybe I'll see you two in the water later this week. I'm eyeing Friday morning."

They both said they'd try to make it. As I turned to paddle for my last wave, which Riva had spotted for me, they wished me a good day. It already was one.

■   ■   ■

About a year later I was back on Cape Cod at our late parents' modest ranch in Mashpee, which my sister and I had sold after deciding that it didn't make much financial sense for either of us to keep it.

We were about a week away from the closing, and Todd and I had rented a van and made the drive up so I could clear the basement of the furniture and home goods from my townhouse life with Eric that didn't fit into the bungalow in Rockaway. We'd already loaded up the van with an outdoor bench that had been one of the wedding gifts I'd kept, along with a pair of Moroccan lanterns, an exercise bench, and assorted furnishings I thought we could use.

I'd gone through most of it when I came across my old bike, a yellow three-speed I'd gotten when I was about twelve. I used to spend hours by myself on that bike—it had given me a sense of freedom and independence from the pressures at home. I'd ride all over our area, along the back lanes, around the pond, and into the woods, searching for wild blackberries in sprawling undeveloped lots and lady slippers in the forest groves. They were all long gone, those hidden places, having been bulldozed and paved and sodded and smoothed to make new expanses of suburban homes. I had some misgivings about letting the bike go. Maybe we could have Mike the Beard, who'd been on the porch with me during the storm and rebuilt vehicles, retool it into something Todd or I could use. But our van was already full, and besides, I didn't need it anymore. I finally had a home I wanted to be in and didn't need to escape from, the beginnings of a life I couldn't have fathomed even three years ago.

It was part of what I was absorbing from Rockaway, a place where a lot of people constructed their lives around their happiness, much as I had constructed a month around surfing, rather than trying to shoehorn a little happiness in between all the obligations. I wanted to try letting things unfold simply, as they would. I was learning how to stop looking beyond the horizon, to stay aware of what was around me, focus on what I could make of it, tap into the energy of the moment, hang on, and relish the ride.

Epilogue:
Safe Harbor

JUNE 2017

It's always ourselves we find in the sea.

— E. E. CUMMINGS, "MAGGIE AND MILLY AND MOLLY AND MAY"

WE PADDLED OUT IN ROCKAWAY FOR NICE-GUY RICH
one Saturday in the spring. I'd never been part of that kind of ritual—born, it's thought, in Waikiki as a way for surfers to honor
their dead. But I'd known Rich a little and thought he'd always lived
up to his nickname. He was one of the instructors at Frank's surf
school who'd put a strong emphasis on teaching us how to behave
at a break—how to tell who has priority on a wave and how to stay
a safe distance from other surfers, whether sitting in the lineup or
coming out from the shore. He was my neighbor for a time; he lived
across the street in the big red house where I'd spent the night of
Sandy with Kiva and Tim. I wasn't even aware that he had been sick,

but when I learned about his death, I knew I wanted to be there, if only to help widen the circle to show his widow how many people he'd touched.

Round-faced and always smiling, he was part of the crew I'd met the first summer I'd taken regular lessons with Frank, and I'd see him from time to time after I'd moved to the peninsula, biking around with his dog or taking the bus to the city. People in Rockaway tend to disappear for the winter, hibernating in their homes or heading to the tropics, so I hadn't thought about the fact that I hadn't seen him in a while until, during a surf session, I ran into Rich's fellow instructor Simon, the local musician who'd been so helpful in my early lessons in Arverne.

Nice-Guy Rich, Simon told me as we rocked gently in water colored taupe and silver by an overcast sky, had moved down to Daytona. He had bought a house and was living the dream of surfing every day, even though part of the draw had been a better environment for his wife, who was battling cancer. Then suddenly, it turned out, he had the disease, too, and he quickly succumbed, on Christmas Eve, at forty-six. Vinny, another of Frank's crew, had been close to him, even visiting in Florida, and was organizing the gathering for Saturday at noon.

That morning I slid out of bed not long after Todd, who'd moved in with me, headed off to the Lower East Side for the regular basketball game he'd been playing in for almost twenty years. A light cloud cover was dissipating as I made some breakfast and checked the forecast and surf cam on my phone: the waves looked small and clean, and with the brightening sun it wouldn't be too cold, so I pulled on a bikini instead of Kiva's neoprene core-warmer under my wetsuit, topped up the wax on my board, and headed into the water.

Riva hadn't made it out that morning and Davina was on duty taking care of her and Brandon's young son, Zephyr, so I was on my own. I sat there, watching the light sparkle off the pale-aquamarine water as it gathered itself into thigh-high peaks, lifted up off the sandbars, and spilled in curls across the break—unusually nice conditions for Rockaway. I chuckled as the thought came to me, as it still so frequently did, *How did I get here?* Of course I knew exactly how I got here and into this life that I never could have predicted or aspired to—even if I still wasn't entirely sure why. But it nonetheless surprised me that it was surfing that had finally managed to push me out of my comfort zone and into this strange and magical place where I found relative peace and joy.

The break was mercifully uncrowded, so I caught a few waves and rode them, happy to be out there, moving through the water, feeling the bob and weave of the current and that ever-mysterious, ever-powerful force of the ocean propelling me forward. I went back home and stowed the board on the side of the house, rinsed off, and pulled down the top half of the wetsuit. Hose in hand, I trudged out to the community garden to water my plot, realizing that I was living my own kind of dream, one I'd imagined in an instant all those years ago when, walking to Bob's from a lesson with Frank, I had stumbled upon the row of bungalows on this block. Nice-Guy Rich might well have been teaching that day, I thought, shivering as I realized how easily I could never have found any of these things —surfing, Rockaway, the house, the garden, Todd—and how easily illness, injury, karma, or really bad weather could take any or all of them away.

But I had them, at least for now, I thought, shaking off the sadness and fear as I finished up in the garden, drank some water, grabbed the board, and took it back down to the beach. A few dozen people had gathered on the hot sand and under a tent, including many of my old instructors from surf school: Frank, who now lived on my block; Kat, the one regular female teacher; Kevin, whom I hadn't seen since he'd become a corrections officer; and of course Simon. Poster-sized pictures of Rich looking happy and full of life were propped up along the beach—on his big-wheeled cruiser, with his dog, playing his guitar. A woman arrived with a shopping cart full of white carnations, and we all gathered around to talk about Rich. Vinny told how they'd become fast friends after a single meeting in the waves, calling him "a good waterman," the highest compliment you can bestow around here. Simon played a flamenco riff on guitar. Rich, a hard-rock musician, "always used to like it when I played something like this," he said. And then Rich's widow talked about how much he had loved Rockaway and how the paddle-out was the one thing he'd said he wanted once he knew he was dying.

Then it was time to hit the water. I offered my condolences, grabbed a flower, and began walking out with the board. It was one of those days when you could pretty much walk all the way to where the waves were peaking, but that seemed beside the point. So I grasped the flower between my teeth and, like some sort of surfboard tango dancer, flung myself onto the deck and began windmilling my arms through the water to get outside. I found a place in the gathering circle and clasped hands on one side with Simon and on the other with a kid I'd never met, and I realized I was exactly where I belonged. We were all so different and yet in that moment all the same: united in the love and admiration for a good waterman who had fallen, but also in the love and admiration for our relationship with the ocean in which we sat. I was part of a real community, minus one member, I thought as tears welled up in my eyes, among people whom I would never have met without surfing but who had helped me transform my life.

Vinny said a few words I couldn't hear and then suddenly threw his flower into the center of the circle. We all followed with a hail of carnations and then started splashing the water with our hands, grabbing fistfuls and throwing them aloft, over and over and over as we shouted out Rich's name. The frenzy died down, and then we all sat there for a minute, looking at each other, toward the horizon, up at the impossibly bright, sunny sky.

"Okay," one of the men yelled. "Go out there and catch one for Rich—and don't kook up the wave."

We all laughed, and then fitfully left the circle and made our way toward the breakwaters. A few caught waves and then came back out. I watched several go by before I saw something beginning to form on the horizon. I spun around and started slowly moving toward the sand, looking back to make sure the wave was actually peaking. It was, but it would take some hustle to get it. *Catch it for Rich,* I thought as I dug my arms in deeper, harder, and faster, hearing Simon yell out, "Go for it—paddle hard!"

I felt the tail of the board lift, and I was in. I sprang up and steered the board across the face of the wave, twisting my hips and torso, my arms floating by my sides, shifting my weight to maintain the momentum. I finished the ride and my duty was done: I'd caught one for Rich. But I didn't yet want to leave the group, so I paddled back out.

"That was a nice wave you caught," Simon said.

"It felt really good," I replied.

But that feeling wasn't just about the wave—or any of the several I caught that afternoon as I paddled among people I could truly count as part of my tribe. It was also about having escaped a life that looked so good from the outside but was the product of so many choices I'd made when I was spurred by notions about achievement and happiness and *making it* that were, in the end, so wrong for me and left me feeling not successful or satisfied but anxious and unfulfilled. I had finally got outside of all that, here in Rockaway of all places, and I never wanted to go back in.

Notes on Sources

In conceiving and researching this memoir, I consulted many sources across a wide range of media, including contemporary and historical books, periodicals, advertisements, photographs, maps, and weather, oceanographic, and surf reports; documentaries; and social media, emails, and blog posts. A number of sources, though, proved especially influential in my retelling of events. They are outlined below.

My understanding of the history of the Rockaways and its Native American and colonial settlements begins with Edwin G. Burrows and Mike Wallace's "Lenape Country and New Amsterdam to 1664," part one in *Gotham: A History of New York City to 1898* (New York: Oxford University Press, 1999). For an overview of the peninsula's relationship to larger cultural and socioeconomic developments in the city and region, I turned in particular to Robert A. Caro's *The Power Broker: Robert Moses and the Fall of New York* (New York: Vintage, 1975), and Lawrence Kaplan and Carol P. Kaplan's *Between Ocean and City: The Transformation of Rockaway, New York* (New York: Columbia University Press, 2003).

For a sense of the evolution of the Holland section of Rockaway Beach and the peninsula's culture, I relied on three local histories: Alfred H. Bellot's *History of the Rockaways from the Year 1685 to 1917* [. . .] (New York: Bellot's Histories, 1918); Emil R. Lucev's *The Rockaways*, Postcard History Series (Charleston: Arcadia, 2007); and Vivian Rattay Carter's *Rockaway Beach,* Images of America (Charleston: Arcadia, 2012). The most significant of the historical maps I examined were the *New Map of Kings and Queens Counties, New York* (J. B. Beers, 1886); *Insurance Maps of the Borough of Queens, City of New York* (New York: Sanborn Map Co., 1912–1922); and *Atlas of Far Rockaway and Rockaway Beach, 5th Ward, Borough of Queens, City of New York* (New York: Hugo Ullitz, 1919).

For the early accounts of Western observers encountering surfing in Hawaii, I have generally quoted from the original sources, but I might never have come across them or understood their context without Patrick Moser's *Pacific Passages: An Anthology of Surf Writing* (Honolulu: University of Hawaii Press, 2008). Matt Warshaw's compilations, *The Encyclopedia of Surfing* (Boston: Houghton Mifflin Harcourt, 2003) and *The History of Surfing* (San Francisco: Chronicle, 2010), also proved invaluable in tracing the sport's path from Hawaii to the United States mainland and to Rockaway Beach.

My understanding of how weather and other physical forces and structures create surfable waves is largely buttressed by Tony Butt and Paul Russell, with Rick Gregg, and their *Surf Science: An Introduction to Waves for Surfing* (Honolulu: University of Hawaii Press, 2004). For the detailed narrative of Sandy's genesis and development, I relied especially on the official government recounting by Eric S. Blake et al., *Tropical Cyclone Report: Hurricane Sandy* (National Hurricane Center, February 12, 2013), and Kathryn Miles's *Superstorm: Nine Days Inside Hurricane Sandy* (New York: Dutton, 2014).

My sense of how Sandy's development was reported in real time depends in part on audio recordings courtesy of WINS-AM.

Acknowledgments

The genesis of this memoir—and the journey it chronicles—in some ways lies with Patrick Farrell, the visionary and deft *New York Times* editor who green-lighted the trip to Montauk that gave me my first live view of surfing and elevated the article that underpins some of the material here. Next was Corey Seymour, the *Vogue* editor who emailed me in the days following Hurricane Sandy with the beginnings of an idea about a personal essay on moving to the Rockaways for surfing and getting slammed by the storm. Years later, Penelope Green, a beloved colleague and friend from *7 Days* and the *New York Times,* suggested that I write about how surfing had changed my life for the *New York Times* Style section, and under the astute and sensitive editorial guidance of Laura Marmor, I developed an article that gave me the first inkling of how my tale could sustain a book.

My patient, creative, and dogged agent, Todd Shuster—along

with a large and dedicated team at Aevitas Creative Management (including Erica Bauman, Justin Brouckaert, Sarah Levitt, Janet Silver, and Jane von Mehren)—helped me, over many, many drafts, to fine-tune a proposal and then found the project a fabulous home. Deanne Urmy, my inspiring, genius editor at Houghton Mifflin Harcourt, saw a better book than any of us had imagined in the material and prodded, nourished, and buffed it into existence. Roz Lichter, attorney and friend extraordinaire, kept me safe along an unfamiliar path.

The knowledgeable and tireless staff of the Map Division at the New York Public Library helped me visualize and meander through the historic streets of the Rockaways. The sharp-eyed Andy Young cleared the content of many errors and offered valuable editorial encouragement and insight. Liz Duvall asked the right questions and erased the shortcomings of consistency, sequence, and sense with precision and grace.

I will be forever grateful to my brilliant, incisive, and generous readers, Shari Goldhagen, Jeff Goodell, and Camille Sweeney, who furnished crucial advice in finessing the story arc and prose. For helping me develop and refine important material that wound up in the book, I appreciate a number of people, especially Joyce Johnson and the members of our workshop, "Writing from Life," at the 92nd Street Y; Patricia Towers, my mentor in publishing (and in life); and Joshua Tyree and my classmates in his nonfiction writing workshop at Stanford University when I was a John S. Knight Fellow.

To the surfers of Rockaway—including those no longer with us, like Tim Hill, who helped shelter me the night Sandy hit, and Tommy Volovar, with whom I began many a day sipping coffee at sunrise on the boardwalk—I offer thanks for easing my way into the community. To my sister, Nancy Cardwell, I'm grateful for a lifetime of unwavering love and support in all my ventures. And finally I thank Todd Muller, who—every day—shares his wit, creativity, decency, righteousness, wisdom, and profound sense of fun. He makes it so.